NEW YORK
STREET GAMES
and Other Stories
and Sketches

NEW YORK STREET GAMES
and Other Stories and Sketches

Meyer Liben

Foreword by George Dennison

SCHOCKEN BOOKS • NEW YORK

First published by Schocken Books 1984
10 9 8 7 6 5 4 3 2 1   84 85 86 87
Copyright © 1984 The Estate of Meyer Liben

Library of Congress Cataloging in Publication Data

Liben, Meyer.
  Street games and other sketches and stories.

  I. Title.
PS3562.I17S8 1983   813'.54   82–10492

Designed by Nancy Dale Muldoon

Manufactured in the United States of America

ISBN 0–8052–3849–2

ACKNOWLEDGMENTS

The following stories originally appeared in *The St. John's Review:* "Lady, I Did It" (July 1980); "King of the Hill" (July 1980); "The Relay Race" (July 1980); "Not Quite Alone on the Telephone (Summer 1981).

The following story originally appeared in *New American Review:* "Suspension Points . . ." (#14, 1972).

The following stories originally appeared in *American Review:* "Brenner's Dream" (#21, October 1974); "One" (#21, October 1974); "The Tolstoy Quotation" (#21, October 1974); "The Garden" (#26, November 1977).

The following stories originally appeared in *Commentary:* "The Pharmacist" (April 1954) Copyright © 1954 The American Jewish Committee; "The Winners" (April 1954) Copyright © 1954 The American Jewish Committee; "Homage to Benny Leonard" (June 1959) Copyright © 1959 The American Jewish Committee; "Past Due" (June 1961) Copyright © 1961 The American Jewish Committee; "Change of Heart" (January 1965) Copyright © 1965 The American Jewish Committee; "Ball of Fire" (March 1967) Copyright © 1967 The American Jewish Committee; "A Note on Chivalry" (December 1974) Copyright © 1974 The American Jewish Committee.

The following stories originally appeared in *Midstream—A Monthly Jewish Review:* "Mr. Mintz Retires" (April 1972); "The Tolstoy Movie" (December 1972); "Minkin Copying" (December 1974); "Pinkham: The Enchanted Isles" (October 1976); "Uncle Benny" (May 1981); "No Sale 1" and "No Sale 2" (June/July 1983).

"You're It" originally appeared in *The Massachusetts Review* (Spring 1960).

"Frimmell's Successor" originally appeared in *New Directions* (Annual 1941).

"The Caller" originally appeared in *Accent* (Spring 1945).

"The Perils of Trade" originally appeared in *Horizon* [England] (July 1949).

"The Intermediary" originally appeared in *Art & Literature* [Paris] (#4, Spring 1965).

Diana Liben would like to give special acknowledgment to Martin Greenberg and Betty Gold.

CONTENTS

FOREWORD

Meyer Liben: A Memoir
GEORGE DENNISON

Quietness is the only way.

I last saw Mike in mid-November of 1975. I was in New York for two days and we spent an afternoon together, as usual walking and talking. When I left for my home in Maine he gave me a copy of the manuscript of *New York Street Games*. I wrote him shortly afterward to say how much I liked the book, but before my letter could have reached him I received a magazine he had sent me in which a new story of his appeared, and so I wrote him again: "I hope you won't mind another compliment. . . ." "Mind compliments?" he wrote back, "My favorite quotation of the year is from Gertrude Stein: (approximately) 'Praise is the highest form of criticism.' "

Two weeks later, at night, just before Christmas, my younger daughter called me to the phone. I recognized the exhausted, saddened voice of Mike's wife.

"George," she said, "this is Diana. . . ."

Her tone told me that something grievous had happened. She paused, keeping her voice under control, and I said, "Are you all right, Diana?"

She said, "It's Mike, George. . . ." and hearing the sound I made, she said very quietly, "Yes. . . ."

He had died the night before, of a heart attack, after a gathering of friends, while walking the short distance to the new apartment on West 15th Street in Manhattan, in which he lived alone.

He had not felt well and had left the party within a few minutes of arriving at it. Something in his behavior had alarmed a friend who knew of his heart condition (he had become frail at last), and she had telephoned his apartment and then had called Diana. For several hours Diana and her son searched the streets of the neighborhood, stopping frequently to telephone the hospitals and the police. In the small hours, still searching, they were told that a body had been identified. Just before daybreak Diana went to the morgue with all three children.

Mike's service was crowded. I recognized a few writers and intellectuals, people I had met at Mike and Diana's place, at their place in Amagansett, or at other parties and functions: people of the Old Left many of them, a few of whom were well along in their drift to the New Right; some poets and painters. I didn't know Mike's family, or Diana's, or business friends, or old school friends. . . .

Mike had been born in New York City; he had grown up in New York, had gone to school there, had married and raised a family, had been in business, had written and published there. The continuities of the city itself had often seemed to me to be apparent in his character, and certainly they had been subjects in his writing. Looking around the crowded room and seeing the three generations and the range of types and occupations, I thought of those things again that I had known in their familiar forms of attitudes, virtues, and anecdotes.

The rows of chairs were filling. The chairs faced a lectern. Near the lectern were flowers, and near the flowers the open casket.

Perhaps in some primitive way the sight of the body verifies the death for us, but in fact I couldn't see Mike in that inert mass in the coffin, and I was unwilling to tell myself that I could. I remembered standing like that and feeling that very thing at the coffin of our mutual friend Paul Goodman. The body in death is not even a body, but something less, something entirely generic and impersonal, unattached to any memory or love. Years later the persistence and sharpness of missing Mike surprised me, and I came to believe, and believe now, that *the-man-dead* and *the-death-of-the-man* are here in my feelings, memories, and actions. We are part of nature for one another in just this way. When we gather at funerals it is not only to honor the departed ones but to achieve their deaths, to make a human fact of death, since it is we ourselves who are its repository and not the earth.

The crowded room grew more crowded still. The air grew warmer. One heard the low, uneven sounds of constrained voices. Soon the rows of chairs were filled. People were standing. I waited in the back with two other friends of Mike's, both writers. The service began. We listened to the rabbi, and to Mike's son Ned, and to Mike's daughter Lucy, who read the poem of his beginning

Sitting in this place, rather than another. . . .

I had come from Maine the previous evening and had sat up most of the night. I was tired and overextended, very vulnerable to emotions, and I am glad that this was so for there now occurred an event so moving as to have become for me a symbol of the love that is left behind by death, and that death releases into a purity that perhaps always belonged to it but was always qualified by relation. Mike's dark, intense daughter Laura, who is short and stocky like her mother, and in whose face one saw flickering alternations of homeliness and beauty, came before the mourners carrying her guitar. She said she had composed a song for her father and could only express her feelings by singing. She began to play and sing, not tinkering as so many folksingers do, but powerfully, so that the massiveness of her emotions came out to us in waves of unabashed love, unabashed grieving, and unabashed praise. That she stood there singing this song, and that her father lay in the coffin behind her, was so deeply moving that many present lowered their heads and covered their eyes. I too. I listened to the whole of this song in a downpour of tears, not only for the death of my friend but for other deaths and pent-up things. I understood at the time, and since then have understood it better, that I was seeing an aspect of Mike I had never known, an accomplishment and profound meaning.

In my eulogy I spoke chiefly of Mike's writing. Most of the people present had read his novel *Justice Hunger* and the stories printed with it. Some, I knew, had followed his stories in the literary magazines for years. Knowing how much of the man was in the work, it seemed fitting to praise it on this occasion, and to cite the praise that other writers had given it.

I was acquainted with Mike for several years before we became friends. Paul Goodman introduced us. I had just come back from Mexico, where I had lived for a year and a half after the breakup of my first marriage. I remember meeting Mike at the corner of 8th Street and Sixth Avenue, in front of the drugstore not far from where he lived. We talked for a while and then parted, and Paul said to me that Mike was recovering from a severe heart attack. This was said not only as a point of fact about his good friend, but to explain why Mike carried himself so cautiously, as if he were trying to move without muscular effort or expense of energy.

Mike was then in his early forties, and (as did Paul) seemed younger. He was of medium height, of an erect and compact physique that was striking for its good balance, the left-right symmetry or equipoise one often sees in athletes. (I learned later that he had played basketball at CCNY on one of Nat Holman's glamor teams. When he wrote and spoke of athletes, of the great lightweight boxer Benny Leonard or of basketball players or runners, it was always *form,* deftness, agility that he remarked, and his own bearing exemplified these qualities.) He carried his head erectly, and occasionally glanced from side to side like a quarterback or play-making basketball center, keeping track of things and keeping cool. There was great intelligence in his face, and decorum, and (I became more aware of this later) shyness. His hair was brown and his eyes were a striking, translucent brown, large and round, and deeply recessed at the top, which accentuated their roundness. His nose was large, with a prominent, bumpy arch, but was not fleshy. His eyelids, characteristically, seemed always half-closed. It was a face that took easily to gravity, reticence, and a firmness that was without censoriousness or severity—and also (I came to see) to a shy, sweet smiling, a deft, droll, and extremely original humor that was based entirely on observation and reflection, not on fantasy or outrageous invention. There was a combination of virility and sweetness in him of a kind that seems to have characterized Camus, virility in the domestic and civilized forms not much noticed in American life.

All of these qualities were tempered by the physical emergency from which he was recovering. He seemed shaken. He was pale, and obviously was convalescing.

The things that I saw in Mike at that time were of a kind that I now find attractive and have come to know are rare. And they were attractive to me then too, but I thought that I had rejected the middle-class world he seemed to live in. He was a businessman (as had been Italo Svevo, whom he much admired). He disliked his business life intensely, and I was unaware of it for years because he never complained of it, and never disdained its people and places as subjects for stories, but wrote at times of salesmen and shops, much as Doctors Chekhov and Williams wrote of their patients and their patients' families.

I was impressed by the friendship between Mike and Paul. They differed vastly in outlook, character, and way of life, yet remained important to each other. Where Paul was often deliberately outrageous, and helplessly or compulsively rude, Mike was decorous, conventional, and courteous. To see first the one man's apartment and then the other was to see a striking contrast in style. Paul and Sally had very little money. They lived on Ninth Avenue over a butcher's warehouse in an apartment put together of odds and ends, like a students' clubhouse, not slapdash at all, but improvised in a characteristic spirit of high principle, wit, practicality, and desperation. One felt that poverty was indeed "practiced as a virtue" here, as Paul once claimed. There was nothing passive or defensive to be seen. It was as much a workshop as a home, a center of wonderfully unencumbered intellectual and artistic activity, and was obviously important in a lively community of friends. One sensed an active principle of expansion and adventure. The door seemed always to be open, and it was as if the street itself might amble up the stairs and walk right in like a shaggy dog.

Mike and Diana, by contrast, lived in a large and substantial building on 10th Street near University Place. Their furnishings were handsome, had been carefully chosen, and were unified in a definite sense of style. There were avant-garde paintings on the walls and books in a quantity that meant something special, but in most ways it was a conventional middle-class home. One knew that there were business suits in the closets and that few if any people were privileged to come calling without an invitation.

Mike and Paul were of the same age, as were Sally and Diana. But where Diana seemed maternal, grave, and steady, Sally seemed like a pretty schoolgirl, a brave and dutiful one, but forlorn at times in the way that a young girl can be forlorn, and at times sullen and oppressed, and then again lively and vivacious. And where Mike, so it seemed, was practiced in the restraint of impulse and desire, as most of us are, Paul was cultivating those very things. He was a poet-scholar who after a brief stint of teaching had broken decisively with university life. On sunny afternoons he roamed the streets like an adventurous urchin, and at home often seemed to be the rival of his own children.

Yet it wasn't hard to see the similarities. Diana's Russian gloom could be dispelled instantaneously by a stroke of wit, and then one saw a merriment so illuminated by intelligence as to be memorable: a *radiant hilarity*. And if there was a schoolgirl in Sally, there was also a strong admixture of the matron, a loftiness, even a severity of spirit, just as in Paul the most striking things were not, after all, the various modes of childishness he indulged in, but the extraordinary quantities of thought, observation, and knowledge that poured out of him, in a style, moreover, of true accountability in the high tradition. Both Sally and Diana were acutely intelligent and acutely discerning, to such a degree that though their literary observations at that time were lacking in scope one preferred them for accuracy and finesse to those of many professional critics, in whose presence both women characteristically fell silent.

Of these four friends it was Mike, so I thought, who was most openly appreciative of others. There were times of bad feeling between him and Paul, but their friendship survived them. He admired Paul exceedingly and didn't begrudge him his extraordinary privileges of behavior. And it was noteworthy of Mike that his own very conventional code of conduct was not based either on simple inhibition or fearfulness, but on virtues in their positive forms. It was this that gave his conduct its irreducible and often luminous quality. At times one felt a wistfulness and sadness in him, but one never felt that these were the effects of an ethics he hadn't really chosen. On the contrary, his way of doing things was impressively right for him.

Occasionally over the years I went to parties at Mike and Diana's place, and encountered intellectuals whose names were prominent in important journals. I remember seeing two short rows of disputants at the end of an evening. They sat in straight-backed chairs facing each other, three on a side, as if some game had commenced, but it was entirely spontaneous. Every one of them sat with his arms folded across his chest or atop his belly, and they spoke together in a relaxed and savoring way, as if the bouts of the evening had ended. It was striking. I had been under the impression that no one listened at these gatherings, though there were several dazzling talkers (no dazzling listeners, as Mike might say), or else they listened by a remarkable process that did not entail the cessation of speaking. But here was an interlude of mutual response and amicability.

Often at these gatherings Paul and Harold Rosenberg, old friends and respectful antagonists, would argue hotly some issue of politics or art. Rival arguments would cease, and disputants would gather round or cock an ear or bend from the waist so as not to miss a word, though there were times when the words of both seemed drowned utterly in the pure aesthetics of dispute. One would hear tones of assertion, tones of rejection, ironic scoffing, demurral, tones of patient correction, tones of impatient correction, tones of amazed disbelief, the extensive armamenta of fact and opinion advanced on both sides so fragmented and intermingled by the mingling of their voices that they no longer appealed to the mind at all, but directly to the heart, like an opera in a foreign language.

Mike's style was not at all like this. One would see him in a group standing with a bowed head, listening, occasionally nodding, sometimes smiling at one or another remark, and now and again adding his own comment. It was not that he lacked opinion or did not take his own opinion seriously, but that the relations and proportions of opinion, ego, observation, praise, devotion, etc., were put together differently in him than in other people— uniquely, actually. He was less like others than they were like each other. In the postfight analyses conducted by those who stayed at parties for a final round of coffee, one would hear, "What Harold doesn't understand is . . ." or "What Paul fails to grasp is . . ." Except from Mike. Mike was capable of pointing out what might be called the physical peculiarities of an argument, something characteristic about the speaker's way of thinking, his way of coming at things. And he was capable of paying a simple compliment, and of enjoying the fact that an argument, especially a heated one, is a marvelously structured form. One finds many such arguments in *Justice Hunger*. They reflect the world's events, the speaker's character, the intellectual fashions and preoccupations of the time. It is delightful to encounter them, and they are of a kind that do in fact abound in life, and that yet for some reason are not much represented in American literature.

Gradually I came to see more of Mike. I read his stories in magazines like *Commentary, Accent,* and the *New Directions Annual.* I wasn't aware of the full extent of his publishing, and didn't know until after his death how many of his things were never published at all. What I did come to see was that writing, for him, was a spiritual activity, a way of being in the world. It was not dependent on publication, was not a matter of career, or even perhaps of choice, but of need, enjoyment, and love of what it was. I asked him once what he was working on, and he said, "I'm always writing something, George." Very likely months had gone by in which I hadn't seen a story of his, and there was an overtone in my question of: Are you working at all? This kind of thing—equating publishing with working—must have been painful to him, as it must certainly have been painful that his published work received no more praise than it did, while inferiors, often crass, enjoyed attentions of all kinds. This problem was exacerbated by Mike's unwillingness to show unpublished things. He was quite unlike Paul in this, who offered almost everything to his friends as soon as it was written. There may have been psychic reasons for Mike's privatism, reasons not evident to observers. But the vocation itself seemed unbroken. We were talking once of Stefan Zweig's book on Balzac, and Mike said of Balzac, "He makes you proud to be a writer." Perhaps I would have remembered those words no matter what the tone of voice, but Mike's delivery made a revelation of them, and also, for me, an inspiration. He spoke impulsively, yet with gravity and his usual quietness; and I heard an ardor and purity of admiration that one tends to associate with boyhood and youth, when the praise of distant heroes is a compound of admiration, love, determination, and hope. But I heard notes of gratitude as well, and dedication. Mike was in his late fifties, already entering old age, not an optimist or a sentimentalist. It was moving to hear that unalloyed youthful voice coming from his lips.

Nothing during that whole period of the 1950s, 1960s, and early 1970s could have been less harmonious with the spirit of the times than the quietism one found in Mike. Some of the painters he knew were in that photograph in *Life* magazine, identified as "The Irascibles." Goodman never ceased attacking the society around him. Rosenberg could scarcely write an essay without thumping a head or two, or several dozen. Artaud enjoyed a vogue both as a martyr and as a theorist calling for a theater of attack, and the Becks found ways of achieving exactly that. The plays of Brecht were widely performed. The Beats appeared with a literature of noisy rejection. Political and social agitation in the 1960s and early 1970s became mass phenomena. Mike was the only person I knew who was quietistic. It was not that he supported the status quo. On the contrary, he would have—and could have—welcomed an epoch of social justice more wholeheartedly than many people whose lives were devoted to bringing it about. It was simply that no style of agitation could have been right for him, no form of contention, or even of anger, could have achieved a voice in him capable of displacing the voice of quiet praise and grateful comment that he already possessed.

Often I was aware of these qualities in Mike because his responses to things acted upon me as correctives to my own impatience and too-ready vehemence. When the work of the so-called Beat writers (it was not their word) first appeared in New York, Mike was one of the few of his generation, and of those circles, to pay much attention to it. I had had some fleeting contact with them, they were my age-mates, and I had looked forward to reading *Howl* and *On the Road.* Both of those books were disappointing to me, were filled with the rhetoric of collaborative make-believe such as one hears among adolescents and finds tedious even there. This was at a time in our country's history when middle-class wage earners, in unprecedented numbers, were complaining from the couch that their lives didn't *make sense*—and here were spokesmen for a new movement extolling the irrational on the grounds that it was antibourgeois.

I would say such things to Mike, say them angrily, and often he would agree, but without the anger, and he would point to some virtue I had neglected to notice in these authors. Years later I came to admire certain of Ginsberg's works (and his public role), and to admire even more Kerouac's late book *The Vanity of Duluoz,* and I remembered Mike's saying to me, raising his eyebrows and cocking his head, his voice cracking lightly on every fourth or fifth word, "Well, it's a remarkable idea to write about your friends. It's not a bad idea at all."

Settled, sober, domestic, urban, engaged in business, paternal, circumspect, judicious, modest, quiet—Mike was everything the Beatniks weren't. But they affirmed their boyish excitability, their boyish freedom from the world of toil, their boyish loyalties to one another; and all this, so I believe, touched a chord in him, and pleased him.

I remember his response to a symposium on Trotsky that we went to together. He knew the panelists and had known them for a long time. All said more or less belittling things about Trotsky and didn't make adjustments for the privileges of hindsight. After it was over, while we were leaving, Mike said to me, "You'd never have known how much they admired Trotsky when they were young."

There had been a general discussion after the panelists had spoken. I said to him, "Mike, why didn't you say that?"

He thought for a moment and shook his head. That his silence had been something other than shyness hadn't occurred to me, but seeing him take the question seriously, I pondered it too.

When he had said to me "You'd never know . . . etc.," he had spoken without rancor, without superiority or moral accusation. Had he spoken those same words in the heat of discussion, the context would have transformed them into an accusation he did not intend and a moral and political criticism that was not his point at all. Nor could the temper of the discussion have credited the equanimity and forebearance of his remark.

That he refrained from speaking appeared to me finally to be another example of the instinctive, day-to-day integrity in small things that characterized him, and that added up finally to integrity of the entire life. Every memory I have of him is of this kind. There simply aren't any in which he has done other than the authentic thing—and I don't believe that he was even aware of this trait at all.

There seem to have been two periods of deep satisfaction in Mike's life, and he writes of them with a natural piety entirely unaffected and convincing, an attitude of praise and thankfulness that one judges to have been second nature to him rather than literary motive. It was this, I think, that in his milieu, in which chiefly *issues* and opinions were brought forward, allowed him to remain interested in the events of peoples' lives, and in, as he said (which is perhaps even more important), "the time between events."

The first of these epochs was the time of boyhood games of which he writes in *New York Street Games*. The second was the time at CCNY, which is the immediate past of *Justice Hunger*, and is the actual background of stories like "The Dream Issue," and of course of the brief memoir called "CCNY," which in its charmed detail, its humor and affection, is one of the finest things of its kind that I know.

In the stories set in these periods one finds a luminous quality of a distinctive and almost mysterious kind. Ordinarily in writings as personal as these, and based as these are on recollection, the objects and people are illuminated by many overt qualities of loving memory: enthusiasm, direct praise, nostalgia, warmth of voice, a sweet vivacity of manner that tends to characterize relations of friendship, love, and innocence. Mike's prose, in contrast to all this, is objective, reticent, sometimes dry, always very sparing in its effects. Where does the luminosity come from? I think it is in the gaze itself that he turns on the past. It is not that the author's gaze is drawn to certain things, but that *everything* that appears in that gaze takes on the quality of a magnetized presence. The gaze itself is charmed, and constitutes a charmed medium. To say this is to say that it has in it authentic vestiges of childhood and youth, specifically the accepting good faith of childhood (that scarcely distinguishes between the routine and the dazzling), and the idealism, committed hopefulness, and naïve decency of youth. These are among the characteristics of that distinctive luminosity. Mike speaks of the importance of "the time between events," and he does often elevate the incidents of ordinary time to the status of events. But in fact, especially in *Justice Hunger*, there is no ordinary space. Every presence is a magnetized presence; their fatalities are not in their relations with each other, but elsewhere. This is an attribute of religious experience, and it seems to me to be an important source of the arresting luminosity of many of Mike's fictions.

As for his religious nature, that would be hard to define. He was not a practicing Jew. He had a skeptical, appraising, worldly eye. Yet no one could be with him any length of time without realizing that in some important and obvious way he was a religious person. What this means I don't know. Surely whatever else it means, it means that the experience of solitude does not constitute a cessation of care or of world presence, but the opposite—a gate of care, and a true essence of the world.

During most of the 1960s I lived not far from Mike and Diana's neighborhood. Our friendship became firmer in this period, perhaps because I was changing in ways that made it possible. I had married for the third time and had begun to raise a family. I was writing more than I had used to. And I was older—old enough to have seen new fashions and new styles in painting, poetry, theater, and dance emerge in New York and somehow combine money-making with the idea of the avant-garde. There were people of genius among the newcomers, especially in theater, but there was a tremendous lot of gloss and blather, and the fashionable consumption of art began to acquire a status almost equal to the productuion of it. It was during this period that I began to understand the importance and historical significance of the generation of New York Jews to which Mike belonged, and whose values and implicit assumptions he embodied in his work. They were the last generation able to take the civilization of the city entirely for granted, and to take for granted the importance of the written word and of literature. They were the last ones to have grown up in the still-functioning neighborhoods of New York, and to take their places in a city at once cosmopolitan and homely, the culture of which was still a function of place and had not yet been reduced to mere cultural servicing. They were the last generation to reach maturity in a world that still used words like *infinite* and *eternal,* and could not believe that technology would appropriate the moon or that mere human waste, mere accident, would corrupt the very oceans. They were the last generation to have produced independent intellectuals in any numbers, that is, intellectuals not affiliated with universities. And much else. . . .

The qualities and experiences of his generation as a whole were especially attractive in Mike, and were among the many things I had come to value in him. Now that I have lived in Maine so long, I'm aware of the extraordinary degree to which, in the city, the medium of friendship is conversation. In the country friends share work and a great many activities . . . but when I think of New York friends I think of conversations, usually long and intense. And there is an image of Mike that is probably the master image of my memories of him, that is not confined to a single event or year. It is an image of him listening and smiling, or talking and smiling. The image is Mike smiling his shy, sweet, quiet smile. He was the only one I knew who did that—smiled with enjoyment because the conversation pleased him.

I stayed with him for a week at the place in Amagansett one summer. It was a pleasant time for me, away from children, gardening, and chores. I had a room upstairs to work in, and would spend the mornings there while Mike worked at the handsome table in the living room where the veranda turned the corner. In the afternoon we would go to the beach, usually Louse Point, where Mike knew everyone. We sat there one day with several other people, among whom was Harold Rosenberg. A scholar friend of his had just published a book on Dostoyevsky and Rosenberg was talking about it. From Dostoyevsky he passed to Tolstoy, suddenly grew impassioned, and delivered a sustained diatribe against him (my idol) so one-sided and arbitrary as to leave me speechless with amazement. When his discourse had reached its fullness, he got with difficulty to his feet, using his cane, and limped grandly toward the water, though "limping" scarcely describes that imperial gait, or the effect of that stiff leg that did not seem like a stiff leg at all but like patriarchal rectitude, manly egotism—a grand and oddly pleasing spectacle.

Mike had been persuaded as little as I by Rosenberg's remarks, but he was not reeling as was I, and he watched Harold's progress appreciatively, saying to me, "He's the least embarrassed person I know."

We went to a restaurant for a seafood dinner, and late that

evening were reading in separate parts of the house when the telephone rang. Mike answered and called to me, and I could hear him greeting Mabel. He handed me the phone, and since it was fairly late (actually, probably just to give me some privacy), went upstairs to his bedroom.

Mabel was calling from Maine. Sally Goodman had just telephoned her. Paul had had a massive heart attack the night before, and that morning had died.

It was shocking to hear this, though I heard it without sorrow. I hadn't felt affection for Paul in years, had tired thoroughly of his obsessively dominating character, had had to defend myself against it—yet to hear of his death was sobering and disturbing. The year was 1972. To lose Paul was to lose a great deal. I told Mabel that I would come for her so that we could go to the funeral in New Hampshire together.

I sat there a while after hanging up the phone, wondering if there were any way I could tell Mike that would soften the blow. Just the previous day he had shown me a story, published years before, that I had never seen, a lovely one called "Mr. Mintz Retires," dedicated "to Paul Goodman, who brought Leviathan into the Hudson." The story was a fine example of a form that Mike had invented, the "dialectical lyric" (the phrase had been used by Paul, after Kierkegaard) and that Paul had adapted so successfully to his own uses that Mike had been accused of imitating him. It was Paul who had told me this, years before, praising Mike's writing to me and recommending that I read it.

Their friendship went back to college days. People who had known them both said that Mike had idolized him. They had been counsellors together at the camp Paul wrote of in "The Break-Up of Our Camp," and were two of a small group of friends, all writers, who had met once a week to read each other's work at the apartment in Washington Heights where Paul's sister Alice—ten years his senior—mothered him and offered hospitality to his friends. One would need to know Mike's modesty and generosity of spirit to understand the openness of his pride in Paul. The early flowering and extraordinary productivity of Paul's genius meant much to him, and I know that he deeply admired the courage and integrity with which Paul lived and worked.

In "The Tolstoy Quotation," a strange and haunting story written not long after Paul died, Mike wrote:

> . . . in the Heights recently, in Fort Tryon Park, above the Hudson, and walking the familiar terrain, I remembered what Paul had written to me a little less than a year before he died: "I certainly don't give out joy to anybody," and I contrasted the sadness of his last years with the incredible joy-giving of his youth and manhood . . . and I recovered the sense of Paul's dazzling movement of thought . . . the driving power of his imagination. . . .

As I went up the stairs to Mike's room I wondered if he had heard the tones of my voice, or phrases, and had already guessed what had happened. I called to him before I reached the top of the stairs, and by the time I reached the landing he had opened the door to his room and come out. I said to him, "Mike, something very bad has happened. . . ."

He said quietly, "What is that, George?"

I told him what Mabel had told me. His face whitened and he said nothing for a moment, then: "He takes a lot of life with him."

I could see that he wanted to be alone. He went outside and stood looking away under the oak trees.

I made several calls to friends who I thought would want to attend the funeral in New Hampshire and to whom I could offer transportation. (I remember Grace Paley's pained, spontaneous, "Oh, what a loss!")

Some of the people I talked with I hadn't seen for years, but I had been close to them in my first decade in New York. Memories and the feel of that time began to come back to me. It was then that Paul had been so important to me, friend and teacher, older brother and second father. I could feel again the strange lingering of my boyhood, of my childhood home and the ongoing quarrels with my parents that had kept them close to me yet achingly distant. I remembered the incredible and so beautiful intelligence with which Paul, in the small-group sessions of his

first weeks as a psychotherapist, had exemplified points of analytic theory with points from philosophy, in which he had been
trained, and from literature, in which he was widely and closely
read—dazzling, dazzling occasions. I remembered his endlessly
inventive wit, his gaiety and high spirits, and the deeply held
principles he wouldn't budge from and that made his pride admir-
able and gave the hours of the day great meaning. I remembered
our poker games and ball games, and the Christmases and
Thanksgivings on which compassionate Sally had mothered us
waifs and strays. That whole period had been a confused and
desperate time for me, yet often an exciting time as well, and a
time lit now and again by youthful good spirits, youthful loves,
affections, and hopes. I called a friend whom once I had cared
much for, but whom I hadn't seen now for a decade, and he
answered the ringing phone in a voice so familiar as to cancel out
the years. We spoke briefly and in a friendly way. I told him Paul
had died—and felt a great wave of sorrow pass through me.

Mike entered the house, still pale and withdrawn. I was weep-
ing. I went out. I entered and he went out. At one point we
spoke briefly in the kitchen, I leaning back against the sink, he
against the counter.

He had been writing something about *secret strength,* and said
that that was what Paul had been for many people, a secret
strength.

I blurted out, "He was dreadful, and he was wonderful!"

Mike said, "Yes, that's true."

I said, "I loved him, and I hated him."

Again Mike said, "Yes."

I cursed and wept, and we resumed our strange walking, as if
we each had become one of Giacometti's striding skeletal figures.

I had hoped that Mike would come with me to New Hampshire, but his health was far too uncertain for such a tiring thing.
Even staying on alone at the house in Amagansett was something
to be avoided. He said in the morning that he would call his son.
I left for New York, where I met one of the friends I had spoken
to, and then turned north to Maine.

Our relationships with the dead go on changing. We make discoveries about ourselves and these alter our understanding of the dead. We come to new appreciations of virtues, new analyses of events. We undergo experiences that open our eyes and reveal the existence of entire ranges of sufferings, or braveries, or abject enduring we had not been aware of. Reciprocity has ceased but the dead have not been removed from our lives, and the absence of reciprocity purifies our feelings; we are more able, perhaps, to take exemplary people as exemplars, and to see defects that loyalty had once obscured. Strangest of all, we become the age-mates of people who are no longer aging, but who in this peculiar way are still subject to time. Mike, when I knew him, was fourteen years older than I. Now he is only seven. I have just read *Justice Hunger* again, and—in manuscript—all of the stories at present intended for print; and I see that he was a stranger, rarer man than I had realized, and that his work, that I always had admired, was even better than I had known, rather *is* better, stranger, stronger, more original. I see too how firmly he is placed in the lineage of storytellers, the line, or meandering path, or networks of paths, or airy whiffs of contact between Chekhov and Gogol, Hawthorne, Hemingway, Goodman, Lardner, to name just a few of whom Mike had been fond.

And I have been wondering if it really is possible that his stories now are better than they once had been. Can that happen?

I know that I have come to value highly—I mean in the world, including literature—certain of the qualities I find in Mike's work. For me, in fiction these occur in their fullness in the work of certain nineteenth-century German and German-Swiss authors, notably Stifter and Gotthelf, and especially Gottfried Keller. What these writers have in common is a quality of voice that is actually, in itself, a spiritual meaning. It is a voice purged of temperament in the idiosyncratic sense, a respectful and chastened voice that is at once civic and independently philosophical, is touched very lightly by sorrow and the awareness of death, yet can be humorous and playful, can give way to sober rejoicing, is happy in the act of praise, and often exhibits a kind of egoless pride that is among the handsomest of human traits. It is a voice that implicitly takes life as a great mystery and a great blessing, and that without special pleading strikes notes of filial piety and of honor for the virtues of the past.

This voice clearly is no mere artifact of narration, like the garrulous, self-hypnotized voice that has become the hallmark of American fiction, but a spiritual triumph, an authentic relation of the author to his own experience, including his experience of literary tradition.

Mike (I almost want to say "Liben" at this point) writes more intimately, more essayistically, and on a smaller scale than the great ninteenth-century figures I have just mentioned, but I hear a similar voice in his work, I find the same matrix of values and the same attitude of respect. No doubt I see these things more clearly in his work now than I did fifteen years ago, or twenty years; and to this extent his work has changed for me because I myself have changed. But I think it is also the case that his work has changed in history and not just for me, is stronger than it was, and more choice. Time has acted upon his stories in such a way as to reveal and make prominent certain virtues of art that needed only to be visible to be admired, just as time has leveled other works, making clear their dependence on fashion or their lack of real subject.

That Mike's work should be especially susceptible to this process is due in good part, I think, to the fact that his subjects were taken from "the time between events," the daily flood of ordinary things that while we are immersed in the life of the city, or the excitements of youth, we take for granted and think to be immutable. But the author, in his strangeness, his genius, and perhaps also his long awareness of death, did not take them for granted, and did not judge them to be immutable. Several decades have gone by since some of Liben's stories were written. Many things have turned out to be vulnerable to history, not immutable at all. And the fact that they were the author's chosen things, his valued things, is now much more visible.

It may be that in saying this one is not so much praising the author's conscious evaluation as the unconscious poetry of his life—though on second thought there really isn't any difference.

What may have been at one time an instinctive motion of sensibility, or characteristic impulse of praise, turns out to be the structural equivalent of wisdom. What once had been charm, goodness, and humor becomes an indispensable topography of the soul. What the poet has praised is what he cannot dispense with, and to say that we ourselves cannot dispense with it either is only to say in another way that he is a poet.

Reading *Justice Hunger* again after the passage of fifteen years, I found myself laughing aloud at times at its drolleries, marveling at its luminous simplicities, and feeling gratitude to a writer motivated to deal with such undramatic events as (for example) the triumph of a shy love over the usual defenses of self-consciousness—though it be more telling to say: a writer who deals respectfully with the usual defenses of self-consciousness under the encroachments of love. There are many examples in *Justice Hunger* of ordinary inconclusive conversations (about Marx, about Freud, about baseball), and it is as if the author were saying happily, "Ah! An ordinary, inconclusive conversation!" He writes of a ferryboat ride across the Hudson, or rain coming down in the city so that everyone seeks shelter and stands there looking out at the rain with an enjoyment too deep and too ordinary to need expression. Ostensibly these things are seen through the eyes of the protagonist, who is a man in love, but the effect is actually somewhat different: they are seen in the ineluctable self-sufficiency with which the eyes of youth and childhood see them, and the love is added to that. I think it is this that unites Liben's simple events with our underlying human condition, and allows us to see them rather as states—states of soul, states of the world, conditions of existence—than as actions carried out or undergone by individuals. His modest, lightly done descriptions of New York street games are similarly remarkable for the complex things they evoke beyond the usual exuberance of growth and play, especially the implicit, serious homage to distant heroes and the ways in which childish play is as much a feat of daydreaming and the imagination as of small bodies in violent motion. Liben does not neglect the hair-splitting and the splitting of split hairs that are such prominent and wonderful features of childhood play; or the background of mothers' voices, family dinners, fathers' graver presences, brothers and sisters, bedrooms, pajamas, and sleep. These lovely things of our lives are very little represented in literature (one thinks immediately of such exceptions as Blake and Wordsworth, and of Charles Lamb's stopping in the street to watch the boys at play: "What a pity that these fine ingenuous lads will one day be respectable members of parliament!"). I feel grateful to Mike for supplying some part of this lack.

I have said almost nothing here of the formal qualities of Mike's work. And there are aspects of it—subjects, effects, antecedents, and context—that I have scarcely mentioned in my concentration on the things for which I feel special affinities. One hopes that the great deal here neglected will be dealt with by other hands.

What I have wanted chiefly to say—aside from memorial praise of Mike himself—is that the work belongs with the parts of American culture that we consider permanent. Or let me put it this way, since *permanence* is a dubious concept: the ongoing, comprehensive anthology of important American work, that exists both in our affections and our judgment, would be radically incomplete without examples of the fiction of Meyer Liben.

NEW YORK
STREET GAMES
Stories and Memories

For Laura, Lucy, Ned

NEW YORK STREET GAMES
Stories and Memories

1. Lady, I Did It

A bunch of us were standing on the corner,

future-bound,

in a moment of dissatisfaction and restlessness. It was a late evening in early spring; darkness swarmed softly over sidewalk and stoop, softly filled in the cracks of light, remnants of a day forever gone.

We had finished an afternoon of hard and concentrated play and had enough of that, prefiguring the days not too distant when our play would be put off as a childish thing, opening up long periods of dissatisfaction and restlessness, for nothing rushed in to fill the vacuum created by the lost possibilities of play.

We wanted adventure, activity outside the internecine play on which we had fed for so many years.

"Let's have a track meet," one of us suggested, but nobody budged.

"Let's find the 115th Street Gang," one of us suggested, but nobody budged.

"Let's play *Lady, I did It*," one of us suggested, and that was just right, being midway between the play we could not leave and the power of the outside world we did not quite dare approach, for the 115th Street Gang was an older gang, all-powerful in the area stretching from the Harlem to the Hudson between 110th and 116th Streets.

So we started to play *Lady, I Did It.*

This is a game which stands midway between the play and fantasy spirit of childhood and the demands of the outer world. It is a group testing of the Reality Principle.

It is a simple and insolent game. Any number can play.

We approached a ground-floor apartment in a house up the block and one of us rang the bell. There was the sound of footsteps, and a woman opened the door, looked out at us.

"Lady, I Did It"

and we ran off.

Though any number (more than one) can play this game, it requires at least five to work up the necessary gang spirit, bravado, and sense of protection of the guilty one to give the game its interest.

Part of the interest is in the woman's surprise at the *number* of kids, also as to the reason for our presence.

This was the insolence of the game, that we stayed to tell her what we had done, that we had done it. This was much different from the antics of the little kids on the block, who played the game of *Ringing Doorbells,* then ran off before anyone answered.

With us the confrontation *was* the game—the band of us, emboldened by numbers, staring down the confused woman in that instant of silence which preceded the disclosure.

Properly speaking, the disclosure did not answer the woman's question (which we rarely gave her the chance to ask), that question being:

"What do you want?"

Before she could ask that question, for which we had no formulated answer, one of us announced his guilt and off we scooted.

The announcement by the guilty one made it no easier for any

one of us who happened to be caught, because we were all
equally blamed.

This was one of the hazards of the game. We came up against
it on our very next venture, when a man answered the ring.

"Mister, I did it," one of us said feebly, for the heart was not
in the formulation, partly because it was an irate *man* facing us
and partly because it was not the formulation and so violated the
rules of the game.

Quick as a flash he went after us, just missed the trailing one
with a kick which, had it landed, would have propelled that
trailer much closer to the front of the line.

Our next ring was answered by a little girl of about three years
old, whose smile and interested surprise was in sharp contrast to
our nervous belligerency. She looked around from one to the
other, pleased at our numbers, unaware of our defiance, which,
under her infant scrutiny, withered fast. We felt very foolish,
standing there with our stored energy directed against a target
insensitive to our needs and power.

When she called out:

"Ma, boys are here," the spirit of the gang softened more.
Grumbling and cursing, we broke up, moved away aimlessly,
disregarded the door which was slammed behind us.

"Baby, I did it," one of us yelled, and we laughed, recovered
our spirits a bit, tried our luck in another apartment house.

Here we were again disappointed, for there came to the door a
very old man. He was wearing a yarmulke, and peered at us
through eyes half-shut, without saying a word.

We were again at a loss, stymied by the presence of another
impervious object, for even had he asked us, in a voice cracked
and torn, what it was that we wanted, and had one of us announced that he was the culprit, the daring bell-ringer, the old
man surely would not have reacted with any resentment or even
any interest to this disclosure, which, for an instant, bound the
guilty one to us with the feelings we reserved for the hero in
danger. But there was no danger. We had nothing to say, and the
old man only looked and shrugged at this unexpected image of
adolescent solidarity, now breaking up before his bleary eyes, for

with mumbled imprecations we again scattered, while the old man swiftly, and in a voice much clearer than any one of us imagined he owned, uttered an incomprehensible prayer, probably of deliverance.

Then, on our next venture, our game succeeded perfectly. We were pleased the way a troupe is pleased when after all the rehearsals, all the fumblings and imperfections, the play is suddenly performed to the utmost limits of its meaning and its form.

We chose, by one of those random universal choices where the inclinations of the warring individuals are for the moment subsumed in a joyful group harmony and solidarity, a top-floor apartment and stood for a moment in front of the chosen door, enjoying the possibility of the imminent appearance of the key figure and the swift completion of our curious game.

During this pause we chose, by an intangible stirring, a movement of the group spirit, a series of lightning calculations, stray memories, movements of withdrawal, by the prominence in the foreground which one of us suddenly assumed, by a curious exigency of space, by the discipline of a gang, by a (finally) unanimous inclination—we chose one among us to step forward and commit, for all of us, the predetermined act.

He stepped forward swiftly, with a courage partly determined by the presence of the rest of us, partly by the role toward which he advanced, and partly by the ordinary amount of the spirit of play which he possessed, and pushed the button. He stepped back into the anonymity of the group and we closed ranks about him, as a protective cover, until the moment when he would step forward and expose himself as the culprit. The bell rang and almost immediately we heard the footsteps, vigorous, of the person coming toward the door, down the long hallway into which were built the bedrooms. We were quiet in the moment before the confrontation, one of us looked back toward the head of the stairs, measuring the distance to safety.

This was in a way a very satisfying moment—the thing had been done, for better or worse; together we awaited the issue, bound communally in face of the danger which we ourselves, by our collective will, had brought into being, for we didn't *have* to be in front of this door awaiting the answer to our insolent summons. We could have been playing in the street, in some violent opposition to each other, or been standing on the corner, talking of the heroes of the world, those who had left their blocks and made their ways in far-off realms, figures shadowy and real, gods we dreamed of approaching and rivaling. Instead we stood in front of this door, our rivalries, jealousies, and dreams buried for the moment in this unified thrust against the adult world.

The door opened, and there appeared in the doorway, slightly harassed, interrupted in household work, a rather young woman, who gazed quizzically, without fear, at the band of boys who formed a semicircle in front of her door.

She was genuinely puzzled, not the suspicous type who assumes that, because strangers are at her door, harm is meant, and shuts the door swiftly before the harm is done.

Nor was she one of those who recognized this game, like the smart-alecky woman who, seeing us crowd her door, exclaimed:

"Lady, I did it"

with the hysterical glee which some show in destroying the pleasures of others.

No, the woman now at the door was genuinely puzzled, could not imagine what it was that we wanted, tried in fact to collect her thoughts, to shake off her household distraction, to concentrate on the meaning of this little gang which stood defiantly in front of her, betraying an excitement which *she* could not understand was created by the imminence of a disclosure which in itself would be rather pointless to her, though certainly annoying.

Then, when the pause had reached its fullness, not too early, before the suspense had been built up, and not too late, after the novelty had worn off, our chosen one, before the lady had a chance to make a comment or ask a question (and it was always more dramatic when *we* broke the silence), shouted out, in a voice of triumphant self-confession:

"*Lady, I Did It.*" And we all beat it down the stairs to the street, where we exulted for a moment in our victory.

2. Hop, Skip, and Jump

The bell rang, and Mrs. Flaxman, kitchened, went to answer it, swiftly, impatiently.

"Hello, Reb Rutnick," she said, guiltily remembering it was the day for Davey's Bar Mitzvah lesson. She wiped her hands on her apron.

She led the teacher down the long hall into the dining room, seated him at the round table, and called out:

"Daaaaavey."

There was no answer; she looked vainly out the ground-floor window, and then apologetically at the teacher.

Reb Rutnick, thirty years old, reddishly sideburned, reddishly bearded, threw his hands up in a gesture of philosophical resignation.

"I'll find him," she said. "Will you have a glass of tea?"

"With pleasure," he replied.

"Daniel," she cried.

From the hall room there appeared a somewhat venerable five-year-old boy. He looked like the lad in the "Barney Google" cartoon strip, with speech out of Euclid, Thucydides, or John Stuart Mill.

"Where is David?" demanded Mrs.Flaxman.

The child answered promptly:

"He's practicing the Hop, Skip, and Jump for the Olympics."

Reb Rutnick, a student of the kabbalah, looked up in surprise.

"This is English?" he asked Mrs. Flaxman.

"Go and find him," she said, and Daniel trotted off obediently.

The teacher sipped at his tea and bit into his apple while Mrs. Flaxman busied herself in the kitchen. The dining room window opened quietly and a head appeared. Another window opened and a second head appeared. Reb Rutnick looked up in terror at these apparitions, then he recognized the features of David and Daniel, who squirmed silently into the living room.

David got his yarmulke, his Bible and notebook from the bureau drawer, and pulled up a chair next to the teacher. Daniel sat himself in a corner, constituting a one-man audience.

On hearing the teacher's voice, Mrs. Flaxman entered the dining room.

"You sneaked in again like Indians?" she asked. "How many times have I told you to come through the door? Is it asking so much of children, to come through the door?"

This last question was more or less directed toward the *melamed,* who said:

"Snakes and cats come through the window."

Mrs. Flaxman was not sure that she approved of this statement, and excused herself.

Davey started to chant his portion of the Law. After a few minutes the teacher stopped him.

"A little more feeling, please. You're dreaming about something."

Spurred by this criticism, the lad began to express himself more vigorously, so that Reb Rutnick broke in with words of praise:

"Fine, excellent, another Yusselle Rosenblatt, if only you try."

Stupefied by this praise, the Bar Mitzvah boy began to fade, and his teacher again had to caution him.

"You're in another world."

So the lesson went on. Then a whirring sound was heard in the room, slowly increasing in intensity. Davey disregarded this sound, but the teacher, wary, sought for its origin and soon found it. Daniel had in his hand a piece of clothesline. Attached to each end was a leaden weight; he was twirling the rope and spinning the weights, creating the whirr.

"Is this necessary?" asked Reb Rutnick.

"Shh," whispered the child, "don't interrupt me while I'm going for my record."

The appearance of Mrs. Flaxman led to Daniel's banishment; he walked cautiously and spun his weights.

The lesson continued in a desultory fashion. The Bar Mitzvah was almost two months off and Davey knew pretty much what he had to know. It was a matter now of some improvements, certain nuances in the chant.

When the lesson ended, he sprinted down the the hall and out the door into the street. Then the door opened and closed again, signifying that Daniel, too, had left.

Mrs. Flaxman came into the dining room.

"How is David coming along?"

"Fine, fine," said the teacher. "He'll make a very good appearance, and he has a good voice. He's a little impatient, maybe, but when the time comes, you'll be proud of him. Of course, he's got to study a little more."

"I understand," she said, accompanying Reb Rutnick to the door. "Mr. Flaxman will have to talk to him."

Slightly bemused, for the three years in this new land had not yet accustomed him to its sights and sounds, the teacher was startled, as he walked toward the subway, to see a familiar figure streak out of a courtyard, leap into the gutter on one leg, and then continue toward the other side in a series of jumps.

"Hello, Reb Rutnick."

It was little Daniel, standing at the curb, his job to inform Davey when the coast was clear of approaching cars.

The teacher paused.

"Watch," said Davey, as he ran back into the courtyard.

"Wait," said the kid brother, "there's a car coming."

"Move back," he said to the teacher, "he'll bang into you."

"Okay, *now!*" said Daniel.

Davey sprinted by, and hopped off the curb, skipped, then

jumped well up onto the opposite sidewalk, and Daniel rushed across the street to chalk the landing mark. Then the brothers ran back together.

"Boy!" said the younger. "Almost thirty-three feet."

"What?" asked Reb Rutnick.

"You see," said Davey, pleased at the opportunity of teaching his teacher, "the record, I mean the Olympic record, is fifty-one feet, seven inches. I'll be too young for the *next* Olympics, but six years from now I'll be just ready. If I can pick up a little over three feet each year, I'll be over the fifty-one foot mark, close to fifty-two. Three feet isn't much."

He took three short paces to show his teacher the distance about which he was talking.

Reb Rutnick, who had seen this boy three times a week for a month now, was surprised by the ferocity of his interest. He had shown nothing like it in his studies—even his impatience was not so genuine. Why, if he applied himself with half the energy to his studies, he could become a Talmudist, a Gaon. What was the secret about this skipping, this jumping?

Hands clasped behind his back, Reb Rutnick examined the distance. Daniel ran over with his tape measure and measured off three feet, which was about six inches less than the distance paced off by his brother.

"It's even less," said Davey happily.

"Very true," said the teacher. "If now it is thirty-three feet, and you improve three feet two inches each year for six years, then it will be fifty-two feet." He smiled and continued on his way.

"Fifty-two feet!" cried Daniel. "Did you hear that? The rabbi says you'll jump fifty-two feet in six years."

In his mind's eye he saw his brother crowned in one of the capital cities of the world.

"I want to tell you something about this event," said Davey to his kid brother. "Most people never even heard of it, or if they did, they think it's a real screwy event, something that got onto the program by mistake. But it's a great event, it gets you so far out from the start. And the variety of it. Do you know what I found out? That the skip is the most important part. At first you want to get over the skip to reach the jump. But the trick is to cover distance with the skip and get in position for the jump, too."

"I want to ask two questions," said Daniel. "How much more can you do in the running broad than in the running hop, and do you jump further in the jump at the end of the hop, skip, and jump than you would in the regular running broad jump?"

"That's something to find out," said Davey admiringly. "Tomorrow when it's light, we can check that."

"Daaavey, Daaanny," came the voice of their mother down the street.

"Just one more," said Davey. "Tell me when the coast is clear."

He went into the courtyard, and at his brother's signal streaked out in the gloom, hit the curb, and flew off into space toward the opposite sidewalk and world fame.

3. King of The Hill

Because of the date of his birth and because of the regulations of the Board of Education (lucky for this story) Davey Flaxman entered public school in midterm, February. He was not quite six, and had been in this strange new world of school no more than a couple of weeks when the teacher, Miss Dawson, announced that the next day, February 22, was a holiday, to celebrate the birthday of our first president, George Washington, and there would be no school. Indeed, the school would be closed (but Davey's best friend Chick, wise in the ways of the world, said that the school custodian, Mr. Ogden, would have to come in to take care of the furnace).

Miss Dawson was not one of the strict ones. She was tired and kind. She said that George Washington was the father of our country, that he led us in both war and peace.

Davey was puzzled by the idea of a holiday. There was no school on Saturday and Sunday, but it was not called a holiday. He was of course aware that not all days were the same, that his parents fasted on a certain day in the year, that firecrackers were shot off on another day. These were some of the unusual days in the changing daily scene, but here after going to school regularly he was told that he would not have to go to school because tomorrow was a holiday, and a Thursday. A holiday meant that you did not have to go to school, just the way, for his father, a holiday meant that he did not have to go to the store. But he usually went to the synagogue on those days.

"Do we have to go anywhere on George Washington's birthday?" Davey asked his older brother Abe.

"Are you crazy or sumpin'?" asked Abe. "You don't have to go anywhere. You just don't have to go to school."

There was an assembly and a big picture of George Washington on the wall. He looked very serious, but not angry.

"If he is the father of our country," thought Davey, "who is the mother of our country?" He asked his brother that, but his brother thought that was very funny. He even laughed, and didn't bother to answer. Davey thought it was maybe because he didn't know, but most of the time his brother answered Davey's questions.

Nor had Miss Dawson said who was the mother of the country, but she had said that our country used to be a *colony*, that it belonged to England, and then came the Revolutionary War to make America free from England.

Davey repeated it at the supper table that night.

"Of course," said his father, "he was like Moses: he led his people to freedom."

"Is there a holiday for Moses' birthday too?" asked Davey.

Although he had only been in school for a few weeks, and although Miss Dawson was not strict like some of the other teachers, but tired and kind, Davey liked the idea of no school somewhere in the middle of the week. He did not find it much fun to sit in one place for about five hours every day.

Mr. Flaxman laughed at Davey's question. It seemed that most questions about holidays made people laugh.

"Passover is the celebration of the freedom of the Jews," he said. "I don't know about Moses' birthday. I don't know if it's written in the Bible or not."

On that day, in that year, February 22 was cold. It had snowed the day before, snowed heavily and steadily, and then in the early hours of the morning it had stopped snowing, a bitter wind quieted down, and snow lay evenly on the streets, with the far-off quiet of snow.

The kids came out early, lured by the snow, the heaviest snow of the season. Some of the bigger kids carried ice skates, on their way to the park, from which news had spread that the lake was frozen. Kids of all ages came out with sleds, the older ones off to Snake Hill in the Park, the younger ones to belly-whop on sidewalk and in gutter, racing one another, or seeing who could cover the most distance (complexities of time and space). In those not-exactly pastoral days, play in the gutter was conceivable, actual.

Davey, like most of the little kids, came out to play in the snow-filled streets; they made curious designs in the snow, wrote their names, and the names of others, in the snow, wrote random numbers or showed their arithmetic powers in more detail, made little houses and other architectural shapes, made snowballs and hurled them at likely targets, including one another.

Snow is not a pervasive element for New Yorkers. Some winters there is hardly any snow at all, not enough to make a firm snowball to say nothing of the minihouse, and to say less than nothing of the great hill which was slowly formed by the work of many hands, a firmly packed hill with a solid base, not so much soaring as rising to a height of eleven, twelve feet—no Mount McKinley, but a fine, even impressive hill in the eyes of Davey and his friends to play on, and what game is more likely to be played on such a hill than King of the Hill?

Of all the simple, basic games in the world, what *can* compare (for basicness and simplicity) with King of the Hill? Someone, by decisiveness or speed, or after formal choosing, gets to the top of a hill, most often stone, but the material is indifferent—snow is just fine. Why should *he* be on top of the hill? Why should he have the greater view? And above all, why should he look *down* on everyone else? Why should he be alone up there, even in splendor, and the rest milling about on the flat earth, hardly possessing that ground, sharing it, certainly not in control, and he up there King of the Hill? These were some of the questions that went through the minds of Davey, of Chick, Richie, Benjy, and the other kids, as they looked up at Allie, secure atop the snow hill, gazing down in disdain at the groundlings, daring them, by his presence and manner (for few on top of the hill will act in a modest or casual way, in an unkingly manner), to dislodge him from his lofty perch.

That is not the most difficult of tasks. It sometimes takes time; there are repulses, for the would-be king can be pushed off, even tumbled ignominiously down the hill; but after a while, in the fullness and necessity of time, by a swift ascent, by curious distractions, by a planned movement, maybe flanking, of two or three aspirants ("You go slow up that side, you start to holler, I'll sprint up the other side") the king was dethroned, and a new king was in command of the height. No one of them was king forever.

Now while these efforts were being made (the succession was always violent, not hereditary), Jerry appeared on the scene. He was one of the big guys on the block, Chick's older brother, a sophomore at CCNY, and a keen and eager analyst of any situation at all. He paused to observe the scene and then to comment on it.

"Some day to play King of the Hill."

"Whaddya mean?" asked Benjy.

"I mean," said Jerry, "that today, as you well know, is George Washington's birthday, and there were some people in America who thought that he ought to be made king, forgetting the nature of the colonial struggle."

Jerry, in making this point, forgot that he was talking to six-year-olds, then remembered that he was talking to six-year-olds, and said:

"I mean, some people forgot that we got rid of one King George by fighting a war, so what was the sense of having another king. It turned out that his name would have been George too."

"A president is better'n a king," said Benjy.

"Why?" asked Jerry, suddenly seeing himself as Socrates.

"Because," said Benjy, "he's elected."

"So what's so great about being elected?" asked Jerry, suddenly seeing himself as the Devil's Advocate.

Benjy seemed puzzled, couldn't come up with an answer, so Chick chimed in:

"If you're elected, it means you know what the president *stands* for—he has to tell you. A king doesn't have to tell you nothing if he doesn't want to."

Benjy made a swift movement up the snow hill, was easily repulsed, just about managed to come down on his feet.

"That's very good," said Jerry to Chick, suddenly seeing himself as the Encouraging Older Brother, rather than the older brother.

"Yah," said Benjy, "all you have to do to be a king is to be a king's son."

Noting that Allie seemed bemused up there on top of the hill, Richie sprinted up, but Allie shook off his bemusement at the sound of approach and thwarted this new challenge, more than ever King of the Hill, though truth to tell, he was beoming a bit bored with the loneliness of his position and somewhat yearned for the company, commonplace though it was, of the groundlings down there. He was no doubt ready to be toppled, but aware of his own vulnerability he showed the greater determination in a fierceness of mien, a stubbornness of posture, to remain King of the Hill.

Jerry was a Freudian, and he thought, watching the game, that here was another illustration of the theory of the Primal Horde, the banding of the brothers (though on a somewhat individuated basis) to topple the father from his throne and then to win the mother, though she seemed to be nowhere in the game (murder, he also thought, is much less of a taboo than incest).

Chick moved up the hill warily, and while Allie covered his movements, Davey sprinted up, pushed Allie (who was ready to be overthrown) off the top of the hill. He slid in a babyish way down the slope, and now Davey was King of the Hill.

Jerry was also a Marxist (it was before the time of the Freudo-Marxists) and he saw this game as another illustration of the endless struggle for power that was going on everywhere, but the kids would soon be finished with this game and start on another, for it was George Washington's birthday, no school all day.

4. The Ball

When Davey came out, the block was pretty empty. There were, of course, adults here and there. Then Chick came out of his house and the block was no longer empty. It was early spring; the weather was on the raw side, but moving in the direction of a more consistent warmth. Winter was gone and forgotten, its trials and triumphs. Davey, who had come out of his apartment house tossing a ball, which he caught one-handed, two-handed, or occasionally with his hand cupped backward, threw the ball to Chick, a long, looping throw which Chick caught without any trouble. He threw the ball back, and there followed a varied interchange—hard fast ones, pop flies, skipping grounders and easy grounders, a couple of high ones— before the friends came together.

"Where's everybody?" asked Chick.

"They'll be around," said Davey. "It's early."

So it was, a little after three—both kids had dashed into their apartments, dumped their books, gulped down glasses of milk, made incoherent replies to mothers' questions, and rushed back into the street, trailing words of hail and farewell.

"Lotta homework?" asked Davey.

"Not much," replied Chick.

"Me too," said Davey, and they got into a game of sidewalk boxball, each in his own lined square, trying to place and cut the ball in the enemy box so as to make a return impossible. Davey won, eleven to eight, and then, walking toward the schoolyard, they tossed the ball back and forth, their conversation interrupted as one or the other ran into the gutter to retrieve the ball which he had either missed or which had been thrown out of catching range. It was always possible to argue the case. Then they continued the conversation.

Before reaching the schoolyard they played a game of points against a desirable wall. One foot on the sidewalk, one in the gutter, the trick was to hit the ledge and catch the ball on the fly, without, naturally, getting both feet on the sidewalk. Davey led, eight to six, then Chick got three points in a row and went on to win, twelve to ten in accord with the rule that if both players reached ten, the winning spread must be two points. The theory is that if you're that close at so late a stage, the winner must decisively prove his superiority. Then they continued their catch, crossed the gutter—the traffic was always light enough for gutter games—and came to the schoolyard.

This yard was protected as though there were untold millions buried inside. There was a long stone wall into which were set iron gratings (they certainly did not grow from that wall) culminating in spikes, and the wall was broken in the middle to allow for an iron gate extending higher than those spikes. That gate was locked, but it had thin iron columns so spaced (somebody had goofed), through which the younger kids, the thinner older kids, could shimmy. Davey and Chick were of the climbing age.

It was now about half past three, and the boys looked for signs of the school custodian. All the doors in the schoolyard were closed. There were no signs of the custodian. So they hopped the rampart and gingerly climbed over the spikes. Who was not aware of the consequences of a mishap? Then they jumped into the yard and Chick ran for the corner, transformed by the expanse of this yard into a fleet end on some out-of-town college football team. Davey waited until the receiver was in the clear and then threw a long lazy pass which Chick gauged and was about to snatch from the air when Davey suddenly hollered:

"Look out!" and pointed to one of the side doors where stood the burly figure of the custodian.

Chick, thrown off balance by the cry, turned to where Davey was pointing, saw the figure of authority, missed the ball (after being in perfect position), paused, went for the ball, scooped it up, veered circularly left, and sprinted for the gate, where Davey was waiting and encouraging his friend. They shimmied through the gate and stood there on the outside. The custodian hadn't moved at all.

The boys looked into the yard, at the scene of an imminent disaster avoided, now swiftly forgotten as they began once again to toss the ball back and forth, in an interlude which was also an activity. Davey was practicing a bounce with heavy English. He flipped it toward Chick and the ball veered, sometimes more successfully than others, away from Chick.

"Pretty good English," said Chuck, though he was not too pleased at the ball's moving away from him that way as though it had a life of its own. That erratic movement somehow violated the character of a catch.

Chick then threw the ball up and tried to catch it with his right hand cupped behind him, against his side. It was a fancy maneuver which was in season, had the character of a catch, but one from which Davey was excluded.

Then they started a game of Chinese handball against the high, outside school wall, where they were joined by Richie and Allie, who appeared first as spectators and then joined as participants. This can be a long game, it was a long game, for the kids were fairly equal in ability, made impossible saves, and so kept the ball in transit until the inevitable killer or faulty return.

A number of other kids had gathered round, first absorbed in the mechanics, in the conflicting loyalties, and then, growing restive, expressed their disapproval at what they considered the undue length of the game.

"Come on, cut the stalling."

"Break it up, let's choose up a punchball game."

The game finally ended, no more quickly than if the players had not been egged on, and then they chose up, not a game of punchball, but one of boxball—genuine gutter boxball, five to a side, a game of grounders, for anything hit on a fly outside the base paths was out. The teams were pretty even, the play was exciting, and then, in the fourth inning, with the score three up, it started to rain. This was none of your indecisive rains—drizzle or mizzle—but the real thing, a downpour that would quickly drench, and the players scattered into convenient hallways.

"Hey," hollered Davey, "my ball."

That object was in the hands of the opposing pitcher, who was preparing to make his throw when the rains came and then started to move toward the most convenient hallway. He could have asked who owned the ball but he did not. The sudden, drastic nature of the rain was a factor in his favor. He threw the ball to Davey, who, as he ran into the courtyard, into the hallway, dried and cleaned the ball; that is, he removed the dirt from the ball to his own hands.

What is more pleasurable than looking out into the rain from a protected place in the company of a group of friends? Bound by so trivial a danger, they talked teachers, girls, and baseball, boasted about fathers, ran one another down (a little pushing, nothing serious), formed and broke cliques, cursed and praised one another and friends not there. The ball was always in evidence. Davey threw it up and caught it, threw it up and somebody snatched it. The ball was passed around, bounced, dribbled, thrown off the ceiling and walls, against steps, now and then went into the courtyard. "Get it." "*You* threw it." "Nah." After a rough consensus, someone finally ran out and retrieved the ball, rubbed it on the floor to dry, so rubbing in the dirt, and tossed it to the owner.

The rain did not stop as dramatically as it had started, but gradually let up. An occasional passerby was seen, either scooting against the building walls or walking serenely under an umbrella. Every now and then one of the kids zoomed out, and finally Davey, Chick, and Allie were left. They stepped into the courtyard.

"It's practically stopped raining."

"Yah, that's just drops coming down from the roof."

They walked onto the street, where it had definitely stopped raining (their dry outstretched hands proved it), and started to throw the ball around. It was a three-handed catch, with the throwers close enough to one another to be able to talk. Then they spread out and threw flies to one another, but that got boring, so they moved into a baseball game, with two fielders and a hitter who threw the ball against a wall ledge. Each fielder took a section of the gutter, which ordinarily would have been divided into three areas, but under the circumstances of wet, the chalked lines could not be drawn, or if drawn, could not be seen, and so they played pretty much by eye—single, double, or triple being called if the ball landed (uncaught, naturally) into one of the three unchalked areas. The hitter did not run. A ball which fell safe on the opposite sidewalk was a homer. Ground rules provided that balls which landed in the cellar across the street were doubles and balls against the building across the street unless caught, were homers. These rules were not invariant; they were agreed on before each game. The hitter was allowed one out, and the fielder who caught the ball went to bat.

This game was interrupted by loss of the ball, which missed the outstretched hands of Allie (the thrower) and bounced into the open window of the apartment of Mrs. Angst, an aged woman who did not take kindly to the pranks or playtime mishaps of children. The kids on the block usually avoided playing in front of her apartment, for she chased them off, even threw water at them. It was for these reasons that the kids sometimes played in front of her apartment.

The situation was discussed, the problem was analyzed, and the boys came to a decision, a mode of action. It was not clear from observation whether or not Mrs. Angst was at home. There were rooms which were hidden from the outside. It would therefore be hazardous for one of them to climb into the window and recover the ball. No one of them was keen to be enclosed in a room with Mrs. Angst under these circumstances. So this is what they decided. Allie would stand at the end of the courtyard, Chick would be in the hallway, and Davey would ring Mrs. Angst's bell. If Mrs. Angst was not at home (her not answering the bell, after repeated rings, would have to be considered proof, if not conclusive, of that fact), then Allie, the smallest and the most agile, would climb into the window and make the recovery. If Mrs. Angst was at home, then Davey would engage her in conversation and Chick would flash the signal to Allie, who would climb into the window to recover the ball. The attempt was to be made under any circumstances, and if Mrs. Angst slammed the door immediately, why then Allie's safety would depend on his speed.

They took their positions. Davey rang the bell, and waited. Then there were footsteps; and the voice of the old lady: "Who is that?" Davey waved to Chick, to indicate that there was someone in the apartment. But Chick, suddenly cautious, did not relay the message to Allie, for how could he be sure that the old woman would open the door? Then Davey identified himself to Mrs. Angst's satisfaction, for she opened the door, first part of the way, and then, in full recognition of Davey, more of the way. At this point Chick moved swiftly to the doorway and waved to Allie who ran to the window and started to climb in.

"What do you want?" Mrs. Angst asked of Davey.

"A raffle," said Davey, and he pulled a raffle book from his pocket and displayed it. "We want to sell you a raffle for ten cents."

"What kind of a raffle?" asked Mrs. Angst suspiciously, and she started to close the door.

"It's for a good cause," said Davey, holding the door without giving the effect of exerting pressure, "the Franklin A.C."

"It doesn't mean anything," said Mrs. Angst. "Franklin A.C.?"

"It's the name of our club. It's named after Benjamin Franklin. All the kids belong to it. If you get the lucky number, you can win a coffee pot."

"Ten cents for a coffee pot?"

"Ten cents a *chance*. If you get the lucky number, your prize is a coffee pot."

Mrs. Angst waved wearily and said:

"Bang me no tea kettle."

"It's only ten cents. What can you lose?"

"I can lose ten cents," said Mrs. Angst, and finished closing the door.

"Wait, Mrs. Angst," cried Davey, ringing the bell again, "open the door, I want to explain something."

"You've explained enough," said Mrs. Angst, and Davey heard her walking away from the door.

Had he stalled long enough? Hard to say. Allie was fast all right, but he had to creep in quietly—the window had to be raised a bit—then walk on tiptoes halfway across the room, find the ball—could be under the sofa—then tiptoe back again and then out the window. Davey rushed outside and there, in front of the house, were Allie and Chuck, teamed up as a battery, Allie winding up, shaking "no" to Chick's signal, then nodding, and burning the ball in, or throwing a drop, or a spitter, or even the famed double shoot, learned (or guessed) from Baseball Joe, the hero of a popular sports series written by Lester Chadwick.

"It was a breeze," said Allie. "She didn't know from nothing."

Somewhat exhilarated by the success of this maneuver, the kids started to throw the ball around, and then up: first pops, then high flies, and one of those throws landed on a roof. And up they sprinted—the building four stories high—to that roof, and in the growing dusk looked for the ball, found it (just where it had fallen), and took a look at the city from this vantage point. They looked south, saw the park, and way down, just beginning to light up, the apartments and hotels of Central Park South, an area as far from them as the castle of Kubla Khan (where is that?). There was no expression from any of the boys on the grandeur of the view which lay exposed. Their age made unseemly any expressions of aesthetic awe. "Let's go down," and they ran down the steps at breakneck speed, though no one was in pursuit.

Then they were back in the street again. Fathers were coming from work. The schoolyard was dark, the walls and gate looked more like the outside of a medieval fort. The lamp posts went on, or more accurately, the bulbs within the lamps went on. Radii of that light extended partly onto the sidewalk, partly into the gutter. It was more of a street for adults now. Throwing the ball around wasn't so easy—the interruptions were human. "See you, Allie." Then Davey and Chick walked on, not far apart, the ball continuing to move between them, mostly low tosses in the air, and occasionally one of them moved ahead, threading his way through the sidewalk crowd and getting into the clear for a pass. "So long, Chick." Then Davey was on his own. He dribbled a ways, looped the ball through the two bottom rungs of a fire escape ladder, caught the ball on the other side, continued dribbling into his courtyard, and so to his apartment, where it was getting to be time for the evening meal.

5. The Record

You have seen figures entranced, or on a frieze? Well, take a good look at Yelly, on the foul line.

"Hey, move back, can't you see he's gawn for the record?"

This from one of the self-appointed overseers, who retrieved the ball, careful to return it so accurately that Yelly would not have to move from his spot. He protected the boundaries, allowing no one into the area being made sacred.

Yelly was quite immovable, except for a slight flexing of the shoulder muscles, kind of catatonic, or superstitious. His feet were on a line, about a foot apart. Those too he flexed. He threw in the approved underhand style of the day, raising his heels slightly, putting the pressure on the balls of his feet, and then onto his toes when he finished the shot. The throw had reverse twist and was aimed over the front rim of the basket. On the follow-through his hands went up past his head, palms upstretched in the approved Holman style, as it came down to the settlement houses and playgrounds.

It was of course impossible to keep the area free. Here a rubber ball bounded through the space; sometimes a boy from some other game, some other world, stumbled back or ran through. Some of these strangers remained, gave up their own games, their own incertitudes, joined the crowd which stood behind and to the sides of the shooter. Once part of the crowd, the newcomers respected the silence and the circumscribed area.

The count was silent; the number spoken would be at least a distraction, at most a jinx. The viewers silently counted, whispered the number to any newcomer.

"What's he up ta?"

"Shhh, thirty-four."

He was going for the block record, which was fifty-eight. That number was nowhere written but universally known. Nobody questioned that record; it had been set on this very court by Mack, an older fellow. Age meant nothing in these records. Way off was the world record for foul shots, in the hundreds, held by one or another of the *Original Celtics*.

Many a streak had been broken by a poor return, that threw the shooter off balance, broke the spell. Yelly had an excellent ball retriever, who threw the ball in an easy underhand flip, then kind of faded. He said no word; his silence was encouraging.

Most everyone was silently encouraging. Who does not like to see a record broken? Enemies reluctantly join friends part of the way in the sweep toward the record, a kind of impersonal thing.

But it is a goal which can be achieved because it has been achieved (records are meant to be broken), so we have the expectancy of the onlookers and the frozen excitement of the shooter.

It was late afternoon; the sun was down, the scene in early shade.

It was an early afternoon, in the hot glare of the sun, that Mack had set the record of fifty-eight.

The onlookers closely observed Yelly's movements, his "form," for if he was to break the record, then the details would be the key elements in the conversations of the next few days.

Yelly turned the ball so that the stitches were horizontal, a bit toward him, then moved the ball back and forth a few times. The pressure was on the thumbs and the tips of his fingers. His palms did not touch the ball.

Swish! Forty-two. Only two of his throws, the fourteenth (which angled slightly off the backboard) and the twenty-first (which teetered on the back rim before dropping), had not gone cleanly through the nets.

There was a moan, a stir of displeasure among the spectators. The Jinx had appeared. He brought bad luck even to his own side. The divisions in the crowd (for despite the seeming unanimity, there were some who wished failure on Yelly, out of animosity, or in admiration for the old record-holder) now closed to make a front against the sorcerer.

"Beat it, Jinx." But he stood his ground, even if that was on the outskirts of the crowd. You couldn't make a commotion and so throw off the shooter. There were harsh looks and gestures of awayness. The Jinx wasn't on, for Yelly survived his appearance and then his presence. He survived too the appearance of Mrs. Angst and the confusion she brought. Mrs. Angst came for her son, a boy of nine, deep in the crowd. She caught sight of him and shouted, the way you do after you've looked and looked and then suddenly found.

"Shhh. Can't you see he's going for the record?"

"What kind of record? Jerry, I'm calling you, *I'm calling you.*"

But the boy shrank into the crowd, waiting for the outcome with all the others, his peers for the moment. Against the hushed warnings of the crowd she fought her way, sullen and oblivious, and reached her son, he in silent movement. The wrath of the crowd turned against the boy. "Beat it, Jerry!" "Take your old lady with you." So isolated, the boy was helpless, angry. He let himself be dragged out of the crowd, out of the schoolyard.

Yelly did not look around, kept the hieratic pose he had adopted once the record was in sight. The first throws had been casual. He moved back and forth from the line, spoke to friends, became more involved when he hit nine and ten. That cut off the conversation and the movement, isolated him in his fixed position.

Some athletes fear to succeed, fear the completion, prefer the role of the loser, the runner-up.

But Yelly was not the losing type. He was not terrified of the victory, went right for it, reached the fifty-eight mark, and then passed it. Setting the new record (once the old is broken) has an easeful glory all its own. Each new successful toss makes it that much harder for the contenders, who are everywhere in the crowd, cheering and denying you.

The sixty-fourth throw hit the front rim and bounced back. He was surrounded.

"Boy! Sixty-three."

"Wait till Mack hears about it."

But Yelly was already beginning to melt into the crowd of record breakers and contenders, winners and losers.

6. The Winners

"Hurry up," said Mrs. Mandel to her husband, "we're already late."

"I'll be ready in a second," said Mr. Mandel. "Benjy isn't ready anyway."

"He's waiting for us outside," she answered, which meant (as she knew) that he had got into a ball game in the street and would probably have to wash all over again. He was nine.

It wasn't usual for Mr. Mandel to be late this way, but he was not too anxious to visit the Josephses who had just moved uptown into a large apartment house, with an elevator, only two blocks away from the Drive. This fact, this location, constituted a challenge to Mr. Mandel's earning power, a challenge which his wife did not fail to hurl at him on appropriate occasions.

Mr. Mandel was a furrier, highly skilled and (in the season) well paid. He and Mr. Josephs had worked together for a number of years till the latter had decided to go into business for himself, a move attended with many perils. After some difficult years, Mr. Josephs established himself in the trade, employing as many as thirty men in the busy season.

"Oh, Benjy," said Mrs. Mandel, "just look at you!"

The boy, who had just run into the apartment, was good and dirty. Particularly outstanding was his shirt, which was darkly smudged, or stained.

"I fell," he explained.

By the time he was readied for the trip, Mr. Mandel had also whipped himself into readiness, and they left.

When they reached the uptown apartment house, they had to ring downstairs and then they heard Mrs. Josephs's voice asking who it was. Benjy was intrigued, but Mr. Mandel refused to be impressed, saying: "Next we will have to prove who we are before we can get into his house."

Then they had to wait for the elevator, and inform the elevator man of their destination, and then walk down a long hall and ring the Josephes' bell.

"Hello," cried Mrs. Josephs, "come in."

And she swept them into the foyer; while she was hanging their coats Mr. Josephs came in and shook hands with the calmness, close to urbanity, which had always characterized his most formal social behavior.

Mrs. Mandel handed Mrs. Josephs the tin of candy which they had purchased on the way uptown, saying, "Lots of luck in your new apartment."

Mr. Mandel muttered something along the same lines and accepted in silence the thanks of Mr. and Mrs. Josephs.

They went into the living room. Carpeted from wall to wall, it had a *set* of furniture, including a china closet gleaming with cut glass.

"Harold," called out Mrs. Josephs, "Benjy is here."

The son, about Benjy's age, came out of a bedroom. He was by no means nattily dressed, and Benjy threw an angry, resentful look at his parents. Harold invited the guest into his room, and the two boys disappeared, but first Mrs. Josephs offered Benjy a dish full of macaroons and slices of honey cake and sponge cake. He chose a macaroon, and turned down the offer of a glass of milk.

"You have a very large living room," said Mrs. Mandel.

"It is very comfortable," said Mrs. Josephs. "Would you like to see the rest of the apartment?"

This is an invitation which few have the courage to turn down.

Back in the living room, they looked out the window and Mrs. Mandel admired the view of the river.

"Yes," said Mr. Josephs, "it gives you a sense of distance, of repose."

He spoke in a rather manorial manner, proud but a little bored with the formalities.

Mr. Mandel could not help thinking that Mrs. Mandel was thinking of their apartment, quite adequate when they moved in, but now grown old and dark, old and crowded with the years.

Then they sat down and Mrs. Josephs placed before them a bowl of fruit, overflowing with oranges, apples, grapes, and some figs.

They picked and chose from this dish, and conversed—Mr. Josephs with Mr. Mandel, Mrs. Josephs with Mrs. Mandel.

They got onto the subject of politics, and then into that wider realm where economics and politics meet.

Mr. Mandel maintained that the standard of living was steadily rising and, given normal expansion, would continue to rise within the framework of capitalist society.

"And what is normal expansion?" asked Mr. Josephs. "Normal expansion is imperialism, normal expansion is war."

The dogged sectarianism of the socialist of 1926 was unflagging.

"You are too young," said Mr. Josephs, "to remember the depression of 1907. Otherwise you would understand how things shrank—capital, production, jobs, everything."

Mr. Mandel did not think that the seven-year seniority of the expanding manufacturer merited that rather supercilious tone.

"You do not have to lecture me about the depression of 1907," he said. "One does not have to experience completely in order to understand. Take death, for example."

At the mention of death, the two women looked up.

"The fact is," said Mr. Mandel, "that we emerged from the depression of 1907 stronger than ever and have been climbing ever since."

"You forget," said Mr. Josephs, "the small matter of the World War."

"Well," said Mr. Mandel, who had been a soldier in that war, "we got out of that too. Life progresses by upheaval, by no easy stages."

"By holocausts," said Mr. Josephs, "by one rigged Armageddon after another, by exploitation and the making of surplus value which then must be *shot* away."

"Exploitation," said Mr. Mandel pointedly, "begins at home."

"Look, Mandel," said Josephs, "in business it is dog eat dog. Do you think I should let myself be pushed into the gutter? Do you think I can act what I believe and *survive?*"

"Pure *fakerei*," said Mr. Mandel. "You know what is the right thing and you can't do it; what would you expect of those who do not know the truth?"

"I am trying to tell you," said Mr. Josephs with an air of patience, "that life and theory do not belong together. It is an insoluble conflict; knowing the good, we must do the bad."

"Knowing what good?" asked Mr. Mandel. "This cockeyed notion of a millennium where the capitalist and the proletarian will lie down together? And meanwhile you milk the cow dry. Is that the good?"

"How many times," asked Mr. Josephs, "in how many ways must I tell you that we must *personally* operate against the greatest good? From this contradiction twentieth-century man cannot escape.

"Tea," he said rather sharply, "let us have tea."

"Twentieth-century man *bubkes*," said Mr. Mandel. "You are only hiding your selfishness and your acquisitiveness behind a lot of high-sounding words. You are ten times worse than the boss who is out to get what he can but manages to be decent to his workers."

This comment referred to wage troubles which Mr. Josephs was having with his employees.

The tea being delivered, Mr. Josephs drank heavily from his glass.

"To maintain the production," he said, "I must strike a certain balance between the profit and the expense."

Mr. Mandel laughed uproariously.

"Surplus value," he cried, "there's surplus value for you!"

Mr. Josephs put his glass down vigorously, so vigorously that some of the tea spilled onto the new rug.

"What are you doing?" cried Mrs. Josephs. "On the new rug!"

"It is only water," said Mr. Josephs.

"And tea," said Mrs. Josephs, "and sugar, and lemon."

Mr. Josephs was upset by the accidental, topical intrusion into the frame of historic necessity.

"All right," he said, "all right."

This little accident had the effect of slowing down the conversation; it was clear that the high point of sociability had been reached and passed. There remained the second glass of tea, the farewell, and the departure.

Just at this time, when sociability had retreated, so to say, to a secondary level, a new diversion was created in the form of a series of cries, the sound of a struggle from the bedroom where the boys had been playing.

All looked up in surprise at this sudden outburst from a quarter which had been far too quiet all this time.

Then the door was pushed open and Benjy Mandel appeared, in the manner of a victor.

"I won the game," he said, "and he tried to take the winnings away from me."

"What game, what winnings?" cried Mrs. Josephs. "Where is Harold?"

Harold appeared in the doorway behind Benjy. He was bleeding lightly from the lip and whimpering. His mother rushed up to him and dabbed at the blood with a handkerchief.

"We were playing Monopoly," groaned Harold, as if in explanation.

"How come *you're* so, so—untouched?" Mrs. Josephs cried to the victorious youth.

"I learned that from Benny Leonard," said Benjy.

He held a make-believe microphone in front of him and shouted: "Hya, Mom. He never even touched me."

"That will be enough," said Mrs. Mandel, in the special tone of the mother of the victorious child, proud and as-if-chastising.

Mr. Josephs and Mr. Mandel stared at each other while the women fussed with the children, Mrs. Josephs binding up the wounds of her child and Mrs. Mandel managing to find some hurt in the victorious child.

Mr. Josephs was stonily preoccupied, while Mr. Mandel, in his mind, was trying to formulate the phrase about the generations and shirtsleeves, got caught up in the rhythm of *from Moses to Moses there was only one Moses,* then smiled openly at the thought of making some comment about the famous triumvirate of *Tinker to Evers to Chance.*

But to his credit he kept his counsel, though Mr. Josephs was not unaware of the smile which passed over the face of his guest, and Mr. Josephs put the worst possible interpretation on that smile.

"Thank you very much for everything," said Mrs. Mandel. "Best luck and *naches* in your new apartment."

There was a rather formal handshake between the men, and then the Mandels left. Mrs. Josephs accompanied them to the elevator.

"Boy," said Benjy Mandel, "is he going to get it."

"Quiet," said Mrs. Mandel, and Mr. Mandel looked agreeably at the child, on account of his victory, and because of the temporary respite from the complaining, the *nudjing,* which would follow as a result of this victory.

7. Homage to Benny Leonard

"What's wrong with him?" asked Mr. Flaxman as Davey got up from the table, where he had sat morosely through the meal, and walked off.

Mrs. Flaxman shrugged, as though to say that she could not choose among the numerous possibilities.

When, a moment later, Davey walked back into the dining room to pull out the ball which was securely lodged between the floor and the bottom of the bureau, his father asked him, "What is it, David?"

It was David's turn to shrug his shoulders. "Nothing, Pop."

"A fine nothing," said his father. "One could die looking at you."

"I'm telling you, Pop, it's nothing," and he walked slowly out of the house.

When the door closed quietly behind him, did not slam, Mr. Flaxman said to his wife, "What is it, they don't tell you anything?"

There was an implied criticism here, the burden for the child's nonconfiding was suddenly put on the mother.

"You were probably no different at that stage, that's how the children are."

Mr. Flaxman was momentarily bemused, as he thought of his far-off childhood, the childhood that is twice as far off for the immigrant as for the native-born.

"To tell you the truth," he said, "who remembers?"

Since the problem had not come into full light, he shook it off, the more so when his wife said, "I wonder what's bothering him. You think he's not feeling well? Maybe I'll take his temperature."

Mr. Flaxman shook the thing further away from him, shook it almost into nonbeing.

The sports pages of that morning's newspaper told the story of Davey's grief. It was the defeat of Benny Leonard, one of the three defeats this remarkable champion was ever to suffer in the ring.

Benny was the boy's hero. On the short side himself, putting his reliance on skill, speed, dexterity, what the kids called "form," it was only natural that Davey should identify this way with the peerless lightweight.

Stories he had heard at home of the old world pogroms and persecutions had created an uncertainty, a fear, which required a defender. This defender was required against no present foe but against some unknown future enemy, even against the monstrous foes of the past—Haman, Antiochus Epiphanes, the thundering Black Hundreds.

It was no accident that at this time (later his heroes were the mighty figures Ruth and Dempsey) he needed the prince-hero, the 135-pounder who could weave, parry, outguess his opponent, jab, feint, dance off, and yet throw the sudden knockout punch, and then come dancing into the middle of the ring, his dark hair unruffled, saying into the microphone: "Hi, Mom, he never touched me."

At this moment Daniel Mendoza would not do, but Benny Leonard would.

He remembered his mother's story. She was taking care of the store in their Russian village. Suddenly the cry "Cossacks!" She quickly locked up the store, ran desperately. How Davey wished he could have been there to defend her. . . .

"Hi, Davey."

It was Chick, also out in the street for that glorious hour between supper and sleep.

"What's eatin' you, Davey?"

When Davey mentioned the fight, Chick was surprised. He couldn't understand that much of a reaction.

"So what," said Chick, "you can't win them all."

Chick was one of those kids who had more easily thrown off his ghetto past. He did not seem to carry within him the ancient walled cities, the nighttime assaults and terrors; he did not dream of the bearded Jew shot to death in the tunnels under the New York Central Railway up on Park Avenue. He took for granted the prevailing freedom, was not drawn to the ancient midnight, nor was he disturbed by vague and monstrous presentiments, menacing shadows. He was well adjusted historically.

This rather flippant attitude on Chick's part both angered and relieved Davey, the anger because his friend did not share his woe, the relief because his friend kept him from sinking deeper and deeper into this woefulness.

It was not yet dark, just light enough to see a ball, so they had a catch, throwing the ball back and forth in a leisurely manner—slow balls, curves, floaters, and an occasional fireball down the groove. Allie and Richie joined them, and they got into a quick game of boxball, playing under the lamp post. Then it was too late to play, and they sauntered down the block toward the candy store.

"Last one down is a rotton egg," said Chick, and the four of them were off in a flash. Allie, a P.S.A.L. runner, won easily, by four or five boxes. Richie, who was kind of heavy, pulled up a game last.

"You're the rotton egg," said Chick, but the satisfaction was not abiding.

Inside the candy store they picked and chose among the sponges, the caramels, the licorices, the creams, in the secure and exciting candy world.

Coming out, at their ease, chewing or biting or sucking or crunching, they paused near a group of the Big Guys who were hanging around in front of the store. They stood close enough to the Big Guys to hear everything that was being said, but far enough away (they hoped) not to disturb them.

Included among these Big Guys was a lad who was not so much a stranger (for he was one of those nomadic types who thought it nothing to wander three or four blocks from his own block) as what you might call a "border figure"; he hung around enough so that he was no stranger, but still he did not belong, because he did not live on the block. There was always an element of suspicion attached to one who did not live on the block. He was called "The Gate," or when he was addressed directly, "Gate." This nickname apparently referred to the figure he once had, wide and formidable. There were some signs of that old figure, out of which he had grown, and yet he kept the nickname (like a tall "Pee Wee" or a gray-haired "Red"). A later school of sociologists may decide that the nickname "Gate" refers to the blocking maneuver, founded on superstition, or suspicion, in a dice game.

Now the conversation of the Big Guys was not of a particularly profound sort. It related to given individuals, mixed praise with the most severe criticism, the foulest maledictions, and was punctuated by expectorations geared for aim or distance. But to Davey and his friends, age conferred, if not dignity, a certain awe, because of that extra measure of experience, the activities just beyond them, so they listened, hoping to get closer to the unknown, the forbidden, and to be initiated painlessly into the mystery of the stage ahead.

But this cynical adoration on the part of the youngsters (for it was not exactly improvement they were looking for) did not predispose *all* of the Big Guys in their favor. Some were pleased, some paid them no mind, but The Gate, who looked around and saw these blemishes on the landscape, said: "Whatta you kids hangin' roun' for?"

At this question the four of them, in a kind of reflex movement, seemed to come closer together, but nobody made a move, for it was clear that the taunter was not serious in his intentions.

The scattered interchange of praise and invective went on; two of the older fellows lit up cigarettes, but The Gate was not one of those two.

"Beat it, you shrimps," he said.

This statement was not yet the one requiring flight (though it was a move in that direction from the previous question) because it was a command, but without a threat attached.

None of the Big Guys showed much interest in The Gate's annoyance. They looked at it as a kind of eccentricity, but with a sure knowledge that there *was* a motive, inexplicable to be sure, but the kind of motive that could induce any one of them, under similar pressures, to behave quite the same way. One of them said, tolerantly, "Aw, leave the kids alone, Gate."

But this friendly admonition only angered him the more. It was as though he was being opposed not only by the silent four, but by these contemporaries of his in whose company he was still somewhat of an outsider, where he still had to prove himself.

"Get goin'," said The Gate, "befaw I roon yiz."

Here was the command, and the threat, but no overt move. The Gate's rhetorical string was played out—his next move was pursuit. Again one of the Big Guys put a cautionary word to him, asking: "What's the diff if they stay here?" implying the acceptance and even enjoyment of the kids' somewhat idle homage.

"Because they're a buncha wise kids, that's what," said The Gate, and it was just then that Davey tossed up his ball, catching it in his backward-cupped hand.

Here, finally, was a reason, an act of insubordination to justify The Gate's wrath. He had been publicly humiliated.

"Aw right now," he said, and then he made his move. His intensions were obviously to disperse this group, swiftly, by this move in their direction, and then to return to the charmed circle, quietly triumphant.

To his surprise (and deepening chagrin), one of the four detached himself from the group and advanced toward him, on his toes, in the approved boxing stance. The taunter was being taunted. In the few seconds between Davey's first move and his near approach The Gate realized in what an absurd predicament he now found himself, forced to do battle with a kid three years younger and maybe thirty pounds lighter. To take on four of the kids was one thing; to find himself isolated with the one was monstrous. A victory could be only hollow and meaningless, a defeat catastrophic. He had no way of coming out at all. He looked longingly at Chick, Allie, and Richie, hoping they would move in to do battle, but they had stopped in their headlong flight, and were watching in fascination as their comrade-in-arms advanced on the enemy.

"Go way, ya runt," said The Gate to Davey, "go back tu da cradle."

In reply, Davey threw a left jab which grazed The Gate's cheek.

Some of the Big Guys snickered. It was quite easy for them to turn against this suspect border figure.

The Gate had to protect himself, for to be hit by the kid was in itself an embarrassment, perhaps not so bad as sloughing him, but certainly shameful enough. The Gate's position was deteriorating fast; he could find help neither from his friends nor from his enemies.

Davey, meanwhile, was desperately trying to remember everything he had read about his hero's style. "Keep jabbin' him," he said to himself, "jab him crazy, look for the opening, and if you don't find it move back. Then jab away again."

He followed his own instructions to the letter. The Gate had to adopt a fighting stance in order to avoid the ignominy of being hit. Davey was fighting against an immovable target, for if The Gate were to start moving forward that would constitute an offensive, and The Gate realized that after he was out of this absurd predicament he would have to be able to say: "The kid went crazy, I just kept blocking his punches."

But that turned out not to be the case, for every now and then one of Davey's blows landed, and each jab was a monstrous humiliation for the older boy.

Davey was in a kind of euphoria, imitating the image of himself, and every now and then realizing that it was all real, that he had fled the imaginary world where victory was dearly but surely won and was struggling here in the street, where the issue was always in doubt. Once more he jabbed at The Gate, struck him lightly under the eye and danced off, but not before The Gate, helpless and infuriated, struck out blindly and hit Davey high up on the cheek.

The Gate advanced threateningly.

"Why doncha grow up?" he asked, but Davey's answer was a long left jab. One of the Big Guys snickered.

This ambiguous bout was brought to an end by a passerby, one of those gents whose sense of justice is outraged by the sight of an obviously unequal struggle (as contrasted to one of those gents whose sense of—exactly what?—is outraged by the sight of an obviously equal struggle).

"Here, break it up, you two."

The Gate turned toward this gentleman with a look of the deepest gratitude. "You are a veritable Nestor," he seemed to be saying, "a depository of the most profound truths buried in the heart of mankind."

Davey was perhaps less pleased with the turn of events, and would have been even more less pleased had his cheekbone not begun to swell and cause some discomfort.

"That'll loin ya," said The Gate, as Davey walked off with his friends, but this remark was meant for what record?

Davey was considerably cheered. He understood as well as the next one that the Big Guy had pulled his punches, but he was pleased with his own exhibition. Looking back, he saw himself in the classic weave, felt the acclaim of his invisible mentor.

"That was nice goin'," said Richie admiringly, and Davey felt also the approbation of the others. Then they walked each other home, and finally Davey and Chick stood together in the early darkness. They spoke seriously of matters of import, of the latest trade in the American League, of the next club meeting, of the distance of the furthest star.

"So long," said Chick, "see ya."

"So long," said Davey, and he sprinted to the door of his apartment, then opened the door slowly, hoping to avoid at least a direct appearance before his parents.

He reached his room without being seen, and raised a warning finger to his lips at his brother Danny, as he opened and closed the door.

"Who socked you?" asked the younger brother.

"The Gate," said Davey, and he gave a blow-by-blow description.

Danny was proud, envious, and disbelieving.

"You don't have to believe me," said Davey, "just ask anyone tomorrow."

Then he got onto his bed and started on his homework. He wasn't at it long when his sister Joan, who was between the two boys in age, entered noiselessly.

"Did you see my *Little Women?*" she asked.

Davey denied any knowledge of the whereabouts of this work; Danny denied any knowledge of the very meaning of the question.

"It's a book," she said, "and I'm sure you know where it is."

The last part of the sentence was directed to Davey, who had been facing the wall, but now turned round to meet the gaze of his accuser.

She gasped with interest.

"What happened to you?" she asked.

"Oh, it's nothing," he said, "but don't tell Mom and Pop about it."

"If it's nothing," she asked, "why can't I tell them?"

"Instead of being so smart," he said, "why don't you think of something that will help?"

"Beefsteak," said Danny, who was steeped in all sorts of esoteric lore, "that will reduce the swelling."

"That's the same as steak," said Davey to his sister. "See if there's any in the kitchen."

She went and returned with a piece of steak in her hand.

"Great," said Davey, and he applied the meat to his cheek.

There was an instant of silence; then he opened his mouth with every intention of shrieking bloody murder, remembered the danger of disclosure, and bit into the meat, his eyes shut in agony.

"What's the matter?" gasped Joan.

"It burns," he said, "real bad."

They both looked at Danny, whose look of puzzlement suddenly passed into the area of understanding.

"Naturally," he said, "Mom salted the meat already."

"You're a girl," said Davey to Joan, "you should know all about these things."

"Don't bother me," said Joan, as she beat a retreat in the face of her brother's repeated admonitions to say absolutely nothing.

"They'll see it in the morning," said Danny sagaciously.

But Davey was not taking such a long view. He asked Danny to bring some milk and crackers, and they ate and drank together.

Then it was Danny's bedtime, and Davey, to avoid discovery and because he was tired, got into bed himself. Deep in his soul he exulted, having fought in the manner of his peerless champion, and for his vindication.

8. You're *It*

It was a little after five, the sun was beginning to lose its power for the day, and the three couples were sitting on the screened porch, in the early summertime, mostly with drinks in hand. They were all on vacation, had begun to soak up sun and surf, and, now, in the established ritualistic manner, were spending the time between exposure and dinner in this social communion.

"You're *it!*" cried Teddy Horton, the eight-year-old child of the host and hostess, and he tagged Danny Levy, son of one of the visiting couples.

From their vantage point, the six adults became, in an instant, the audience of a most ancient game. The five children—three from neighboring houses (for the Thurlows, the final couple, were childless)—who had been playing in a haphazard manner, with occasional struggles of a short-lived though sometimes dramatic character, were suddenly transfigured, being chosen for parts in a drama of unusual intensity.

The four fled from Danny as though he were the carrier of a plague, one whose touch meant danger, desecration, humiliation; they fled from Danny to avoid the touch that transmitted the nameless horror.

Teddy, Barry, and Jackie scattered in various directions, but Gus, who was the youngest, made for the scrub oak. This tree was a sanctuary; holding it, one could be tagged with impunity, for then nothing baleful could pass between the *It* and the tree-toucher.

Seeing Gus safe at the sanctuary, and scorning, moreover, the thought of going after the youngest (although he would have carelessly brushed him if he were in the open), Danny lit out after the others. As soon as Danny disappeared, Gus, who had been holding onto the tree quite firmly, now became rather bold. He walked away from the tree, sat down on the grass, followed with fascination the flight of a bird— but all the while he was on the lookout for Danny's reappearance. Tempting the fates this way, he nevertheless strolled back to the tree occasionally, made contact with it, sat down at a point midway between temptation and absolute safety.

When Gus moved away from the sanctuary, he was taking the chance that Danny might suddenly reappear from an unexpected quarter (conceivably behind him), touch him, and transmit the awful thing. But the temptation made the game: by running for the tree and holding on for dear life, the four could put an end to the game—for what self-respecting *It*, under the circumstances, would not have walked off in disgust?

Suddenly Barry appeared from around the corner of the house, Danny Levy in close pursuit. Roused, Gus ran to the tree and reached it a step before Barry, who, breathing heavily, encircled the oak and gazed triumphantly at his unsuccessful pursuer.

"Safe," he cried at Danny, who paused, keeping a lookout for Jackie and Teddy while resting within the shadow of the sanctuary. Then he went back in pursuit.

"That's not quite how we used to play the game," said Mr. Levy, who was a trifle upset that his son had been so ignominiously made *It*, and continued to be *It*. "We had no tree; if you were *It*, you just ran till you tagged someone, and then that person was *It*."

He wished that his son would tag someone, for he felt *It* himself, some of the untouchableness had passed into him. Quite by accident, he brushed Mr. Horton's sleeve as he reached for his drink. Mrs. Levy thought it unfair that the young host should have tagged *her* child when there were three strange children playing, but she said nothing.

"There are different ways of playing the game," said Mr. Horton. "We used to play just this way, except that we'd use a lamp post for *safe.*"

He tried to think of other variants of the game, for he saw himself at the moment as the analyst and historian of the game of Tag, but nothing more came to mind.

"It's a fascinating game," said Mrs. Thurlow, "so simple and kind of . . . awful."

Just then Teddy Horton broke into view, in a mad rush for the now deserted base (for Gus had gone into the field), but Danny was close behind, made the tag, cried "*It,*" turned round, and was off. The chase must have been a long one, for Teddy was winded; he sat down next to the tree which he had vainly tried to reach.

"You see," said Mr. Thurlow, "how the sanctuary receives the unclean as well as the clean."

"I beg your pardon," said Mrs. Horton.

"I mean," went on Mr. Thurlow, "that the notion of a sanctuary interests me. I remember reading in St. Augustine that, in the sack of Rome, the barbarians recognized the churches as sanctuaries, made no move against the Christians or the pagans who took refuge there. It is one of the more noble features of human society that there should be a place so recognized, even 'mid the horrors of war, when all restraints are thrown aside, in which man, relieved of conscience, destroys in a fury of anonymity, all sanctions gone. Why, even in the last war there was a *tendency* to avoid the destruction of certain buildings, call them, if you will, hallmarks of civilization."

The three couples on the porch were not well known to each other; Mrs. Horton, who was a friendly type and believed in bringing the world closer together, had met the Levys at the house of a mutual friend and the Thurlows at a museum opening in town. She never hesitated to invite to her house people whose acquaintance she had recently made, a habit whose social consequences were unpredictable. Until now the conversation had been scattered, for the group did not share enough close friends for serious gossip, and had somehow not been able to hit on any subject that brought them together.

Mr. Thurlow's remarks, however, did have the effect of starting up a fairly spirited discussion, touching on the importance of a room of one's own as a sanctuary from domestic confusion, on bird sanctuaries, on the modern pressures—as shown in Hitler's extermination of the Jews and other examples of genocide—to destroy the concept of sanctuary, a pressure finalized by the appearance of nuclear weapons, whose total destructive power made a mockery of the ancient notion of sanctuary. Then the conversation moved on to nuclear testing and the possibility of its abolition, sane nuclear policy, the French nuclear blast in the Sahara and the awesome possibility of *small* countries becoming members of the Nuclear Club, the problems of detection in underground testing, the hazards of fallout, with particlar emphasis on strontium 90, the feasibility, architecture, and cost of shelters, concluding—after a slowly diminishing masochistic thrill at the prospect of being involved in so inconceivable an orgy of mutual destruction—on a note of futility.

Nullified by contradictory elements and their sense of "What can I do about it?" the conversation died, and they all looked with interest as little Gus suddenly appeared from nowhere (out of the brush) and sank down beside the tree, happy that he had been out there on the battlefield, and happy, too, that he had been able to return in safety. And all were happy for the child— for his courage in testing himself against the older ones, some of them strangers, and his good fortune in avoiding the awful touch.

"Safe at home," sighed Mrs. Thurlow, and then Teddy appeared, trying to pass the thing on to Barry, who dodged and turned, made a dash for the tree, but was overtaken just before he reached it.

"He's *It!*" cried Mrs. Horton, triumphantly.

"It's rather curious," said Mrs. Levy, "that the neuter 'it' is used, as though the person tagged has become a thing. Why not: you're *He* or you're *She?*"

But the question answered itself; they all laughed at the prospect raised.

"It's one of those disguises," said Mr. Horton. "The neutrality of the name (I just can't get myself to use the word 'neuterness') was an attempt to cover the horror of the content, but then the word itself took on the unknown horror, and so was despoiled of its neutrality."

"I can remember when *It* meant sex appeal," said Mrs. Thurlow, but the other women said nothing, either because they did not remember when *It* meant sex appeal or did not want to acknowledge that they remembered when *It* meant sex appeal.

"I am reminded," said Mr. Horton, "of, shall we say, the social difficulties of the lepers in the Middle Ages, who moved from town to town and were denied admittance out of the darkest fear of contagion."

"And the medical fact is," said Mr. Levy, "that the disease is not at all as contagious as was thought. Modern miracle drugs are said to be very effective."

"We know," said Mr. Thurlow, "that such fears tend to be irrational. I need only point to the prevalence of syphilophobia only twenty or thirty years ago. You remember the phrase: 'The Syphilis of the Innocent'? But when it became known that salvarsan was able to cure this disease, the fear of syphilis declined; it is hardly of any significance today."

Whether the fear of syphilis was irrational *before* the introduction of salvarsan was not discussed.

"Well, then," said Mr. Horton (the women were discussing, for the moment, another matter), "this game carries on in the tradition of the ancient uncleanness—the tagged person is become a leper, his touch brings contagion; what is there to do but flee?"

"But did the leper pursue the nonleper?" asked Mr. Levy.

"The healthy ones," said Mr. Thurlow, "always feel that they are being threatened by the diseased ones, and in this game of Tag or *It,* we have a dramatic confirmation of that feeling."

"The fear of the diseased one, by the way," said Mr. Horton, "relates to all sick people, not only to those with contagious or infectious diseases."

"I think that you're going too far there," said Mr. Levy. "I think the fear is confined mostly to infectious and contagious diseases."

"I agree with that," said Mr. Thurlow. "You'd be surprised how many people there are who, after shaking hands (even with a close friend), will not eat till they wash their hands. That also refers to doorknobs, old books, and other objects."

"That's getting into the area of mental disease," said Mr. Levy, who gave the impression that he did not prefer to get into the area of mental disease.

"Well," said Mr. Thurlow, "you are dealing here" (and he waved toward the game, where Barry had just come up noiselessly behind Jackie and put the hex on him) "with the realm of the unconscious and irrational; the kids don't know *why* they're afraid of being *It.* This is a game that they pick up from the older generation, and the fear seems to come along with the game."

"It would be fun," said Mrs. Thurlow (for the women had rejoined the conversation), "if we could play this game sometimes."

The thought of the six of them rushing off in all directions to avoid one another's contact made them laugh, and Mr. Horton said, with a bit more sageness than was absolutely required, "In a certain sense we are playing that game all the time."

"Haven't you ever been touched," asked Mrs. Horton, "in a way that makes you feel absolutely filthy for days—you can't wash it away?"

She hurried off to get some more ginger ale, the conversation subsided, and the adults looked out more closely at the game.

Jackie, who was *It,* was not pleased with the distinction (but some were, loved and sought to be *It,* enjoyed the significance, if not the desecration—and that was another way of destroying the game). He was very anxious to be rid of *It* and moved as swiftly as he could to transmit the unpleasantness. As is often the case, he was betrayed by his anxiety; the others dodged and escaped him in a way they never would have been able to had Jackie been playing in the style of the games where he was not betrayed by his anxiety. Jackie slipped, he ran past his prey, he lunged and broke his stride when in another few steps he would have caught up.

"He certainly is worried and anxious," said Mrs. Levy, in the absence of (not instead of) Jackie's mother.

"He seems actually frightened," said Mr. Horton. "Something seems to have gotten *into* him."

"True," said Mr. Levy. "He's behaving as though something awful will happen to him if he doesn't rid himself of this . . . this incubus."

"The Devil," said Mr. Thurlow. "Casting out of the Devil."

(Mrs. Thurlow giggled, for the three men had given the effect of a kind of academic vaudeville team, each delivering his set piece. She thought it would have been more appropriate if they had risen, advanced a few steps, and then said their pieces.)

Mr. Thurlow's mention of the Devil opened up a new conversational vein: the game was viewed as a self-exorcizing chain, requiring no Black Mass, no Witch's Sabbath or incantation (unless the "You're It!" was the incantation). All that really was needed to rid oneself of the Evil One was simple contact—touching one who was involved, but touching a stranger was useless. This led to a discussion of the history of Satanism, a glancing reference to *Paradise Lost,* a comment on the remnants in popular speech of devil worship ("You Devil, you," said half in admiration, or "You lucky devil!"), mention of the Evil Eye (which Mrs. Horton said had been cast on her by a stranger in a passing car the day before), a rave remembrance of Dreyer's remarkable film *Day of Wrath,* and so into witch-burning, Salem, Miller's play, the rise and fall of McCarthyism, conformity (especially of the young), the unusual tensions that might account for that conformity, the desire for hedonistic and material satisfactions in view of possible universal holocaust, and so back to the hydrogen bomb and a sane nuclear policy.

"Oh," gasped Mrs. Thurlow, "the little boy is *It!*"

Swiftly side-stepping the anxious Jackie, Gus had headed for the oak, tripped over a branch, and been fallen on by Jackie, who had either tripped over the same branch or had just plainly fallen on the small boy to make the tag as complete and indisputable as possible.

"He couldn't be more *It,*" said Mr. Thurlow, as the child rose from the ground, angry at his bad luck, missing very much the security of the oak, for, tired of the constant dodging and shifting made necessary by his short legs and his inability to cover ground as quickly as the others, he had planned a long stay. But he pluckily set out to divest himself of the unwanted thing.

"I hope he's not *It* long," said Mrs. Thurlow, who had adopted the child as her own. Indeed, they all felt a certain sympathy for this six-year-old among the eights and nines.

"What puzzles me," said Mrs. Levy, after a pause long enough to create the need for a new beginning, "is how the game started, suddenly, without warning."

She had not yet recovered from the shock of that unexpected tag that had started the game and catapulted her son into the unwanted commanding position.

"Why," said Mr. Horton, thoughtlessly, "I guess the kid who made the first tag had that *It* feeling and wanted to pass it on."

"Nonsense," said Mrs. Horton, who had not forgotten that it was their son Teddy who had started the game. "Kids get tired of one game and they decide to start another, the way we get tired of one conversational area and move on to another."

"That's true," said Mr. Levy, trying to bury deeper Mr. Horton's unfortunate remark. "I don't think we ought to make a mystery of everything. Take this game, for example, about which we've talked so much. Haven't you ever felt like wanting to get rid of something, and in a hurry? An old suit that you're sick and tired of looking at, although it has plenty of wear left; a piece of furniture that has suddenly become a burden, you can't look at it anymore; some old thought or scheme that you want to get rid of, forget once and for all? Maybe this game dramatizes that desire to get rid of unwanted things, a kind of efficiency kick."

"You throw out a piece of furniture," said Mrs. Horton, "or you give it to a charity and do not know its final disposition, but here the excitement is in passing the thing on to a specific individual."

"One child passes on his own particlar fear," said Mrs. Thurlow, "and the child who is tagged replaces that fear with his own."

She was wondering what fear little Gus was struggling with, and was saddened as she watched the boy outdistanced by his four tormentors, who came up close to him and, as he made his move, scattered and opened up a space with their unfair long-leggedness.

"Of course," said Mr. Thurlow, "he doesn't *have* to play with kids two and three years older."

"How brave he is!" cried his wife. "He seeks the difficult task."

The absolute contradiction between these two points of view created a silence, and the adults watched the flashing figures, listened to the medley of cries—playful, fierce, and honeyed.

"Of course you've got to give him credit," said Mr. Thurlow, realizing that his wife's position was the nobler one, "but there's such a thing as taking on too much, more than a body can bear."

There was general agreement on this too.

Somone asked where Gus lived, and Mrs. Horton replied that she wasn't quite sure, but thought that he came from a house down the street. At least that was the direction from which she had seen him coming one afternoon. She didn't know his second name, and thought that he might live out here all year. All this uncertainty added to the pathos generated by his diminutive size, his current *It*ness, and his difficulty in passing along the stigma; all this created, most certainly for Mrs. Thurlow, the image of an orphan, a waif, but there was no real reason to think that he didn't come from an absolutely secure home—a point someone would undoubtedly have made if Mrs. Thurlow had voiced her gloomy sentiments.

But Mrs. Thurlow's gloom was suddenly dissipated when little Gus, hidden behind a bush, lured his colleagues into the open (they came stealthily, but into the open) and sprang on Danny, who was closest, and so transferred at last the accursed thing.

Then he sprinted to the sanctuary and hugged that tree as though it were a spar in a tumultuous ocean. (He had learned the great danger of being retagged, so in making the touch he was moving away at the same time.)

This dramatic change in the circumstances of the game led to a new conversational spurt, this time on the question of the underdog. There was talk about those who made it against the most severe hazards, of long shots in horse races, odds against poorly rated contenders, of David and Goliath, the haves and the havenots, of big and little nations—and this led, imperceptibly, to the possibility that these little nations might get possession of hydrogen bombs, or at least obsolete atom bombs, and that led right to the shelters and a sane nuclear policy.

Mrs. Levy was not as disturbed this second time as she had been the first time that Danny was *It*, but she was disturbed, partly because he *was It* and partly because he was *It* for the second time, being therefore the first one *It* for the second time. But, like all the others, she was somewhat impressed, even a bit mellowed, by the fact that the game had now come full circle, underlining the elegant statement of Copernicus:

for the circle alone can bring back the past

They sat waiting for the game to end, for that would give a formal character to the departure envisaged by the two visiting couples, one end leading to another, although it would be more proper for the Levys to make the ceremonial move than for the Thurlows, whose sentimental adoption of Gus did not quite qualify them as parents.

While waiting for the game to end, Mr. Thurlow could not forbear a final probe into the nature of the game they had been watching.

"When kids that age (I mean Oedipus-wise) harbor a guilt, a shameful thing that they want to share—for passing the guilt from one to the other is a kind of sharing—can we exclude the Freudian interpretation?" Nobody took a strong stand excluding the Freudian interpretation, and he went on: "Parricide and incest, that is the stuff of their guilty imaginings, and the band of brothers transferring and sharing this guilt."

"That was concise," said Mr. Levy, admiringly.

Out on the field the game was over, the kids were milling around, making comparatively meaningless contact, and Mrs. Levy said, in the prescribed ceremonial manner, "I think the kids are sort of tired. We ought to get started."

Which they did, and, in the cool dusk, they heard Mrs. Thurlow say softly, *"The world's slow contagion."*

9. The Relay Race

On a late afternoon in June 1924, a group of kids were coming to the end of their track meet on a street in the north Central Park area. It was a contest between the *up-the-blocks* and *down-the-blocks,* not one block against another, but these internecine struggles can be the bitterest of all.

It was close to the median point between the end of the war (not *which* war) and the beginning of the depression, and these are always the greatest points. Calvin Coolidge was filling out Warren Harding's term, and jokes about the New Englander's teciturnity were heard:

"Mr. President," said a woman reporter, "I've wagered that I can make you speak three words."

"You lose," said the unsmiling Cal.

But these youngsters were more interested in the Olympic Games which were coming up in Paris, and were following avidly the exploits of Jackson Scholz, DeHart Hubbard, Harold Osborn, to say nothing of Paavo Nurmi, the "Phantom Finn," who, stopwatch in hand, was running all competition into the ground.

Considerations of a technical and human nature restricted the scope of these street track meets. The high jump, for example, proved impractical in competition because it was not possible to trust the steadiness (or the neutrality) of the two rope-holding lads. And nothing could be *thrown.* That cut out the javelin, the shot-put, the discus, the hammer. But most everything else was in—the sprints, the jumps, the middle- and long-distance runs, the relays, even the marathon (which was omitted in this particular meet for lack of time, it being a race ten times around the block). The pole vault had not yet penetrated the popular athletic consciousness.

Though Davey and Chick lived in the middle of the block and considered themselves *middle-of-the-blocks,* for purposes of competition they allied themselves with the *up-the-blocks,* partly because that area was less populated than down-the-block, for up there was the Yiddish theater, whose side wall took up space which otherwise would have been taken by apartment buildings.

The meet was over, except for the relay race, and it had been very close. The running broad jump had just ended, and the contestants were crowded around the scorekeeper, who was keeping count, chalking up the score in the gutter.

"What's the score? What's the score?"

"Lemme alone, lemme figure," said the scorekeeper, Pimples, who had been chosen not so much for his arithmetic ability, but that he was one of the older guys and therefore in a sense above the battle, and mostly because he was around and willing to take on the job. The starter and judges were picked out of the same complex of reasons.

Pimples was scribbling away furiously. The scoring was spread 10–5–3.

"It's 84–78," he said, "the score is 84–78."

"Favor who?"

"Favor the *down-the-blocks,*" he said, "who do you think?"

What he meant was that anyone who had been keeping score wouldn't be asking such an idiotic question, but certain of the *up-the-blocks* argued, from what he said, and from the *tone* of his voice, that he was obviously on the side of the *down-the-blocks.*

"What's the difference who's ahead?" asked Davey. "It all depends on the relay anyway."

That was because the relay counted ten points for the winners, zero for the losers. This procedure had been agreed on, that is, it had ostensibly been agreed on, for now there came forth a champion from the lists of the *down-the-blocks,* one Wally, to ask since when did the relay count ten points, when from time immemorial the relay had always counted five points.

But Wally was so obviously trying to pull a fast one (the combined weight of the scorekeeper, the starter, and the judges being against him) that even his own teammates pulled him back.

"He's just kiddin'," said one of them, but nobody took it very humorously.

"Cut the stallin'," cried one of the spectators, "and let's get the relay started."

There were spectators: girls, nonrunning boys, older kids, even a few stray adults. They sat on the curb or stood on the sidewalk. There were viewers too, from the apartments; they leaned out the windows, silently watching, or crying out encouragement to their favorites.

The relay race was a four-sewer race, each contestant running one sewer, which was 33⅓ yards, that is, if three sewers made up 100 yards, which was the popular notion. This notion rested on a legend that many years back someone (long grown and moved into the great world off the block) had actually measured three sewers—though it was pretty clear that the sewers were equally spaced—and had come up with the 100-yard figure. It was, of course, a fine figure, the classic sprint distance and all that. We always thought it was pretty intelligent of the city authorities to figure the distance between the sewers that way.

So this relay wasn't much of a race from the point of view of distance covered. But two sewers to each man was out because there weren't enough sewers on the block. There was another possibility: each man running two sewers and then the third man doubling back. But this had led to many arguments in the past—the third man tended to overextend his welcome to the oncoming runner, meeting him before he had completed his stint.

There was another reason why this double-back relay, where you ended up at the start, was not favored. It lacked a significant character of a relay race, whose primary charm is the fact that distance is cooperatively covered, that the precious stick had been carried farther into the distance. The circular track, of course, has helped to destroy this aspect of the relay race.

They were getting ready for the relay race. There was jockeying for position—both sides trying to anticipate the other's line-up, to put a strong man up against a weak man, etc. The general procedure was to put your fastest man last; in the case of *up-the-blocks*, that would be Benjy, a stocky lad who ran like a streak, with absolute absorption, everything propelled him forward— legs, arms, and heart. Davey was a brilliant starter and the obvious choice for lead-off man. In so short a race, a slow start could be fatal. Chick and Allie were running second and third, in that order, though it was difficult to say what motivated this choice. Allie was the faster runner, so you had double strength at the end of the race, but it was as easy to argue that it was more important to get off to a strong start and then depend on the last runner to make up for the third man's weakness. The line-up of the teams always led to interesting, and sometimes vehement discussion, with undertones of character analysis. There always seemed to be one weak man on a relay team.

"Why don't they get started?" asked a bystander.

"They're getting the sticks," said another.

The "sticks" were tightly rolled sections of newspaper. The officials were rolling these papers, making sure that both "sticks" were the same weight and the same length, for they had to meet the extraordinarily detailed scrutiny of both teams.

"I hate the relay race," said one of the kids watching, and there was some agreement. They thought it was somehow not a real race, it being the only nonindividual event in the track and field program. After the first runner, it became a kind of continuing handicap race.

"You're making a great mistake, kids," said Chick's older brother Jerry, the sophomore at City College. He had just come out of the candy store with a pack of cigarettes in his hand; he lit one of the cigarettes with the awkward nonchalance of a beginner. He was seventeen, having skipped twice and then gone to Townsend Harris Hall. He was standing down the block, near the finish line.

"A great mistake, kids," he said, "the relay is something special."

"What do you mean *special?*"

By now the "sticks" had been analyzed, measured, and approved, and the eight runners were moving slowly toward their places at the manhole covers. Some of the runners were limbering up.

"I mean," said Jerry, and you could see he was torn between not talking over the kids' heads and showing off his newly won knowledge and vocabulary, "that the relay is a cooperative event, people working together for something."

"What's so great about that?" asked one of the kids.

"Plenty," said Jerry. "That's how things get accomplished in the world. Take science—one scientist does the work, and then he dies. So another scientist carries it on. It's like a relay race. Copernicus to Galileo to Newton to Einstein. What a team!"

"I'll take the Yankees," said another kid, who was working with a softball, trying out different positions with his fingers, for curves and drops, perhaps dreaming of the fade-away and double shoot.

"Where do you think the word *relay* comes from?" inquired the young collegian.

There was a pause devoid of expectancy.

"It comes from the French," he went on. "It has to do with relays of dogs and horses. You've seen in the movies how a team of horses and carriage comes into an inn, the horses are exhausted, foaming white spit, then a new team of horses takes over. It's a relay."

"Now that we have autos," said a youth, "who needs those relays?"

"That's not the idea," said Jerry, "it's one man taking the load from another, carrying on. And let me tell you, it's much faster too. Do you know what the mile record is?"

"That's Nurmi's record."

"It must be about 4:11."

The kids were interested.

"That's pretty close," said Jerry. "It's 4:10.4 and it's held by Nurmi all right. And let me tell you what the mile relay record is. It's 3:16.4. Almost a minute difference."

"Well, naturally," said one of the kids, "there's four guys running."

"That's just it," said Jerry, "doing it cooperatively, cutting down the time almost a minute."

He introduced the word *cooperatively* in a rather gingerly way, but nobody paid too much attention, because up the block you could see Davey and his opposite number, Mitch, take their places at the starting line.

Now the relay race we are about to describe is one of those events where the description will surely take a longer time than the duration of the thing described (unless, in the utmost baldness of narrative, we were to say simply: the *up-the-blocks* took the lead, kept it on the second leg, lost it on the third leg because of faulty passing of the stick, and then regained the lead on the anchor leg to win the race; that is what happened, and takes less time—to read or write—than the what? thirty seconds it takes to run this race).

In the first place there were two false starts, one by Davey, the other by his opponent. This was blamed on the starter: seasoned observers contended that there was too much of a pause between the *Get Set* and the *Go,* that the kids were too nervous and bound to "break" in the long interval. Then, as they got set for the third try, an automobile turned the western corner of the block. Now there were guards at each end of the street, and had the race started the car would have been stopped (as cars had been stopped during the running of the other events) until the race was over, but since the relay had not started the car was allowed to proceed, and then all the runners started limbering up again, some of them quite desperately, as though their muscles were undergoing some unusual tensing as the car traveled over the stadium.

"No more cars," cried the starter. This message was heard by the traffic official up the block and was relayed to the one at the other end of the street.

"It'll get dark by the time this race starts," grumbled one of the spectators, but he was talking of a race whose duration was—what? thirty seconds?—and the afternoon sun, though sinking, was quite a way from its home in the Hudson.

The starter cupped his hands around his mouth.

"On your marks . . ."

"Get set . . ." and taking to heart the criticism which had been hurled at him, he pushed ahead of his natural inclination, with a swift

"Go"

and off went the two lead-off men. They got off to a pretty even start. Mitch, a little taller, had a longer stride so he took the lead. But Davey was a fleet lad, a form devotee; he would not hesitate to see a movie through again so as to get back to the newsreel which showed Charley Paddock streaking off to another sprint victory. Davey flailed his arms, plunged forward toward the waiting Chick, whose hand was outstretched. In such a short relay the handling of the stick is, of course, fundamental. Moving slowly away, Chick took the stick smoothly (the fruition of long practice between the friends) and tore off toward the third· man, Allie, with an edge on his rival. This was an edge that Chick maintained, but when he came to pass the stick there was a moment of confusion. The handling was not smooth—either Chick was anxious, or Allie held on, the timing was bad, the transitional instant was prolonged, so that Allie was a couple of steps behind his opponent. He strove valiantly, ran with a kind of stubborn chagrin, picked up a step, and then made a perfect relay to Benjy, who tore after his rival as though he had been shot from a gun, and, head bobbing, came even with him, passed him in the last few yards, and kept running almost down to the end of the block. Then he turned around and ran springily to the finish line for the plaudits of the crowd.

That was how the *up-the-blocks* won the track meet; then most of the kids stood around in front of the candy store, discussing the various events, the turning points, the key performances.

"You kids ran a terrific relay," said Jerry, "and that pass from Allie to Benjy, that was perfect."

"Yeah," said Chick to his older brotheer, but the relation between affirmation and agreement was not clear. "Benjy ran some race."

He was in this way lowering the importance of the passing of the stick (because of his difficulty in that maneuver) and contradicting the cooperative point of view of his brother by fastening on to the exploit of the anchor man. He was also just contradicting his older brother.

Jerry waved off his kid brother.

"What do *you* know?" he asked, in the immemorial way you treat a kid brother who is disputing you in public.

"Plenty," answered Chick, in the immemorial way a kid brother stands up to an older brother who is putting him in his place in public.

"The worst thing that can happen in a track meet," said Jerry, "is when one of the runners drops the stick, particularly when it's a close race. You don't realize how important that stick is till you drop it. The runner is ashamed, angry, the crowd's sympathy is spontaneous. And when the runner picks up the stick and starts on his hopeless quest, the crowd is with him."

"For a minute," said Davey, "then they forget him."

"Certainly," said Jerry, "their attention falls on the ones who are carrying on their task victoriously. That's natural."

Then the kids began to drift home, for supper.

10. Trick or Treat

"Trick or treat," said Benjy, age nine, and without a word the woman at the door put a penny in his hand. It was hot.

"Ow!" screamed Benjy, and his friends were amazed at his sudden outcry.

"It's hot," cried Benjy, throwing the penny into the air. The coin rolled along the floor, and his friends approached it cautiously. They waited a full minute, kicking the penny along, stepping on it, and blowing at it from a distance. Then Joel picked it up.

"Warm," he said. "It's still warm."

"Ow!" cried Benjy, wringing his hand, then waving it to stir up some cool air. "It still hurts."

Up to that time it had been a pleasant Halloween night for the children. In their costumes of hobgoblins, witches, and raggedy nondescripts, they made the rounds, knocking on every door and awaiting the outcome.

How generous many of the inhabitants were! One had stacks of little packages, carefully prepared. Another offered a choice from a box of cookies. An elderly man, somewhat befuddled, smiled and emptied his pockets of coins.

For every person who rejected them, graciously or rudely, there were a dozen who passed out little gifts to enrich the holiday.

They wandered in bands, passed other bands, strangers passing one another in the dusk, creating the illusion of adventure in far places.

The act of begging answered some obscure need of these children from fairly comfortable homes; roaming the streets and knocking on the doors of strangers, in a world dusky and unfamiliar, they could give into feelings of being unwanted, abandoned.

Yet every now and then a familiar figure answered the door, laying a kind of security under the orphan feeling.

Then this world of make-believe was suddenly destroyed by the hot penny which caused Benjy to scream out in pain, and was now bringing the children to the store of Mr. Bennett, the neighborhood druggist.

The druggist looked at the curious round burn and then applied some Butesin Picrate ointment.

"That'll make it feel better pretty soon," he said. "How did it happen?"

He looked up incredulously when the children told the story.

"No," he said, "you're making that up."

When they assured him that this was the simple truth, that a lady had given Benjy a hot penny, the druggist did not know whether this story was a part of the Halloween prank, and shrugged his shoulders.

"Nobody would believe it," said Joel. "Nobody in the world would believe such a thing."

"Big people stick up for each other," said Zeck.

"I wonder how she did it?" asked Joel. "How come *her* hands weren't burnt?"

"She had gloves on," said Benjy. "She knew it was hot."

"But how did she get them hot?" asked another kid. "You think she put matches to them?"

"She probably fried them in a frying pan," said Zeck. "She keeps them there on a low flame, and then when the bell rings, she takes them out while they're still hot."

This was somehow accepted as the official explanation of the mechanism of the deed.

By this time they had come to the apartment house where Benjy had been burned. They stood in the vestibule, for on this night they were free to go anywhere; only the most irascible of supers would have driven them off.

A gang of kids entered the house.

"Stay away from 5N," said Joel to the strangers.

"Why?" asked one of the newcomers.

Joel pointed to Benjy's bandaged hand.

"There's a witch up there. She hands out hot pennies."

The strangers looked incredulous, and went on their way.

About ten minutes later, when they came down, one of the strangers said:

"There isn't even anybody home in that apartment."

Joel and Zeck and the others looked at Benjy's hand, half doubting the truth of the monstrous story.

But had they not heard the cry, had they not seen the penny, had not Joel picked it up while it was still warm?

"Let's see the penny."

Benjy produced the coin from his pocket, and the kids examined it. The date of the coin was 1909.

"Boy, it's old," said Getch.

"What did she look like?" asked Zeck.

"Well," said Benjy, "she was pretty old, and had a kind of mean look. Anyway I didn't see her very well."

"She was very tall," said Joel, a confirmed myth-maker. "She had to *drop* the penny into your hand."

"We ought to get even with her," said Getch. "Why should she get away with that?"

This notion was carefully considered in silence, not from the side of its correctness but of its implementation.

"Let's ring her bell and run," said Mushkie, a timid child.

His proposal was treated with the scorn they thought it deserved.

"We can give her the hot penny back," said Joel, "the same one, even a little hotter."

"She'd never fall for that," said Getch.

"I'd like to do something to her," said Benjy. "She shouldn't get away with that."

They gravely deliberated, in their council of war, the adequate reprisal.

The conventional forms of retaliation for this day—a pin in

the doorbell, a chalk scrawl on the door—were considered inadequate.

"What's the good of hanging around here?" asked Zeck. "Soon it'll be too late to have any fun at all."

The question of the treachery which Benjy had suffered was weighed against this consideration.

"Bust her windows," said Getch.

Nor was this proposal of direct action found acceptable, and the gang of beggars stood and pondered on the quality of revenge, while Benjy felt the cold penny in the palm of his hand.

11. Armistice Day

At 11 A.M. all the kids were asked to stand and observe two minutes of silence to commemorate the Armistice which had put an end to the First World War. At the time it was called the World War, or the Great War. The inability to name the war which followed twenty-five years after the commencement of that first war (despite a kind of contest to name the war) led to its being called World War II, in the manner of another musical opus.

How did Armistice (now Veteran's) Day differ from Memorial Day? It celebrated the end of the war, and thus the saving of lives which would have been lost had the war continued. Memorial Day was to honor the dead of *all* wars in which the country had been involved.

It is a good thing to celebrate the absence of the continuation of bloodshed, but always a bugle was blowing in the distance, harbinger of new wars, new woes.

Then the class was told to sit, and the work continued. The meaning of the silence had been explained by the teacher earlier in the morning.

"It is in honor of our heroic dead," she explained, "who gave up their lives on Flanders Field and the other battlefields of the war. Silence is a sign of respect."

Later in the day there was a ceremony in the Assembly Hall. "The Star-Spangled Banner" and "America" were sung; there was a color guard, a recitation of "I Have a Rendezvous with Death," and a short speech by one of the assistant superintendants of schools.

"Children," he said, "we are come together to celebrate the courage of our brave soldiers in the war against the infamous tyranny of the Prussians. We sacrificed our finest, spilled our dearest blood so that the democratic ideal might continue to flourish. Take heart from these brave men—Christy Mathewson was among them—for it may be your turn some day to take arms in a similar cause."

He, too, said nothing about the saving grace of this holiday, the end of killing.

Davey was impressed by the martial note—he saw himself on foreign fields, another Sergeant York, fighting off the swarming enemy from a trench hole, alone, or better, with a wounded comrade. Then the assembly ended.

He had a dim remembrance of the war—the table talk, the black newspaper headlines—but mostly he remembered his cousin who had been gassed in the war and then came back to America to die as a result of that gassing. He died a few years after the war ended.

The war ended exactly at eleven o'clock in the morning, he thought. A minute before that a soldier could have been killed; a minute after that the killing could have been a mistake. He remembered the Armistice—the whistles, the newspaper "Extras," the excited relief. People were cagy, remembering the False Armistice. But this was the real Armistice—the soldiers stopped trying to kill one another. And the Allies had won. The Germans had surrendered, laid down their guns, and held up their hands. *Kamerad.* Before there is an armistice one side usually has to surrender, unless both sides decide to call it off because it is a draw. But here Germany surrendered—sometimes the enemy was called the Central Powers. He liked much more the sound of *Allies.* That was our side. They wore their hats to the sides of their heads, at an American angle. The Germans had spikes in their helmets and they marched very stiffly. Now years had passed and our side was friends with the Germans. After a war the two sides become friends, just the way two kids fight, then shake hands, and become friends. But sometimes when you fight with a kid it is never the same again—you keep on being mad. And we used to have wars with some of the Allies. England. But not with France. Lafayette helped us in the Revolution. And then General Pershing said: "Lafayette, we are here." So the war ended, all the posters disappeared from the walls ("Uncle Sam Wants You") and now every year at eleven o'clock on November 11 (funny about the elevens) they stood in silence in all the schools on account of the Armistice. In those two minutes of silence he thought of the battlefields full of ruin and fire and smoke, and then the word came to the soldiers that the war was over. Everything quieted down, the battlefield was changed to a field again, the smoke lifted, the holes were filled in, flowers grew again. The poppies on Flanders Field. After a while the farmers would come back to that field, but it would always be an old battlefield.

"You'd think we'd get a holiday out of it," said Davey's friend Chick, who had caught up with him on the way back from school.

"All those soldiers dead and wounded," he went on, "and we just get two minutes of silence."

He pulled a well-worn bunch of picture cards from his pocket.

"I made a good trade today," he said.

"What did you get?"

"I got a Rube Marquard and a Marshall Joffre."

"I've got two General Haigs," said Davey, "a Three-Finger Brown, and an Eddy Rickenbacker."

"I'll trade you Marquard for Haig."

"Okay. Do you have an Iron Man McGinnity?"

"No, but I know who's got one."

"I'll trade the other Haig for McGinnity."

At the moment pitchers were more important to Davey than generals.

It was the Card Season, and after school the block was full of kids matching, trading, gambling. One kid's favorite was another kid's bust. Obscure loyalties made themselves felt—to players on distant teams, to heroes in distant lands.

"I wonder," said Davey, "if the German kids trade cards.

They'd have Hindenberg, I mean Von Hindenberg, and what is the name of their ace? Richtofen."

"They don't have baseball or anything," said Chick.

"They're good in skiing and ice skating."

"You call those sports?" cried Chick. "I wouldn't trade a sub on the Giants for the best skiier in the world."

And he thumbed through his cards, looking at his sport and military heroes, figuring which he wanted to keep, which he wanted to trade, and which he was not sure about.

That evening after dinner Mr. Flaxman turned to his son and asked:

"Well, what was new in school today?"

"Nothing much," said Davey, "except we had two minutes' silence for Armistice Day, and Assembly."

His father nodded his head seriously, and turned to Davey's uncle Ezra.

"Always war," said Mr. Flaxman. "First you fight the war and then you honor the dead."

Uncle Ezra had a philosophic approach, in the Talmudic style.

"It is the way of the world," he said. "Man is not a perfect creature. How could he not be perfect, being made in the image of God?"

He paused, and then answered his own question.

"The *image* of God is far from God. And image itself is a forbidden thing."

"Well," said Mr. Flaxman, somewhat wearily, "we do what we can; there is nothing much to boast of here, we are far from the perfection of angels."

Davey saw the conversation getting away from him, but sometimes he liked to listen to conversation which was beyond him. Usually he was bored when the talk was beyond him, but sometimes it was fun to reach out toward what he partly understood and wished to understand more.

"The psychology of angels," said Uncle Ezra, "must be very much different from ours. They suffer differently; they enjoy differently."

"Who knows?" asked Mr. Flaxman. "Are we supposed to understand such matters?"

"They are beings of another dimension," said Ezra. "They are God's messengers."

"It is for the Prophets and Sages to look into these matters," said Mr. Flaxman. "Our own problems are difficult enough. And when it comes to suffering, Amos suffered enough."

He was using the Hebrew name of Arthur, Davey's cousin who had been gassed in the Great War, later died in a Veteran's Hospital in America.

Davey had known the soldier quite well. Of all the dead people, he knew Artie the best. Most of his cousins were his own age, but Artie was one of the older cousins. Davey's mother had explained this matter to him. He had a very old uncle who had married young. That's why his cousin was so much older. Artie came to the house quite often, and talked to Davey, even played ball with him. He seemed more like a young uncle than a cousin. He rarely spoke about the war, but when he did, it was in a half-joking way. He never spoke about the killing; he spoke of other soldiers, the camaraderie. Sometimes it didn't sound like a war at all. But Davey knew that his cousin had fought at the front, had won a medal for heroism. When he returned from the war, he went back to work but had to quit for long stretches because of the effects of the gassing. He coughed a great deal. He was a man of good spirit.

"He suffered enough," agreed Uncle Ezra, "but he would never let on."

Even in the hospital, where Davey once visited him, his cousin smiled and joked with him. A few days later he died.

When they had stood in silence for those few minutes, Davey thought of his cousin. Every year on Armistice Day he thought of his cousin. The war continued to kill soldiers even after it was over. Artie had died of the war three years after the war ended.

"May his soul rest in peace," said Mr. Flaxman, and Ezra nodded "Amen."

That was what older persons always said about the dead. Then they talked of other matters. There are apparently more things to say about the living than about the dead.

"You think about the dead more than you talk about them," thought Davey. "They are buried inside of you."

Standing at attention on Armistice Day, he felt sad about the absence of his older cousin. Every year he was getting closer to his cousin in age. In about twelve years he would be the same age as his cousin. Then he would be older than his cousin. He missed the games they had played together—Artie was a good boxer and had taught Davey how to handle himself. One day Artie brought a punching bag and set it up in the doorway. They feinted, jabbed, and slammed the bag. "There's the old one-two," said his cousin. The boy came to understand that these games and talks were not to be continued. His cousin was forever dead at the age of twenty-four. Davey had not been taken to the funeral so he did not know where Artie was buried. One night he dreamt of a great battlefield, and his cousin, buried on that battlefield, a field full of crosses, and some stars. But Artie was buried in Staten Island. Every year Davey remembered his cousin a little less clearly, but felt him deeper down. Because he was deeper buried, he was less recognizable. "Someday," thought Davey, "I may even forget what he looks like. By then, he will be buried very deep inside of me."

It was about 7:30 in the evening and Davey had some homework to do. If he finished early enough, maybe he'd have time to meet the kids outside for a little while. He left the room to get started on his work.

12. A Dream of Collaboration

Last night I dreamt that I was walking along an unfamiliar block with a familiar-looking man. That was the first impression. Then, slowly, the block turned very familiar, being the block of my childhood. The familiar-looking man became vaguely unfamiliar, then vaguely familiar. He wore his clothes, which were in the contemporary style (including a long, skinny tie with square ends) as though they did not belong to him, or as though he were an actor in a period piece.

But what impressed me most was the swift, penetrating, extraordinarily intelligent way in which he was looking around, swallowing every detail. He was listening, smelling, his senses aflame. I then realized it was Brueghel who was walking with me, and I was pleased, rather proud, that we were walking together.

I was upset, too, by the way he was looking around, by the competitiveness, the self-assurance, as if to say:

"This may be your block, but I assure you that by the time we walk this block from end to end, I will know more about it than you ever dreamed. It will be mine forever."

Did he really know that it was my block, was he adopting a personal hostile attitude, or was this the way he acted everywhere?

I accepted the challenge, saw myself as the defender of the twentieth century against this formidable Peasant Knight.

And with the supreme advantage that this *was* my old block, the block I knew like the back of my own hand! the block I had traversed a thousand times, in actuality, in retrospect, in dream.

But such a formidable knight, so overwhelming a master of detail, iron scrupulosity, prescientific obsession!

And me out of the frame of modern impressionism, searching for the essence rather than the detail.

And his advantage in objectivity, in seeing for the first time scenes with which I was saturated.

As a gambling man, I would have hesitated to bet on myself. We walked silently, westward. I narrowed my eyes, determined to miss nothing, realizing that I had already spent too much time in looking at my competitor rather than at the activities of the street.

Three little girls were jumping rope. They sang:

> *Teddy Bear, Teddy Bear, turn around.*
> *Teddy Bear, Teddy Bear, touch the ground.*
> *Teddy Bear, Teddy Bear, touch your shoe.*
> *Teddy Bear, Teddy Bear, please skidoo.*

I automatically memorized the words. Does he understand English? Answering the question which I did not ask him, he said: "A very charming song."

The accent is curious. I consider it an amalgam of more than three centuries of speech, of language.

"Vertical cosmopolitanism," I hazarded, but he was listening to another jump-rope song, faintly heard:

> *Charlie Chaplin went to France*
> *To teach the ladies how to dance.*
> *This is how he taught them:*
> *Heel, toe, over we go.*
> *Salute to the captain,*
> *Bow to the queen,*
> *Turn around like a submarine.*

and then:

> *Eighteen hundred and ninety-four,*
> *Shut the door and say no more.*

"Wouldn't that song sound better," asked Brueghel, "if it went:

> *Nineteen hundred and eighty-four*
> *Shut the door and say no more?*

"A very contemporary touch," I said vapidly, but all the time I was thinking:

"Is his hearing as strong as his fabled sight?"

I looked around carefully and saw four kids at play, two on a side. The player up was throwing a high-bouncer against a rounded molding on the wall of the apartment building, in a game of baseball indigenous to this style of architecture. The ball comes off the point into a chalked field in the gutter, defining first, second, and third. The opposite sidewalk is a home run (if the ball is not caught). There is great skill in placing the ball so that it cannot be caught without a bounce. Occasionally you fire away, reaching for the house or cellar across the gutter.

Two boys were playing immies along the curb, in the hit-and-span style.

Two others were racing matchsticks down the current made by the Department of Sanitation truck which had just flushed the street.

A *Johnny on the Pony* game was reaching its climax, with four boys piled on, trying to weigh down the weak link they had chosen to bear their accumulated weight.

Two fruit boxes, piled on ends, were being used in a game of *King of the Hill,* that curious game of exclusive possession and a world full of enemies.

Two boys were in the classic pose of choosing, working their tightly gripped hands up a broomstick, and a group of little girls, preparing to play tag, were choosing *It:*

> *Ink-a-dink*
> *A bottle of ink,*
> *The cork fell out*
> *And you stink.*

There was some dispute over the choose, so they started again:

Engine, engine, Number Nine
Riding down the Chicago line
If the train goes off the track
Do you want your money back?

Yes.

Y–E–S
Spells Yes
And out you go.

We passed the school wall, on which was chalked a tic-tac-toe game, also the spelling game where the first and last letters are given and the others must be filled in, and the game of dots, that interminable creation of squares which you initial and which then belong to you.

Inside the schoolyard a boxball game was being played, and a girl was watching the game and jumping rope:

Policeman, policeman,
Do your duty:
Here comes Gloria,
The American beauty.
She can wiggle, she can waggle,
She can do the split.
But I bet you one thing,
She can't do this—
Pull her dress above her knees.

I was so preoccupied with my own observations that I had almost forgotten about my companion. I looked at him out of the corner of my eye. He was watching some kids who were playing with a paper basketball, shooting fouls through the fire escape rungs, and I noted how his sharp eye took in the lad who was gravely vaulting over the fire hydrant.

Did he notice the boy practicing his running starts in the court-yard, or the chalked game (nobody playing at the moment) of *Girls' Names* on the sidewalk?

What a question! His eyes, under the shadow of a Stetson hat whose brim was snapped close to the breaking point, roamed everywhere. Moreover he seemed to make no distinction be-

FLOWERS	COLORS
CARS	GAMES
BOYS' NAMES	CIGARETTES
GIRLS' NAMES	GUM

tween foreground and background, and brought to light what was buried in the landscape.

It struck me that he was too businesslike in his approach.

"Do you get any fun out of this?" I asked.

"Fun?" he asked, in his curious across-the-centuries inflection.

I was sure that during this brief and unsatisfactory interchange he had picked up a few observations on me.

A child was being taunted:

> *Cry baby, cry baby,*
> *Stick your head in gravy.*
> *Wash it off with bubblegum*
> *And then go join the navy.*

and then:

> *Eight and eight are sixteen.*
> *Stick your head in kerosene.*
> *Put it in a magazine.*
> *Send it to the king and queen.*

"Kids are pretty cruel," I ventured.

He shrugged his shoulders in a pre-Freudian manner.

We were coming to the end of the block, still walking slowly. I felt exhausted, wasn't used to this kind of concentrated activity. He was wearing me down with his insensate observation. I had a mad desire to challenge him to a three-sewer race. But I refrained, foreseeing his glum reaction.

A group of little girls (the block was full of groups of little girls) were playing a *clap hands* game, singing:

> *I am a pretty little Dutch girl,*
> *As pretty as pretty can be.*
> *And all the boys around the block*
> *Are crazy over me.*
>
> *My boyfriend's name is Fatty.*
> *He comes from Cincinnati,*
> *With a pimple on his nose*
> *And three fat toes*
> *E–I–O spells Fatty.*

The meniton of *Dutch* brought the trace of a smile to his face, the first evidence of his famous drollness. What a relief to see these saturnine features light up, if even for a moment! Perhaps some of his Rabelaisian gaiety would now show up. His features hardened back into the original grimness and suspicion. I felt that we might have some pleasure out of this walk yet.

In my dream I tried to tell myself that this *was* a dream, but managed only to incorporate the effort into the dream itself.

I wondered, if I were in *his* dream in the sixteenth century, walking up some village in Flanders, how I would make out.

I took a last, somewhat despairing look at the various games of ball, the various games of tag, the seasonal games being played simultaneously (checkers, immies, buttons, and cards), the hopscotch, and the dice games.

It struck me that he was not looking for these street games at all, but making a study of the faces, or of the architecture, so that all my observations, competitively speaking, would come to nothing.

When we reached the corner we shook hands. He grinned. "Perhaps," he said, "we can collaborate. I will paint, you will write."

I was overjoyed, suggested that we walk back down the block, but he waved this suggestion aside and walked briskly northward, while I hesitated on the corner.

13. The Race

Looking carelessly out the window after the rain, I became interested in the play of two children—they were playing one of the favorite games of my childhood.

This is to race matchsticks down the stream, along the curb, into the sewer.

No sooner had the rain stopped falling, or the Sanitation man turned off the hydrant, than we were in the gutter with our little boats, ready for this stern competition.

It was most exciting when the stream was swollen—we had to run along, watching our craft sail around obstacles, through debris.

We know that all serious play (no contradiction here) is the symbolic recreation of real situations:

Breathing on the neck of this worried lad (the one I see through the window) is a younger brother—bright, ambitious, he is tearing day after day like a wild man through the educational system. First the interloper, then to be outdistanced by the interloper. The older brother worries his matchstick along.

An obstacle! he curses his luck. The other boat is unaware of the obstacle, floats around it, moves majestically into the open waters beyond.

"There is always something in the way," cries our pursued youngster.

Let us not worry our image—this stream, this cloaca, this race of the siblings, this birth in reverse.

Let us play seriously with our image.

Look! a new source of anxiety and pleasure. The sticks are under a parked car. They come from underneath, close together, into the clear again.

The game has caught on—other pairs of kids are playing, up and down the block, recreating in this gutter game the trauma of birth, the growth tremors.

14. New York Street Games, An Essay

For years Norman Douglas's *London Street Games* had been one of my favorite unread books. Then my wife made me a gift of the book, which I read through almost immediately, making notes as I went along. What follows is an amplification of my notes, and whatever further material memory and analysis bring to light.

In my story "You're *It*," I made a point of the implausibility of the tagged one in the game being referred to as *he* or *she,* but at the very begining of *London Street Games* a game of *Catch* is described in which, if the ball is caught by the boy in the middle, "the throer goes Hee." Indeed, Douglas claims that "all touch games are 'he' games," which is certainly not the case in our game of *It*, a classical touch game. Apart from the psychology of the tagged one's being It, something outside the human frame, we avoid the grammatical awkwardness of saying "He is he."

Douglas mentions hundreds and hundreds of street games, most of which are unfamiliar to me, but that may be due partly to the fact that the games are usually not described, and may have names different from our own games.

A number of the games, however, have similar names, and are presumably the same games.

Through the Mill (what we call *Under the Mill*) is a kind of punishment game. If the player does not succeed in what it is that he has to do (I forget what that is), then the other players line up close together, legs apart, and the failure crawls under (or through) the opening as swiftly as he can, for the straddlers are striking with all possible vigor at the moving ass. When the failure reaches the end of the line, he rejoins the community, play is resumed, and then after a while another player fails (maybe to catch a ball) and he goes under the mill. It is a kind of domesticated *Running the Gauntlet:* the failure being one of skill, there is no criminal blow struck against individual or society.

Nearest the Line Takes, which Douglas describes as a money game, is clearly our game of *Pitching Pennies.* I know nothing about the construction of London sidewalks (was once there for a brief spell, but just didn't notice), but our sidewalks are divided (we do not have a continuous run of stone), the sidewalk is boxed, or lined, for ease of repair, I suppose, the way windows are divided into panes, it being less expensive to fix the smaller area. So you'd pitch pennies for the line, and the one whose penny came closest picked up all the pennies. *On* the line is out. There were endless and furious arguments, naturally, as to whether the penny was touching or not ("it's *just* touching") and impartial judges were brought in to make the decision. An impartial judge was one who was a stranger to all the contestants, generally a passing adult. Why would he be biased? But if you pitch pennies against the wall, then the penny that touches the wall is the winner. If two or more pennies touch, the winnings are divided. The theory behind this is that one penny cannot touch a wall *closer* than another penny. But there can be arguments about the closeness of a penny to a line. One of the functions of rules of games (such as calling in a stranger, and therefore an impartial, when the issue is in doubt) is to cut down on arguments—there will always be arguments—and finally destroy the argument, so that the game can go on.

Douglas is not much concerned with the Rules of the Game. He writes:

"The particular rules of all these different games don't strike me as very important, or even interesting."

That strikes *me* as an astounding, wrong-headed remark, for the Rules of the Game *are* the game. There could be no game without rules, which contain and limit the activity, a game being a contained natural activity. The rules have the function of laws in society, with this difference: society's laws can be broken for principled reasons, and punishment accepted, but there can be no principled reason for breaking the rules of a game, which change nevertheless over the years.

Another familiar game from Douglas is *I Spy,* which with us was a game of earliest childhood, a primitive form of *Hide and Go Seek.* In *I Spy* one must only *see* the hidden one, then cry "I Spy." Then the discovered one becomes the seeker. In *Hide and Go Seek,* the hiding is more elaborate, and the seeker must see and *touch* the hidden one.

Douglas mentions *Hopping,* and we played *Hopping* in a couple of ways. The classic way, of course, was to have a hopping race (wonder if there were any lefty hoppers?), and that was surely an odd sight, on sidewalk or in gutter, to see a bunch of kids hopping along, some tripping, banging into one another, pretty well blocking up the sidewalk (and unable to swerve easily, the way you can when running).

A more favorite hopping game of mine was the fight, in which the contestants (usually two, or it could be a team) would fold arms and then try to knock the enemy back onto his two feet. That was how you lost the game, becoming solidly earth-based. It was a game which could last for a long time if the hoppers were expert and strong (though balance and agility were more important than strength—the trick was in the feint: to hop off in one direction, then swiftly catch the rival off guard; he'd sway, stumble, teeter awkwardly, and maybe land on his two feet).

Hopping is of the category of games (like *Blind Man's Buff*) where the rules create artificial handicaps and the contestants work within the limits of those handicaps. The hurdle race is a fine example of such an imposed handicap. I don't know how the sense of taste, or of touch, or of smell, could be excluded to create a game, but the sense of hearing might (practical considerations make such an exclusion difficult, and I know of no such game).

Follow My Leader (which Douglas calls a "Duty" game) is of course our *Follow the Leader*. Indeed he calls it that on another page, and calls it also "the only really dangerous game we have." There is a pause in the street life, a gathering of psychic forces, and suddenly one of us hollers: "Follow the leader." He is announcing the game, he brings it into being, he is the leader, and the succession is established by the place you achieve in line (through agility, not wisdom). Then the leader starts moving down the street, at the head of a single file. He rings an apartment bell and asks if Jackie is home. The others follow suit. One of the charms of the game, its dénouement, is the moment when the receiver catches on, with whatever intensity of dawning surprise (an intensity of dawning surprise!), of chagrin or anger. The leader goes into the candy store and asks for a glass of water. There is no great profit for the proprietor here, but a customer is a customer. The leader raps thrice on the ground-floor window pane. He opens and closes a car door. He stares for ten seconds at an old woman seated on a folding chair, sunning herself. He hollers "Maxie" at a passing taxicab. He hops seven times on one leg and three times on the other. He rushes down a cellar and hollers "fire." He makes an obscene gesture (reduced in scope and of Neapolitan origin) at a passing girl. He does a standing hop, skip, and jump. He shakes an unattended baby carriage. He clasps his hands behind his neck. He feints, jabs with his left, and crosses with his right. He clasps his hands above his head and moves them back and forth, in the classic gesture of the victorious prizefighter. He spits on the sidewalk. He rings the ground floor doctor's bell and runs. He hollers "Go, team, go!" He sprints about twenty yards, stops short, and jumps up and down five times. He raps two longs, three shorts, on a ground-floor window pane. He goes into the grocery store and asks if his mother has been there. He thumbs his nose at an approaching motorist. He honks the horn in a parked truck. We all *Follow the Leader* until the game trails off out of boredom, exhaustion, or the suggestion and then the beginning of a new game.

Robbers and Coppers (known on this side of the Big Pond as *Cops and Robbers*) is a game that never interested me very much. That being the case, I hardly remember playing the game. I was never fond of the more literal imitations of adult life (*Playing House* is of course a girls' game, and *Playing Doctor* never fascinated me). *Cops and Robbers,* like *Cowboys and Indians* (I don't know what the London kids call that game; I do know— Douglas says it is called *Germans and English*) is played by rather little kids, and they are somewhat loose-ruled, but allowing a wide range of movement and solid identifications. There are other games of identity, of adult occupations—*Office* and so on— whose charm for kids is that they are as if living in the world of their parents. But some identifications are livelier than others.

Douglas refers to *Rotten Eggs* as a game played by boys and girls. I assume he means boys and girls together. Well, boys and girls rarely played together on our block (there was of course the phenomenon of the tomboy, which no doubt has received extended treatment elsewhere), not on the street itself, occasionally in homes on rainy days, and later on, of course, there were the games at boy/girl parties. But that gets us quite a way from street games. And *Rotten Eggs,* for us, was not exactly a game at all. There were various ways of getting to a place together. You might walk, or jog, or trot, or run, or, having decided that you were going to the candy store, someone hollers "Last one there is a rotton egg" and off you sprint, the earlier arrivals waiting for the last to come, and shouting "Rotten egg, rotten egg." It is not exactly what Adlai Stevenson called "talking sense to the American people." But there it was, and there it probably still is. It is a ridicule game, a way of denigrating the slowest or weakest, the way chickens destroy the feeble or crippled.

When I read the title *Please, We've Come to Learn a Trade* (a guessing and chasing game) I thought immediately of another game—this one played by boys and girls (separately, I guess, or could it have been a girls' game, a ball-bouncing game?), an untitled game, really a kind of round, moving in the direction, over and again, of total identification with a stranger. One starts with the first letter of the alphabet, call it *A,* and clearly announces:

"My name is Alice, I come from Atlanta, and I sell artichokes."

The next player says:

"My name is Bernice, I come from Buffalo, and I sell bandannas."

You do catch the intent of this game, this round: to identify yourself (first name only), to make clear your origins, and to explain how it is you beat the game, baffle the poorhouse. Toward total identification. How precious little they are telling of themselves. Why not:

"My name is Olav, I am an Obsessional Neurotic . . ." or

"My name is Henrietta, I am a Hysteric . . ."?

But the rules of the round are self-limiting—first name, place of birth, and occupation (how come everybody *sells* things?):

"My name is Carol, I come from Chicago, and I sell Crêpe suzettes."

Any number can play; miss in one of the categories and you're out.

Throwing the Beanbag is a game that London girls played by themselves, as did New York girls. I well remember that game, the tossing back and forth of the canvas bag, so lightly and delicately (not the hard peg from centerfield), and we boys watching, secretly inflamed by all that lightness and delicacy (like the girls in Homer tossing the ball on the beach), that girlish grace, we grinning and making wisecracks ("What a terrific throw, better'n Bob Meusel"), all the time secretly exulting in that lightnesss, that prebosomed beauty, harbinger of womanly passion and womanly wile.

Douglas refers to *Buzz* as a girls' game, but in America it is a game played by all children (and desperate parents) mostly in moving automobiles, conceivably in hallways out of the rain, to speed the passing time (along with the game *Geography,* where you mention a geographical entity—continent, country, city, river, etc.—and the player after you takes the last letter of the word, say it is "Alabama," and utters the name of another geographical entity, say, "Arkansas," and the third player takes the last letter, *S,* and utters a geographical entity starting with that letter, say, "San Antonio." And it goes on that way until a player fails to come up with a geographical entity—"Come on, Canton starts with a *C,* not a *K*"—and then the survivor, the one not at a loss for the name of a geographical entity starting with the last letter of a preceding entity, is the winner).

Buzz is described in Douglas's book as follows:

"One player counts one then the next says two and so on. Every 5 the player instead says buzz. . . ."

But in New York we break up the counting by sevens (lucky number) and say "Buzz" not only every seven numbers, but whenever a 7 appears in a number, and make a special thing of the 70s, saying "Buzz 1, Buzz 2," etc., and saying "Buzz Buzz" for 77. But I repeat that *Buzz,* like *Geography,* is becoming more and more a parlor and car game, and that is true of *Ghost* too.

Our author has an extensive section on girls' songs. Most of these songs are unfamiliar, though I know a few from the play of my daughters, particularly *Polly Put the Kettle On* and *Loobee-loo.* Many of these songs, of course, are accompaniments to skipping games (or vice versa), but skipping for us was a more serious business. It was common knowledge that skipping rope was one of the best ways of getting into condition, for legs and wind, and in the movie newsreels we saw the boxing champions and the contenders skipping rope at a furious clip, doing all sorts of tricks, like crossing the ropes, and we were astounded by their nimbleness. It seemed so far from the rope-jumping of the girls, though some of them, we had to admit, were pretty skillful.

Some of us became experts; we had to move as swiftly and as nimbly as the boxers so that no one would think that we were playing a girls' game.

Douglas, in writing of games that smaller boys and girls play together, refers to those that come "at fixed seasons," and he mentions *Tops, Marbles, Pictures, Buttons*. Exactly (with the addition of *Checkers*) the games of my childhood, but we were not "smaller" children at all, for we played these games until we were thirteen or fourteen, though we started earlier. And the seasons for us were not exactly fixed, in the sense of perennial recurrence, but suddenly it was *Tops* season, or *Buttons*. These seasons did not follow one another in any particular order. I don't know how a particular season started up—somebody coming across an old stack of pictures, or maybe in the mood to play checkers. But these seasons extended beyond a given block: they were neighborhood phenomena (maybe the toy manufacturers, in accord with their production schedules, loaded up the candy stores, and *that* was how the seasons started).

Tops of course was a game you could play alone, just to see how long you could keep the top spinning (though there was no official record, we never *timed* a spin), or aiming at a circumscribed area, to get it spinning just there. Some kids were virtuosos, could get their tops spinning in the most unlikely places, on window sills, for example. But the most fun was in the competing with other kids, and the classic game was one of duration. The top that spins the longest wins, but it is not always easy to say just when a top stops spinning. At what point in its wobbling and wavering does it cease to spin? Justice was not even-handed; the approximations were rough. We also played a game where you had to knock the competitive top out of a circle and keep your own top spinning. The pleasure in spinning a top is to put an object in motion and then watch it live on in its own way. What you have put into movement then has an independent existence. The *Yo-Yo* gives a similar kind of pleasure, but it remains part of you, while the top is something you have thrown away (holding on to the string, the umbilical cord) and then watch with a certain interest, even fascination, as it spins in its own orbit, struggles with other tops in a test of endurance, for it moves until it wavers, wobbles, staggers, and drops.

The game of *Marbles* is what we called *Immies,* for Marbles, to our view, was a kind of rural game—it required earth, and the only earth we saw on our block was in the cracks of the lines which divided the sidewalk boxes. But if marbles need earth, immies need cement, and we played our game along the curb. These immies had an intrinsic value, one kind better than another—a "pearly" obviously very good, a "glassy" obviously not so good. So in playing, the competitor carefully chose the immy to risk (a hostage to the fortunes of the game) depending on what it was he owned at the time (everyone was a kind of hoarder or small-scale merchant, as will be seen more dramatically when we get to *Pictures*), on his estimate of the caliber of the opponent, and on his own mood (always the mood!). We called these immies "shooters" and gave them up when we discovered flaws or felt they were unlucky—they entered slowly into the market circulation. The game itself was quite simple, with very few refinements. The first player rolls his immy along the curb, and when it comes to a halt, the second player (though more than two could play) rolls *his* immy, according to the prearranged rules of Hit and Span. The players roll in turn until they accomplish the hit or span. A lad with big hands has the natural advantage in the span. It is a game involving a certain skill and accuracy. The hazards of the game were the sewer gratings, into which many an unwary immy disappeared forever, and the parked cars, which made a clear view of the curb from way off quite difficult, and under whose bodies complex feats of spanning were achieved.

My dictionary does not show the word *immy,* but does show a word *immarble*—"to convert into marble," but that would be a long shot in word origins.

Checkers was rather a quiet game, as befitting the object itself, which is no great beauty and has little intrinsic merit, one checker looking like another checker. There was no trading of checkers, which are quite earthbound, hug the immediate space, do not roll with the marvelous ease of an immy, whose free movement conjures up images of travel, though it has rolled only a hundred yards or so. The checker is close to the ground, all of it all of the time; to move it (one rarely pitches a checker) is quite awkward—you have to squat, thumb on the ground, middle finger moving up against that thumb until it makes contact with the checker and sends it on its way. It is a somewhat unnatural movement. My favorite checker game was the one where we chalked out boxes, at given distances from one another, and numbered them; then we moved our checkers from one box to another, the first one to reach the last numbered box being the winner. You were permitted to hit checkers in your way, to hit them, indeed, as far as possible out of the way. Your checker had to land inside each numbered box, not on any of the lines. There was, in fact, something pretty awful about lines, some superstition about boundaries, the way a kid might sometimes walk down the block carefully stepping over each line. But another kid might carefully step *on* every line.

Buttons were not much exchanged by us, though they were much more attractive and more varied than checkers, which were just about never swapped. These buttons showed political figures, political slogans, sometimes funny but rarely weird (no "Frank Merriwell is a Junkie"), as well as the features of military and sports figures, some of them heroes. Small and light, nothing but tin, you could carry many dozens in your pockets, where they jangled reassuringly. We did what everyone else did with buttons—pitched them against sidewalk line or wall, winner take all. It was more fun to pitch against a line, for then if your turn was toward the end, you had the chance to knock the leading button past the line, and with luck take its place as the leading contender. The more players, the more interesting—you'd pitch the prearranged number of buttons in one turn, or maybe in rotation, one button at a time. We played the same game with pennies, a more serious kind of money.

Pictures was the game which appealed mostly to the hoarding and commercial instincts or interests. Some kids saved their pictures; others took their pleasure in playing or exchanging them—Silas Marner or the mercantile princes. The fact is that most everyone had a few pictures he would never trade—perhaps an ancient sports hero put aside by the gum manufacturers who included these pictures in their packages as an incitement, we buying the pictures and chewing the gum which happened to be included. The value of these pictures (again mostly sports, political, and military figures, as well as movie stars) naturally varied enormously, according to the history, the style, and the dreams of the individual owner. In our play we flipped the pictures, the idea being to match a head or a tail. It was pretty much of a luck game, it being difficult to flip by effort a head or a tail, though I suppose some kids won more consistently than others. In this play one tended to use only his duplicates, for why risk a rare picture for a prevalent one when you never knew what the other kid was flipping? No, the rare ones, the solitaries, you saved, either never gave them up or traded them for other pictures on which, at the moment, you had your heart set. It was all kind of tricky, for you were at the mercy of the market, never knowing when a Christy Mathewson or a Bilie Dove might appear on the scene in overwhelming numbers, this season or next. These pictures, so much clearer than the buttons, were the most personal of the objects with which we played, being tied up with loves, identifications, ambitions, so we were trading the most precious parts of ourselves, and that was sad but more generous, more humane, than holding onto a picture which anyway in another day, another season, might be a drug on the market.

On the London streets which Douglas describes, boys would not be seen playing *Hoops*. The same went for our block—111th Street between Fifth and Lenox Avenues—about a decade after the period Douglas is describing. I guess younger boys *might* play with hoops, if they were *very* young and if no one were looking. It was definitely a girls' game, and thinking back on it, I don't see why. The manipulation of hoops requires great agility; they can be moved at terrific speeds, one can obviously swerve with them, take sharp turns on the run, even throw the things high up and catch them. Nevertheless, only the girls played this game, another psycho-sociological mystery.

Our author refers to the dying out of stone games because "there are not enough stones about nowadays." On our cement street we never saw a stone from one year to another (had to go to the park), certainly never played with them, but I imagine marbles are a kind of substitute for stone, except they are so round and regular and fabricated, obviously not as much fun as the irregularly shaped stone, the machine product so different from the rough-hewn natural object.

A piece of chalk! what wonders can be accomplished with this humble object, wonders not only of art (there was many a gifted draftsman on the block, creating the lovely arabesques washed away by the first rain) but also in one of the highest forms of sociability, the game. I recognized, among Douglas's chalk games, *Hopscotch* and the game of *Dots*. *Hopscotch,* together with *Beanbags,* was the girls' game par excellence. Our way of making fun of *Hopscotch* was to play it, swiftly, furtively, and unceremoniously, mimicking the shrill cries and the curtailed movements of the girls. *Dots,* if it is the game I have in mind, is more of an indoor game with us, played on paper, a page being filled, equidistantly up and down, with dots, and then the players, in turn, drawing lines between dots in order to create boxes, initialing those boxes. The one with the most boxes wins. It could easily be played on sidewalk and gutter, and sounds like the London game, for Douglas also refers to it as *Dot-Boxes.*

With that piece of chalk—either snitched from the forbidding school blackboard or bought in a box (the chalks either all white or varicolored)—we could create, in a moment, the most elegant boxball field. How easy it was for a couple of us to make the boundaries of the field, the bases, maybe a line showing the position of the pitcher, and close to the curb, or on the sidewalk, the inning diagram, chalked in bold utilitarian strokes and a hundred times more familiar to us than the shape of the Milky Way in the heavens we sometimes looked up to at night to guess what the weather might be like the next day for the scheduled Big League ball game

There was plenty of room for extra innings, and the teams were generally labeled by the names of those who had chosen sides, in itself a kind of game with rather subtle shadings. Who are the chosen, and why? And in the choosing, must not the chooser make his choice not only on the basis of skill, but on the basis of friendship, of favors done, of ties of loyalty deeper even than victory and loss? Yes, yes, in the ceremonial of choosing, the skill of the players chosen is one factor out of many, though for some choosers, who cannot abide loss or the possibility of loss, who do all they can to forestall that possibility, skill is the only factor.

And with this piece of chalk we played our word game (an exercise of the intellect after much physical exertion), you writing down the first and last letters, with dashes in between:

$$A \_ \_ \_ \_ \_ \_ \_ \_ M$$

and the other trying to guess the missing letters, to make the word. But you are playing the part of a hangman, for each time your opponent misses a letter, you fashion, stroke by stroke, the plank, the rope, and then the figure of the hanging man:

He guesses; you make your strokes; he is hanged or not, depending on his skill with words and the anatomical details of the hanging figure. For example, do you show the ten fingers and the ten toes individually?

There is an occasional familiar name among the many hundred that the London kids were playing in the early years of the twentieth century, and one is *Red Rover* ("Red Rover, Red Rover, Jackie come over"). Could that refer to Eric the Red? I don't recall that game nearly as well as one which I think is similar. It is called *May I?* (a bit too grammatical for our tastes, but the names of games are not soon changed) and is a game which dramatizes the caprice and abuse of power. The number playing is limited to the area chosen. All start on a given line, except for the leader, or caller, who faces the others from a distance, signals one out, and says: "You may take two little steps." But the player so addressed may not move (or he forfeits any space he may have previously been granted) but must ask "May I?" Then the leader answers "Yes, you may," or "No, you may not." It is all a question of authoritarian whim. The winner is the one who first reaches the line from which the leader calls his instructions. I think that the players are allowed to make a run for it on their own, defying "the arrogance of power," but are stopped at the point where the leader cries out the theft, and must move back a given distance ("Take seven giant steps backward"), even back to the starting line. It is a rather unpleasant game, and illustrates the horrors of unchecked power.

"If you want to see what children can do, you must stop giving them things."

This accurate observation is followed by a critique of ball-playing, particularly cricket, a game with which I am unfamiliar but I'm sure has lots going for it else it would no longer be played, and I don't know how ingenious the London kids were, or are, with a ball, though I doubt if there would be any national characteristics at play here, a ball being an object of universal interest. To me there is something near-miraculous in the way a New York kid can spin and reverse that ball.

I have closely questioned distinguished linguists on the origin of what the puzzled Douglas calls "A-Lairy" and what we call "larry," meaning "last licks," but have not come up with any revealing answer. I'd also appreciate hearing from any linguist in the house on the origin of the word *chickie,* meaning "beat it," "watch out," "danger," "trouble," and of the expression *lay chickie,* meaning "stand guard."

Johnny on the Pony is a game based on finding the weak spot and exerting maximum pressure there in order to cause a breakdown. A player on the defensive team stands with his back to the wall. A teammate bends over and puts his head into the standing player's stomach. Four, five, six kids (depends on who's around) crouch behind him so there is a horizontal layer of backs, somewhat irregular because of the varying heights and shapes of those who constitute this pony, this human chain, in which each player holds on to the sides of the one in front. The vertical player, the one with his back to the wall, hollers: "Johnny on the pony, one, two, three," and the first of the players on the offense makes a run for it, puts his hands on the back of the last defensive player, and springs forward, landing on one part or another of a crouching lad (or on parts of two of them). The task of the offense is to collapse the defensive team at any given point. The task of the defense is to hold the full weight of the attacking team. The offense naturally seeks to put as much weight as possible on one body, preferably the weakest one. But that one body (weakest or not) may show surprising strength, so the offense seeks another weak spot. And then some kids, bypassing the obvious strategy, just like to show how far they can leap, and will jump as far to the front as they can, flying over the crowded areas. Then there are personal elements which may interfere with the grand strategy. You might jump with special intensity on the back of a player toward whom you are particularly antagonistic at the moment, though he is not the prime target. The individual animus betrays the need of the collectivity. The collapse of one or more players on the defense ends the game. That is the moment of confusion, exaltation, and chagrin. If, however, the defense is able to bear the full weight of the jumpers, and holds that weight while the standing man (a kind of quarterback or coxwain with very little to do) hollers: "Johnny on the pony, one, two, three. Johnny on the pony, one, two, three. Johnny on the pony, one, two, three. All off!" the teams change sides.

King of the Hill is a game requiring the height that can be surrounded, assaulted, and defended. Lose that favorable position on top of the hill and you lose the game. Take undisputed possession and you are the winner (though immediately in contention).

There are activities on the street which are not exactly games, but pleasurable nevertheless. *Spitting* is one. There is a certain perfection of form, to create a symmetrical globule and to deliver that on target. Then, apart from the structural excellence, there was a pleasure in the unceasing quality of the spitting (what our parents used to call a habit, like *Winking*), the kid standing there and spitting idly, to punctuate a phrase or an epithet, or working hard to make what we called an "oyster" a perfect sphere of spit that maintained its shape throughout the duration of its flight.

Obscene Gestures filled up a certain amount of free time. One kid was an absolute whiz at making up variations of the classic Neapolitan gesture signifying "fuck you" or "up yours," that gesture being a hand placed on the wrist of the other arm, which arm moved vigorously back and forth while the hand slapped the wrist, moved up and down that arm. The boy I have in mind moved both his hands with bewildering speed over all parts of his body, up and down his arms and legs, on top of his head, around his neck, the arms jabbing away, moving with snake-like sinuousity, a hand (his own) suddenly appearing through his legs, always winding up in the crude gesture signifying hostility and separation. A curious way indeed of filling up the empty time, movements out of idleness choreographed by the bitterness of the soul's needs.

A game which was a particular favorite of mine has no formal name (true of lots of games). You started to play it by adopting the stance of the game, and then inviting, or challenging, some likely prospect, or just anybody who happened to be around—"Come on, whaddya say?" The opening stance of this game (it is like the hopping fight, in the off-balance category) is simple—feet spread apart, solidly on the ground, hands raised, palms out at about face level, the hands a couple of inches away from the face. The other kid does the same (only two can play). The feet must not move, and the object of the game is to throw your opponent off-balance by striking or pushing against his outstretched palms. There is a good deal of feinting, jockeying, as-if movements, and so on. Only the palms must be struck—contact with any other part of the body means disqualification. The trick is to make contact by a swift movement, when the enemy is a bit unwary, a bit off-balance, or plainly to be quicker and stronger in your thrust than his defensive powers will accommodate. You sway back, hold your position, and then if he falls back, if he loses position, you are the winner (how difficult it is to describe these simple, taken-for-granted movements). There are naturally arguments as to what means winning and losing—how far is back?—but the decision is made one way or another. A common way of losing the game is to miss the enemy's palms (his dexterity, your awkwardness) and then you lose balance and move forward against him. Lose your position and you lose the game.

Every block has a number of features which though they were not built for use in street games are nevertheless taken advantage of for that purpose. The *molding,* or cornice, on the building wall was a natural target for various ball games. The curb, besides dividing sidewalk from gutter and providing a seating area, made a fine edge against which to throw a ball, and was essential for Immies and the game of Racing Matchsticks during and after rainfalls. The *window ledges* were perched on, used for keeping score of some sidewalk games, the writing of slogans, comments, directives, the joining of names, though the walls, sidewalk, and gutter were used more for these purposes. *Sidewalk* and *gutter* were used in so many different ways, and constituted for the younger kids areas of safety and danger ("Keep out of the gutter!"). The *sewers* were hazards, but the *manholes* were logical bases, for the beginning and ending of races (though sometimes the boys based there would be lost in the steam or smoke which poured out of the openings). The *roof* (without which no building is complete) was a place on which to lose balls and from which to drop bags full of water. *The fire-escape rungs* were quite perfect for a species of basketball shooting using whatever round object was at hand; moderately empty garbage cans were used for the same purpose. Rather shallow wall *recesses* were used for climbing, sometimes to impressive heights ("The Human Fly," Harold Lloyd, the star of the film with—I think—that name). The *courtyards* were used for all sorts of games as well as for conversations, meetings which required seclusion, secrecy, even a kind of conspiratorial surrounding (the *hallway* was even better for that). The *stoop* was a natural ball-playing target. The *cellar* had a rear courtyard, which was pretty much out of bounds for us (clotheslines were there), and a front area, down into which we'd dash— generally for a ball—with a speed related to the gruffness of the janitor. The *lamp post* was used as a base for sidewalk games (like Hide and Go Seek for the little kids) and as a hangout for nighttime conversations. The *schoolyard,* a particular blessing on our block, was used for a variety of games and practice (set shots, lay-ups, and fouls in basketball; all modes of handball shots), and attempts at records, which we were always trying to set wherever we played, in the way of distance, duration, and all manners of consecutiveness.

The *automobile*—moving and motionless—is an important factor in street games. I have read that in the days of the horse and wagon the streets were quite crowded, but that would have been mostly in the commercial areas. The coming of the automobile not only clogged many residential streets with moving cars, but filled the streets with unmoving cars. (This is not exactly news to anyone, but it is necessary to describe the already-known in order to get on with the thing.) People take their cars home and leave them on the street. It was the kind of thing you couldn't do with a horse and wagon for too long a period of time. A horse has to be fed and there is no antifreeze for him.

So the car creates a double interference with street games—the movement of traffic, which interferes with the team ball games, track meets, all gutter games; and the stationary cars, which interfere with curb games such as Immies, and with sidewalk games, the ones played against building walls which require movement into the gutter. In the time I am describing it was possible to play games in the gutter—we'd keep an eye for approaching cars (no one-way streets yet), sound the warning, and stop the game until the car went by. The interruptions were not frequent enough to make the game impossible. The flow was not endless, and in the daytime there were very few cars parked. Most residential neighborhoods aren't much more crowded with pedestrians than they ever were, but the movement and the presence of cars makes the sidewalk a less pleasant play area.

Blind Man's Bluff, for example, which Douglas mentions as a street game, would be a pretty rough enterprise for today's streets. It has indeed become an indoor game, and not the only one that's been affected that way. Brueghel's famous picture (*Children's Games,* 1560) gives a sense of street play in the days before the internal combustion engine. The scene is a street but there is no sign of a vehicle. It is a marvelous and remarkably informative picture. The catastrophic effect of the automobile (fumes too) has no doubt been tempered by the ingenuity of the kids (are there any games which used parked cars?) but they (the kids, not the cars) are being pushed into playgrounds, settlement houses, gymnasia, and parks. These areas will never replace the marvelous freedom of street play, the games on the familiar terrain of your own block.

In the way of record-setting, *Pick-ups* was a game you played by yourself in the sense that you tried each time to break your own record, or maybe the block record (in which case it was advisable to have a witness). You threw the ball against the wall and caught it just after it hit the ground; that is, you trapped it, and knew perfectly well when it was too high for a pick-up, nor was there any sense in lying to yourself and forging a record about which you would be forever dubious. And how many times in a row could you hit the molding (whose function seemed aesthetic) and catch the ball on the fly? How many times could you make complete rotations of the weights tied to the end of strings? How many yo-yo returns? How many boxes could you jump? How many paper aeroplanes could you keep in the air at once? How many, how much, how long, how far? Setting records was an important part of street life, we struggling for fame against time, distance, and difficulties real and contrived.

Who remembers *Chinese Handball?* Theoretically any number can play, but three or four players are the most interesting number. There is a staking out of territory, a sidewalk box for each player (what would we have done without those boxes?). The ball must be hit into the box of *another* player on the bounce rebounding off the wall. If it lands in your own box, you can try again to hit it into an enemy box. Sometimes you hit a killer into your own box and lose the point, but the more usual way of losing the point is to hit the ball out of bounds. A way of winning the point, the cleanest way, is to hit a killer, or the closest to it, into an enemy box. A killer is a ball that cannot be returned, for it lands at the point where sidewalk and wall meet, so that there is no bounce: the ball is dead. It is more a game of losing than of winning in the sense that a point is lost if the ball is not returned to another box: lose a given number of points and you are out of the game. The one who is finally not out of the game is the winner. The losers have fallen away and left him isolate. He is the survivor. I don't know why the game is called Chinese Handball. The name obviously has something to do with the required bounce, which distinguishes the game from what we sometimes called *American Handball,* but what the relation is between the bounce and China remains a mystery. Could it have something to do with the weird notion some kids had that if you dug far enough you'd reach China? And the bounce is a downward movement?

The structure of games has a meaning and a fascination all its own. I have looked into the notion of the Beginning of games and will add a few words about the Middle and the End. The middle of a game has the charm and power of all ongoing activities, when the indecisions of early choice are behind one, with victory and loss not yet close (though many a game is wrapped up in the early moments). Aristotle put it in his weird amalgam of the plain and elegant: "a middle is that which both supposes something to precede and requires something to follow." Now how are you going to beat that? The middle is the time of utmost absorption, the play carried out for its own sake, the effort in a way the purest, for the game's sake. Now the contestants are in the fiercest struggle, the physical enjoyment now the keenest, the moralities of struggle almost forgotten. But the end looms soon enough, as the innings pass or the score mounts. The elements of victory and loss come to consciousness, pride and revenge emerge as factors, the pleasures of play are mixed with motives no longer related to the exploitation of the rules of the particular game but to the pleasures of victory, to the pain of loss, feelings common to all games. So much for the Beginning, the Middle, and the End.

Although we heard rumors of criminal activities of some of the big boys up-the-block, even that one of them (his name lingers in my mind) had been electrocuted as a convicted murderer, *guns* played a distinctly minor role in our play. We had *cap guns* (with the roll of caps sometimes more fun to burn as a unit for the firecracker effect), but we outgrew them quickly; they were part of the little kids' world of *Cowboys and Indians, Cops and Robbers.*

Water pistols were more in use. The problem here was water supply. That could be solved by shooting from your apartment window, particularly from the lower floors. Otherwise you could bring a bottle of water (it was precontainer time) into the street. Or more likely, use the water pistol only after the rain, sucking the water into the pistol from the ponds formed in the gutter breaks now known as potholes. It was a random activity, wetting one another, strangers too, by surprise or in formal battle. You could have targets, go for distance, but the guns didn't have that much power, the stream of water further of course than we could manage with spit or piss, that extra distance maybe part of the charm of the water pistol.

Nor were *kites* much of a factor in our street play. Occasionally they would appear, the flying a kind of solo activity, the kites often landing on roofs, tangled on fire escapes.

We had the usual methods of moving faster than our feet would take us—*roller skates,* and those same skates under boards, cartons, or fruit boxes, getting us to our destinations with ballbearing speed. On these skates we were most of the time not racing at all, merely moving around according to our inclinations, even in a tropistic manner, drawn or warned off, picking up speed, swerving, making long sweeping turns (most always someone to impress), reaching self-appointed destinations in sudden lonely sprints. On *sleds,* too, the great joy was the ease of the uninterrupted movement down the slopes in the park a few blocks off (the way Samuel Johnson thought the greatest joy in life was to roll down a hill).

On some days the street games were spread thin, kids playing alone or in small groups up and down the block. On other days some great event took the center of the stage—that event might be a stickball game with a team from another block, or a *track meet,* a kind of curtailed imitation Olympic Games. There were few field events (no chariot race). We had races of one, two, and three sewers' length (a sewer being the distance between man-holes); standing and running broad jump; standing and running hop, skip, and jump; marathon run (around the block a given number of times); and relay races. We divided into teams, kept score, and the meet often grew quite exciting, lasted sometimes to dusk, to early night, the young athletes laboring mightily, cheered on by one another, by strangers attracted to these efforts, by fathers on their way home, even by indulgent mothers subduing their pleas that food was on the table, waiting patiently for the last event.

There were imitative games (a kind of hockey on roller skates), aping the world of professional sports, and there were (on this block at this period, and at this time, say four o'clock on a Thursday afternoon) great varieties of individual and group movement, in the way of play or its more organized form, called game, the effect random, the way it is in Brueghel's painting. But you need only isolate the given activity in your field of vision to catch the specific quality of the movement: A tug of war, four kids to a side, each team pulling to get *them* over to their side, the losers/prisoners immediately released, nothing more to the game than that. Various kinds of entrancement, where one plays alone with an object which you throw away from yourself and then if comes back to you, could be the yo-yo, which *has* to come back to you, difficult *not* to catch; or the cup and attached ball, the latter thrown naturally up, but not that easy to catch in the cup, or has a way of jumping out after being caught; what you throw away from you (call it a lasso) and it comes back maybe with an object attached, could be human, not there previously. Aware too (now from the perspective of one of the players, not a spectator) of all the girls' games going on, such as potsy, a retrieval game of, say, a folded piece of tin from a series of chalk-numbered boxes, singing prison games ("take the key and lock her up, take the key and lock her up, my fair lady"), the classic ring-around-the-rosie, a discomfiture game. Aware, too, of the big guys, cards on stoop or ledge, pennies against a wall, games opening into the money world.

Circumstances change, and these games, for they answer to universal needs, will go on in one place or another. They will live whether they are chronicled or not, but it has been a pleasure for me to recall them, the way it was for Douglas, and will be for some future chronicler who will look into these games and see the beginnings of individual struggle, the cruelties and fulfillments of socialized life, the beginnings of the Community.

STREETS AND ALLEYS

For Diana

BALL OF FIRE

Eleven years ago—I remember the date because of an occurence which is not pertinent to this account—an old friend, that is, someone who used to be an old friend ("he used to be a very good ex-friend of mine") mentioned the name *Oblomov*. I had heard the name before, its mention now (eleven years ago) struck a chord familiar but unclear. I knew, for example, that the name related to a book, but I was not sure whether Oblomov was the title of the book or the name of the author. I knew it to be the name of a person rather than a place, and so if it *was* the name of the book it would refer (presumably) to the main character in that book. Because of the Paperback Revolution (which I will come to in a moment), my readers undoubtedly know that *Oblomov* is the title of a book, even that he is the main character in that book. It is not unusual, by the way, for the title of a book (even where the author is known) to be more familiar to the public than the name of that author. Is not *Don Quixote* better known than Cervantes? And would it be *too* surprising if, say 500 years from now, *Hamlet* were better known than Shakespeare? Explanations take one far afield, but this phenomenon—of the created object becoming more memorable than the creator—has some bearing on the value that mankind puts on the process of creation. So many worship the world over the God who made it, forgetting His name. But explanations take one far afield.

A little more than a century and a half after the French Revolution came the Paperback Revolution. Books that you could buy for a quarter, put in your pocket, read on train or bench, and then throw away if you felt like it, now began to sell for $2.45, and mostly too big to fit a pocket. That was the Paperback Revolution. True, all sorts of books began to be published (Out-of-Prints, Hard-to-Gets, etc.), and among these books was *Oblomov*. There were dozens of the books in a store in which I was browsing, for the economics of the situation demanded that these books be printed in five, even six figures. At any rate I bought a copy. (There is no better price in buying more than one copy.) Though my ex-old friend had praised the book rapturously, he had not offered to lend it to me, and I did not ask to borrow it, because I am the kind of person who finds it difficult to return books and does not like to be asked for them, which the admirer of *Oblomov* never hesitated to do. I remember asking for the book along Fourth Avenue (the one they have not yet succeeded in having people call Park Avenue South), but the booksellers had never heard of it, or it was out of stock, out of print, and so time wore on and I more or less forgot about the book, which joined that group of books that one plans to read. Many books are praised, and, generally speaking, books praised by those who know what they are talking about should be read, and the recommendations of friends are generally more interesting than the recommendations of reviewers and critics. One thing leads to another, circumstances and situations change, there came the Paperback Revolution, and I bought *Oblomov,* at an airport newsstand, where the choice of books is beyond understanding, almost beyond confusion.

I was on my way to St. Louis on a business trip. I started to read the book on the plane, and after a few chapters I fell asleep. That was the perfect physiological, even esthetic, reaction to this work, and I am sure the author, I forget his name at the moment, would have been pleased at my behavior. I do not mean that he was a propagandist for somnolence, but he surely saw it as a kind of Lesser Evil.

To those of you who are acquainted with this book, the idea of reading it in a jet plane, traveling at the speed of 500 miles an hour, is preposterous enough. I do not want to spoil the work for those who have not yet read it ("don't tell me how it ends"), but I can't be giving much away by pointing out that Oblomov is the essence of inertia, procrastination (the scene wherein he puts off everyday tasks is most amusing), the very apotheosis of ennui—that French neurological ailment, of a kind of golden boredom. Not altogether to my surprise, I discovered, in the introduction, before I fell asleep, that "Oblomovism" has a generic meaning in the Soviet Union, that the famed theoretician Bukharin (I am not quite sure whether he has achieved posthumorous, that is, posthumous retaliation, I mean rehabilitation, or not) used the word in criticizing the bureaucracy.

True, sleep was an ideal bit of criticism, but I was exhausted too, for I'd been on a very rough schedule for weeks. I am a keen contender in our famed rat race, but understand the importance of the cat nap, which is one of the marks of the successful man of affairs. Because of the time elapsed and the intensity involved, this sleep of mine turned out to be much longer than the typical cat nap. Indeed, I was plainly asleep, and it was the instruction of the stewardess—a charming girl with a delicate Irish accent, from Kerry maybe, or the Aran Islands themselves—"safety belts on, we're about to land," that woke me from my stupor, which is to sleep what sleep is to a cat nap. We were circling over the landing field and it was quite a beautiful sight. This was a night flight; I had completed a busy day, and my appointment in St. Louis was for nine in the morning. It would have been more sensible to leave earlier in the day, but the press of business forbade. I could have taken the train too, slept the night in pullman or roomette, but the fact is that I travel *only* by plane, become very restless in the slower vehicles of communication. The sight of the city not quite asleep was impressive, to say nothing of the circling lights, those searchlight rays on the field itself. My plan was to get right to the hotel and go to bed, and that I did. However, I was not able to fall asleep (because of the long nap, or short sleep on the plane), so I picked up *Oblomov* again. But it was not a good choice, because the author writes too engagingly of somnolence, one becomes entranced (my sleep on the plane was due, basic-

ally, to exhaustion), the way a master describer of the state of
boredom puts the reader in a state of excited awareness.

Oblomov does not like to move, he has plans that he shelves,
he gets into ridiculous arguments with his man-servant about this
detail or that, he thinks of his house and serfs in the province, of
work that must be done, of letters that must be written (the way
they had to be written yesterday and the day before). He smiles
and falls back in a benign coma of indifferentism—one of the
better kinds of coma. This is a task that can wait—if not today,
tomorrow will do just as well. Here is a task that *must* be taken
care of immediately, he lifts up his pen, is baffled by the demands
of grammar, sentence structure, puts down his pen, the message
loses its urgency, it too can be put off till tomorrow (but no
later!). He is happily somnolent again, has made a clear decision
to procrastinate, a powerful exertion of will, something to be
proud of. How nice that matters can wait, and then, if they are
left waiting long enough, can be forgotten. Oblomov dozes,
dreams cozily of a shelter, a Utopian childhood, but I realize—
there in that St. Louis bed—that I have neglected some necessary
work, work that I should have taken care of on the plane, that I
had *planned* to take care of on the plane but instead I had started
to read the book, and then the cat nap had turned into a nap, and
the nap into the genuine article. . . . I leaned over and picked up
my briefcase, which I always keep at the side of my bed, just in
case I should wake up in the middle of the night with a business
thought which I might have to check against the figures, for if
one goes back to sleep it is difficult in the morning to remember
just what it was you thought. You might forget a given number,
or the commercial complex in which the number has a meaning,
and these night-thoughts, so often forgotten, can be the most
significant ones, so I have trained myself to wake, jot down the
thought or number, and go right back to sleep. I don't require
much sleep anyway. Thomas Edison's four hours are about my
speed; too much sleep dazes me, puts me at a disadvantage for
the exigencies of the day. I took the papers out of my briefcase
and began to work on them.

Then, before I knew it—I am among those who generally

know when they are falling asleep—I fell asleep. I fell *off* into sleep with a suddenness which would have surprised me had I known that I was doing it. Then I went immediately into a dream that proved to me, even while I was dreaming, that I had read *Oblomov,* all of it, and very likely before it had been so highly recommended to me. There was Olga, in the dream, and Andrei Stolz (my somewhat altered ego), the not very bright, selfless Agafya, her villainous brother Ivan—all these, and others, appearing not at all according to the contours of the book but in my own form of distribution. And this night, on the plane, I had only read to a point where some of these characters had not even appeared! So I had either read the book before or, in the dream, created characters similar, name and all, to those in the book. A quick look at the book, past my placemark, showed me that the names I had dreamed were indeed the names of the people in the book, that I had not, as we say, "dreamed them up."

I do not consider myself a mystical personality; I stayed with the laws of probability, and the overwhelming evidence was that I had read the book before and forgotten that I had read it. Either it had had no effect on me, or, more likely, it had a powerful effect which I was interested in burying. But now the return had come in a dream. I moved (in the dream) among those maddeningly familiar figures in an atmosphere of anxiety. Oblomov was sadly reclining, removing himself from life's responsibilities, from its pettiness, coldness, and horrors. And there was Stolz, running through Europe like a madman, promoting one deal and another. I saw him in Prague, around a conference table (one of those covered with green baize in fact; it was a pool table), driving home a point, for the deal was in the balance, the crushing point had to be made. It was just then that I awoke and looked at my traveling clock, with its phosphorescent face. The time was ten after two, and I was wide awake.

Then I did something quite unprecedented (for me). I got out of bed, dressed, and went downstairs to the hotel bar. I had stopped in this hotel before and knew its bar. Had it been necessary to leave the hotel in order to get to a bar, I should probably not have dressed and left the room, because it was chilly out, but since there was a bar in the hotel I did not hesitate for a moment, and made my way down there. I felt that a change of scene might help me to think more clearly, and I did want to understand why Oblomov had been so completely erased from my mind; the fact is that I knew perfectly well, but wanted the comfort of whisky and a few strangers.

There were a few strangers down there, a precious few (as though a remnant, and therefore precious), and given the day (Monday), and the hour (already given), that was no surprise. There was a moody chap in the corner—they do tend to move to the corners—and a couple of men, either friends who had nothing much to say to one another (either because they never had, or out of exhaustion of subject), or men who had met for the first time that night and now had nothing much left to say to one another. At the one occupied table behind me a man and woman were discussing personal matters in rather loud voices—"You never did love me," "Don't tell *me* who to marry." It was warm, and comfortable, the way I had expected it to be.

The thing is—did I need this whisky to tell it to me?—that I am by nature indolent: to this day I must make an effort to get up in the morning, to get started. Once moving, I never stop: my reputation as a ball of fire is well deserved. But I move, as do so many of us who do not know the meaning of change of pace, out of anxiety, out of fear that if I don't start I'll never move, that if I don't move I'll never start, and if I don't keep moving I'll just stay put. As a kid I was as lazy as they came; I returned from school (on days that I wasn't able to beg off, feign illness, etc.) and liked nothing better than to lie down, with a book or magazine—something to incite my dreams—and spend the afternoon that way. My mother often tried to get me out of the house. I was, and remain, an only child, and she was pretty busy during the day, didn't mind having someone in the house, but at the same time she had my interest at heart, made efforts to get me out, where I could move around, mix in the life of the street, that perpetual movement from which I recoiled. Out on the street—for my mother sometimes struck a kind of insistent note which I was bound to obey—I usually wound up sitting on the stoop steps or on the curb (as a last resort, for there was no support for the back), watching the mad whirl. I never wanted to be chosen in, the kids after a while didn't want to choose me in, accepted my laziness, not without jibe and stricture, but now and then, out of desperation, where an extra man was essential, I was forced into the action, to the chagrin of the team to which I was assigned. I was not the stuff out of which the immortal heroes of the playing fields are made. My Eton would have led to *our* Waterloo. I was lazy in school too, kept looking out the window toward the freedom, not of movement in far places but to dreams undisturbed, for here in class I was sometimes brought up sharply, by the insistent, even the insolent questionings of the teacher. . . .

My father worked hard, six days a week, often not home till late at night, and he took it pretty easy on Sundays. At first he used not to be upset by my Sunday indolence, figured maybe I needed rest, the way he certainly did. He wasn't looking for trouble, but then things began to get to him—remarks by the neighbors, made directly or overheard, a note from the school which he happened to see, though my mother tried to protect him from these difficulties. One day he came home early from work and found me fast asleep. Another day he watched in amazement from our apartment window as I sat dreamily on the stoop steps, watching a punchball game from which I had artfully extricated myself. I had to explain to my father that I had come out into the street late (homework to do) after the sides had been chosen. I was getting to be kind of fat, something hard to imagine if you look at me today.

Well, my father slowly came to understand what was going on, and finally he raised the roof. He accused my mother of protecting me, indulging me, said I would become a drone, a parasite, and they got into a furious fight, my mother taking the position, which she did not altogether believe, that I had my own special way of doing things, that not all kids were alike, more about "specialness." "No kid of mine is going to turn into a bum," he shouted, "I'll see to that." Since I was his only child, he must have been referring to me. And he certainly did see to it. He had to get up before I did, but he made sure that I was up and dressed before he left the house. When he came home, he demanded to see my homework, cuffed me sharply if he was not pleased, was not averse to putting the belt to me. He wanted to know how I had spent the day and applied the corrective measures if he didn't like what he heard or didn't believe what I told him. That went on for six months, maybe a year, and it certainly got me moving. I haven't stopped since. And all on my own too, for I have up to now avoided marriage.

So it was not difficult to understand my forgetting Oblomov. It was a fear of returning to that old indolence, those golden hours of forgetfulness, all that avoidance of growth and responsibility, which the author of *Oblomov* has so unforgettably described. That is one way hot shots, demon salesmen, promoters, wheelers and dealers, operators forever on the way develop, that is one of the elements in the creation of the rat race, the orgy of restlessness with which we are all too familiar.

I guess Oblomov is a kind of secret hero of mine; one must admire the courage, so to speak, of his laziness, to say nothing of the lovable qualities with which his creator endowed him—his sweetness, his innocence, his absolutely unconniving nature, his loyalty, his infinite trust.

Not difficult, I thought, to understand why it was that I had read a book, forgotten that I had read it, and then realized (through the mechanism of a dream) that I had indeed read that book. But for the life of me I could not remember when. I no longer had a copy of that book (could I have lent it to the friend who had so unreservedly recommended it to me?), couldn't remember the shape, the texture, the color or binding of it. Was it a library book? Maybe. But what difference did it make? Yet I was puzzled. One doesn't like to imagine that whole areas of experience have disappeared like islands into a sea. Why, I thought, that is a kind of death to unremember what it is that has happened; it makes experience unreal, almost meaningless, means that what I am doing now may well be forgotten, that this moment at the bar, trying to remember, may itself disappear. And why shouldn't it be forgotten? Do you call this experience? Here, a stranger among strangers? The couple at the table behind me were making a phony effort at reconciliation. It was probably because the man (maybe husband) wanted a little action in bed that he was coming to agree to matters in which he didn't have much interest, meaning: we're together, we're friends. What if they were making a phony effort at reconciliation? I mean, what difference did it make whether these strangers got along or didn't get along? Somebody else's experience. We oughtn't to live off the experiences of others. The moral note.

It was pretty late, and I had to get up pretty early. The fact is that it is not easy for me to get up in the morning. I have trained myself to let the alarm wake me, but at the moment of waking there is a powerful urge to return to sleep. Now this is not uncommon, and most of us give in to another few minutes sleep. These tend to be the most delicious moments. But my habit is to throw the covers off immediately and jump out of bed, as though there were a demon beside me. There is such a demon, the imp of indolence, urging me to return to dream, to the softness of bed and sheet, to the warmth and darkness. Prenatal you say, and I would not deny it. But I am a true son of the West, my father saw to it. I am deaf to the siren murmur of prenatality, to the charm of Oblomovism, but at the same time I take no chances and go right for the cold shower (nothing like a cold shower to destroy the morning remnants of prenatality), rub myself vigorously, look out the window to see what the weather has in store for me, so that I may choose from my carefully chosen wardrobe. Of course the weather is only one element in this choice—it is more a matter of who it is I am going to see, the impression I feel I ought to make, etc. Then downstairs for a quick but nourishing breakfast (for I have come to believe what the sellers of breakfast foods want me to believe, that breakfast is a key meal, sets me up for the day). Many a day I have completed my business in the first hours of the morning, taking advantage perhaps of the somnolence of the man across the table, the sleep is still in his eyes, I lay out the papers, I talk fast, convincingly, his mind is off somewhere, he is shaking out the night memories, the night horrors, and I am fresh as a daisy—the shower has paid off, also the brisk rubdown, the intelligent breakfast.

But here—in this bar—it is close to three in the morning and I am not sleepy. I must be up at eight in the morning. How nice it would be if I could sleep through the day. And then I hear Stolz say: "Where are you? What have you become? You must come to your senses! Is this the life you prepared yourself for—to sleep like a mole in a burrow?"

But why is Stolz talking to me this way? Why is he saying that "in another four years there will be a railroad station there" (on Oblomov's estate which Stolz has been managing) and that "your peasants will be working on the line, your grain will be carried by rail to the landing stage. And after that school, education . . ."

My peasants—what an idea! I, who log seventy or eighty thousand miles a year of air travel! Well, of course Stolz is not talking to me, he is talking to Oblomov, thinking about Oblomov. It is time for me to get to bed, for I have a rough day ahead. How come that ex-old friend, that old ex-friend, hadn't offered me a copy of *Oblomov* (assuming of course, that he hadn't borrowed the book from me in the first place)? Not too nice of him, was it? Water under the bridge, ships that pass in the night.

In reading a book where an "I" is telling a story, I have often wondered how it is that the writer expects his readers to believe that a person who is not a writer by profession should be able to write in such a persuasive, even brilliant manner. The narrator may be a worker, a farmer, a merchant, a lawyer, and yet (as in Dostoevsky) one is quite carried away by the style. The writer, of course, is acting, and we the readers must accept the double role—we know that there is a writer behind the farmer, and we more or less accept the convention, wondering, meanwhile (for we forget that there is a writer behind the narrator), how a merchant, or a lawyer, could write in such a persuasive, even brilliant manner. Sometimes the writer, recognizing that his narrator is not a professional author, tries to write clumsily, the way a farmer, or engineer, trying to be a writer, might write. But that effort at *complete* identity rarely works; it is somehow better when the writer treats the narrator as though he were a writer, recognizing that he is not a writer, doubling up, so to speak, on the fiction.

Sometimes the "I" is the writer himself, writing in an autobiographical way, an as-if autobiograhical way, an imaginative autobiographical way, etc.

Sometimes, too, the "I" is indeed the writer himself, but he is not a professsional writer, in the sense that he does not work steadily at writing (though all those who work steadily are not necessarily professionals). He can be one who "wants" to write, or a blocked writer, or a failed writer, or even what I believe the Italians have called a "ceased" writer, one who has tried and given up, who does not plan to return.

I bring these matters up because I am not a professional writer, though indeed, like so many in my line of work, I fall among the as-ifs, the blocked, failed, and ceased. I am in the book business; it is possible that a keen reader might have guessed the "line" I was in by the knowledge I showed of the book business. Yes, I am in that line (it is abundantly clear by my manner of expression that I am not a professional writer), am a salesman of books, and as I've pointed out, a very successful one. I knock down twenty-five, thirty Gs a year, even more in an exceptionally good year. I suppose that I was drawn to the book business because I've always wanted to write, have worked up a few things on and off, but in a very sporadic way and never with any sense of the work having any real worth. Unfortunately, I deal in classic texts a good deal, sell to the colleges and universities, so I am always comparing my work to the best (that may be an error; perhaps it is proper to compare your work to the best *you* can do). At any rate, I've faded away from writing, done nothing at all for ten years, but this Oblomov business somehow stirred up my writing interests, and I've been moved to set down these happenings.

I left the bar just a few minutes before it closed (don't like to be in places when they close), and going through the lobby on my way to the elevators I saw a great automatic book-vending machine, lit up like a jukebox. This machine was filled, it goes without saying, with paperbacks, selling mostly for $2.45. The machine makes all manner of change (may even, for all I know, accept checks, money orders, letters of credit), and the book comes zooming down at you. It is not quite like picking up a dusty book off a shelf in a used-book store. *That* book you can examine at your leisure and return. *This* book you must choose and buy before touching. No browsing here. And no way of returning it. How is it possible to return a book to a machine? The title *Literature and Revolution,* the author Leon Trotsky, caught my eye, caught both of them in fact. One of our serious competitors—I mean a competitor who published serious books—had issued this volume, which was not calculated, sales-wise, to make furrows on the brows of the publishers of Ian Fleming. I felt that I ought to read this book and went to the hotel cashier, conveniently located near the machine, and got the necessary change (for the change machanism on the machine looked tricky, and I prefer to do business with people). The book came down at a terrific speed, all fresh, new, absolutely sanitary. It seemed to me that the vending-machine manufacturers had missed a bet. Why not a strain of music corresponding to the work purchased?

I then went upstairs to my room (having first to waken the drowsy elevator man, slumped over his stool in the corner of the cab, next to the controls; in this hotel, the selling of books was automated before the elevator). I went into bed and glanced at the book I had just bought.

I was nine years old at the time of Trotsky's death, so he is for me a figure out of history. Any person about whom you have not read in the daily papers, where his current activities are de-scribed, is a figure out of history. Russian politics have never particularly intrigued me, but I was, of course, aware of the significant, even tragic role of this man. Some of my older friends have a passionate attachment for him, though they seem to have slowly given up any political allegiance, and even seem to have lost interest in his political position, or meaning. But I had heard a great deal about his literary style and verve, and I felt that he would create a dialectical opposition to the Oblomovism in whose quiet backwaters I was somewhat fearful of being immersed. A little too much of that immersion would make me a dead duck (by drowning) in my country, in my time.

I looked through the book idly, and there, sure enough, was the statement: "One has to put an end to the romanticism of Oblomov and Tolstoi's Karataiev."

I was not familiar with the name Karataiev, obviously not an outstanding fictional figure because the name of his author had to be mentioned. But the name Oblomov stood alone—no need there for the author's name.

Then, a little earlier in this book this passage drew my attention, because it was what I wanted to read:

> Futurism is against mysticism, against the passive deification of nature, against the aristocratic and every other kind of laziness, against dreaminess, and against lachrymosity—and stands for technique, for scientific organization, for the machine, for planfulness, for willpower, for courage, for speed, for precision, and for the new man, who is armed with all these things.

True, true, just what I wanted to read, just what it was necessary for me to read, to avoid the perils of Oblomovism, this feudal swamp into which one can sink, and vainly struggle, and slowly die. This was modernity, even "futurism," which I vaguely recognized as a literary movement of the past. Of course, there is no need for an American to struggle to write this way, for we have no tradition of Oblomovism. There is a laziness approaching sloth, even sloth itself, but this is an individual phenomenon, not a social, nor even a group characteristic. In our business world the qualities of willpower, speed, precision are taken for granted (only the word *courage* strikes an odd note). These qualities have been, so to speak, internalized, and coming out in favor of such qualities would be, in the U.S.A., a tautological absurdity—if all tautologies are not absurd—telling people what they have been brought up not to believe but to live. Dreaminess and lachrymosity are not serious problems in our land; it is indeed the excesses of speed and precision that draw the criticism of some of our social observers.

But the Russians had Oblomovism to contend with, and after (even while) putting down the book, turning off the bed light, I thought of this problem as an individual, if not a social, hazard.

There were hints of it in my own psyche, a tendency toward the vegetative.

The attraction of Oblomov is, however, more than that of stupefaction and death, for he was, to repeat, a kind of hero—he was trusting, he recoiled from all conniving, the working of the angles, the sly washing of one another's hands, the subterfuges, the psychological elisions which go along with the speed and the scientific organization.

Yes, I thought, staring up at the hotel ceiling, hearing through the window (so I imagined) the flow of the mighty Mississippi, ours is a society of the morning, most of our work is done before noon, we rise swiftly from our beds at the sound of an alarm clock (think of it, having to be roused by an *alarm*), while Oblomov, fearful of this tricky morning speed, rose late and fell back, worried about those intricate responsibilities not yet internalized, then shaking off the worry in a species of somnolence, as though what is put off does not exist. He was a good fellow, ready to do anything for a friend, but seriously deficient in a sense of responsibility to the immediate. He almost achieved the responsibility of love, but not quite, and that drove him back to the fantasies and comforts of childhood, if not of prenatality. He found a wife who was also a mother—more a mother than a wife—an angelic creature, and she, in her own innocence, cradled him against the storms of reality. And so he died:

> However vigilantly the loving eye of his wife watched over every moment of his life, the perpetual peace and quiet, with one day sluggishly moving onto the next, gradually brought the mechanism of his life to a halt. Ilya Ilych apparently died without pain, without suffering, like a clock that stops because someone has forgotten to wind it. No one witnessed his last moments or heard his dying breath.

My eyes closed, the long day took its toll, I wooed sleep, found and conquered sleep, then fell into dream. I was in a pine glade, shady and warm, as comfortable as could be, half-asleep, looking up into a patch of blue sky. I had no place to go, nothing in prospect (I had in fact buried my appointment book deep in an unmarked place in the forest), I was quite unanxious about the passing of time. A little way through the woods was a lake, whose gray glint I could glimpse. Then I walked to that lake, which was frozen, and I skated on it, first gliding at my ease, then with mounting anxiety as the ice began to crack under me. "What an absurd mechanical dream," I thought to myself in my dream, very critical of my dream, as though I were a movie critic unhappy at what was being shown. Meanwhile, the ice continued to crack very insistently, and I woke to the insistent demand of my alarm clock. I jumped out of bed and tore into the shower, rubbed myself vigorously, then swiftly dressed, for I wanted a good breakfast before my early appointment. I put the two books on the bureau, the one by Trotsky, the other *Oblomov* (by Ivan Goncharov, translated by Ann Dunnigan, with a foreword by Harry T. Moore. A Signet Classic paperback published by the New American Library, 1963. 95¢).

PINKHAM: THE ENCHANTED ISLES

It is because my business is so well regulated, so stable, that the antics—how else can I describe them?—of Pinkham (some people don't seem to need first names) so much intrigue and sometimes annoy me. He has the office next to mine, and although the building is an old, solid one, I hear much of what goes on in there. It is simply that his enterprise is a noisy one, for I hear nothing at all from Mr. Worthington, who has the office on the other side.

The answer is not in the varying thickness of the partitions. I do not hear the telephone ring on either side, but Pinkham answers his phone with a roar. He must seize the instrument with the fury, the desperation of one who expects everything from this call, and that is the kind of man he is. Everything seems to depend on what he is doing at the moment; there seems not to be, in his life, any sense of an ordered future. With him it is all or nothing all the time. He seems not to be saving any energy for future contigencies, is ready to consume it all in the transaction of the moment.

Pinkham is a broker in the stationery line. He buys and sells mostly without seeing the merchandise. He has no inventory for he does not buy until he has sold. Once having sold the merchandise offered to him, he gives shipping instructions to his supplier, and bills his customers. That is fundamentally the nature of his business, which he carries on pretty much by himself, with the occasional help of a woman who comes in a few days a week to take care of the billing and of his office records.

He has no samples in his office, for he deals in job lots, his deals are one-of-a-kind, in items of every conceivable sort: 9500 boxes of discolored paper clips; 4800 rubber stamps on which the letter D in C.O.D. unaccountably appears as an E. Who could buy such a stamp? A good question, and Pinkham has a ready answer:

"There is a market for everything."

Job lots is one way of describing his business. *Distress merchandise* is more accurate. So much of what he buys and sells has been through fire, flood, all sorts of natural and social catastrophes: 5200 reams of corrasable typewriter paper that had been flooded when a sprinkler system went off by accident in a warehouse; 12,000 composition books that had unaccountably (the word "unaccountable" figures much in his buying) lain for some twenty-seven years in another warehouse (first in, last out) and the pages of which notebooks had turned a kind of dull gray, but otherwise in excellent condition. 35,000 envelopes with the mucilage missing; 90,000 large-size file cards, each one with a pronounced smudge the size of a half dollar right in the middle; 14,500 wall pencil sharpeners with the largest sharpener opening blocked by a kind of metal sliver.

All these oddities I heard about through the walls of our adjoining office. But sometimes the knowledge came through more personal contact. One day, for example, he rushed into my office carrying a box with maybe 100 pencils in it, which he gave to me.

"Look," he said.

I looked at one pencil which had the name of a restaurant in a small Indiana town and a Muck Avenue address.

"It was supposed to be *Luck* Avenue," said Pinkham. "I bought 65,000 of them for something like half a cent apiece, and believe me they're terrific Number 1 pencils, made by one of the top manufacturers in the country."

"Thanks very much for the pencils," I said. "Why didn't the manufacturer block out the whole name and address?"

"To run all those pencils through again?" hollered Pinkham. "That would cost a small fortune. It's cheaper for them to sell it to me."

Pinkham coming into our office is like a hurricane whirling through a room where all is neat and in order. Though I rather like him, often enjoy his company, his presence disturbs me, as though his habits of disorder, a kind of chaos which he carries with him, will disrupt the smooth functioning of my business.

I am in the belt business. I handle a number of lines of men's belts, some women's belts. I have been in it for many years, have dealt with the same manufacturers, have pretty much kept my customers. I get excellent terms from my suppliers, have a prime credit rating with the bank because the bankers like my financial statement, because I've been doing business with them for a long time, and they've never had any trouble with me. If I have to borrow money, my payment is prompt.

I know pretty well where I stand in my business all the time. I think I'm fair to my workers. The enterprise moves smoothly, a minimum of friction. We have our good years and bad, but usually keep the profits at a decent level.

If anything, I err in the direction of caution; when some deal comes along that has a speculative ring to it, I tend to shy away; I'm not *much* of a gambler, would rather work with tolerable profits than take the chance of doubling my money or losing half of it.

I've studied some psychology books and I think I understand pretty well the nature (if not the causes) of my prudence and need for order. And I sometimes think of Pinkham as the Unconscious roaring into the living room of my ego; it is perhaps a fancy way of putting it, but that's how it sometimes strikes me. 4700 of those pens that wrote underwater submerged in error for nine years when some testing procedure went wrong, and who bought them? Who but Pinkham?

And the rubber bands, which, because of some manufacturing distortion, came out so huge that the band, when stretched, was big enough to circle, or enclose, an ordinary-sized desk. Pinkham came in one day and showed me on my own desk! He bought

600,000 of these rubber bands without the slightest hesitation, to say nothing of the incredible number of erasers which plainly wouldn't erase, and the 140,000 office sponges which didn't hold water very long (unaccountably, no doubt). Why would he buy all these products? But I've already explained his reasoning.

I often discuss Pinkham with Mr. Worthington, who occupies, as I've already stated, the other adjoining office. He is a lawyer who specializes in bankruptcy cases, and believe me, I hear some hair-raising stories from him about people who don't run their businesses properly, carry too much overhead, don't make the proper judgments about market trends, who take unnecessary risks. I find the subject quite fascinating, like to hear the details of the bankruptcy cases in which Mr. Worthington is involved. He gets to know a good deal about the people involved, their characters, how the family is affected, all sorts of private matters.

He has a certain confidence in Pinkham's ability to survive the storms and stresses of his commercial life, although, as he pointed out, he's known him for less than three years. That is as long as I know him, for it was then that he took the office next to me.

"Do you know," Mr. Worthington said to me one day when he dropped into my office, "Pinkham told me that he's just bought 3700 postal scales which are defective, off by a half cent. He said it was a terrific buy, that since the scale was exactly one-half cent off, that made it easy for the user to figure. Not that he wouldn't have bought the scales if they were off some other amount. Mad as he sounds, he's a pretty shrewd man, and I doubt if I'll ever be doing business with him."

That statement chilled me a bit, made me wonder if perhaps, in the inflationary times we were living through, I was being *too* cautious in my business dealings, not marking up the merchandise enough, for example. Indeed, in the last few months my profit margins have been quite slim, I need money to meet my bills, all expenses are up, the interest rates are fantastically high. But God forbid I should learn *anything* from Pinkham on how to run a business. And it wouldn't surprise me that much if one of these fine days Pinkham was in the toils of the bankruptcy court and running to Mr. Worthington for advice.

Not that I wish him any bad luck. Why should I, considering that he's not a bad fellow, and except for his noisy telephone conversations, a good office neighbor (ours is a small office building, and I am well enough disposed to him to call him *neighbor).*

I found out more about Pinkham the other day when I went into his office to leave word that the telephone repairman had not found anyone in and had left word with me and that he'd be back in a couple of days (I wondered whether Pinkham's screaming had damaged the phone mechanism, but didn't ask the repairman about it).

Pinkham was not in his office, but the woman who worked for him, a Mrs. Jacobs, was. She appears to be in her mid-sixties, reserved in manner, almost serene. She said that she had been working for Pinkham for about two years, that she preferred the part-time aspect of her job. I knew that she was a widow.

"It's hard not to know something about your business," I said.

She smiled and said that Pinkham wasn't the quiet or secretive type.

"Is there *anything* that he won't buy?" I asked.

"I've yet to see him turn anything down," she answered. "In the last couple of weeks, if you haven't heard, he's bought ten gross of clipboards whose clips don't quite hold the paper against the board; 14,000 lined 8½ × 11 yellow pads every other line of which is missing and down whose sides run two heavy verticle lines; 30,000 Number 2 pencils whose points tend to break when sharpened by machine but which take well to knife and razor sharpening; 7700 scotch tape holders whose cutting edges are extremely dull, in some cases nonexistent; 1800 boxes of greeting cards which had printed *Happy Mew Year* (Pinkham said that catowners and fanciers would be interested, that he'd sell the cards to pet stores!) and some 2000 boxes of cards with the imprint *Reason's Greetings* [with which Pinkham said he'd circularize college and university Philosophy Departments]; 1350 zipper-style key rings each with a couple of teeth missing."

"Do you understand how he got into such a business?" I asked.

"Well," she replied, "I gather that he's always been interested in buying and selling, that he left home as a boy, peddled merchandise in the streets, never worked for anyone, always in business for himself, I'm not sure how he got into the stationery line, but he seems to enjoy it. I don't think it makes much difference *what* the line is."

"Perhaps his upbringing," I said tentatively, not wishing to put Mrs. Jacobs in the position of talking about her boss in any kind of private or intimate way, but I was curious nevertheless.

"I don't know much about his upbringing," answered Mrs. Jacobs. "I have the impression that he's from a fairly poor family, grew up in Brooklyn."

She paused, and then went on:

"You know, some individuals grow up in conflict with their upbringing, live an opposite kind of life; others go along with their upbringing, even exaggerate what it is they accommodate to. More of the same."

"And Pinkham?" I asked.

"I don't know," she replied.

The phone rang and Mrs. Jacobs answered it, said that Pinkham was due back within the hour. She took three or four of these messages during the quarter hour of my visit.

In her unruffled, serene manner, Mrs. Jacobs told me that Pinkham was married (something I had not known), that he lived with his family way up in Westchester County, and that though the office was noisier and more chaotic than I imagined when Pinkham was there, and that his fanatic business interest and involvement sometimes got on her nerves, he was nevertheless not a difficult man to get along with, was indeed quite a generous boss, and with a kind of sweetness under that commercial ferocity. . . .

And now, this very morning, Pinkham stormed into my office, carrying a box which he threw on my desk. In the box were six men's belts.

"I've got something for you," he said. (But Pinkham never "says"—he "cries," "hollers," "screams," "shouts," "speaks excitedly.") "These belts just came in from Hong Kong. They're a terrific buy. Tell me what you think."

I had long imagined the possibility of this situation, and now that it was upon me, thought to play it cool, warily.

"This is not exactly your line, is it?" I asked.

"Not in my line!" exclaimed Pinkham. "Why not in my line? A high-class stationer carries wallets, belts, key rings, and so on. Anyway, why do I have to sell to stationers only? True, I have extensive contacts in that line, but when a deal like this comes along, I don't just turn it down. I want to give you first crack at these. 400,000 can be bought. They're laying right now in a warehouse in Hong Kong."

I had been carefully examining the belts, and under the spell of this close examination Pinkham paused, waited with the tense expectancy of a patient facing the noted diagnostician.

"Well, what about the belts? What do you think?"

"You know," I said, speaking very slowly, "there is something wrong with these buckles."

"Well, what do you expect at the price I haven't told you yet? Perfect merchandise? What's wrong with the buckles?"

"They're not properly fastened into the leather, and with some wear, they'll probably break away."

"So what's so terrible? If a man buys a bargain, he's not going to expect wear forever. Are the six belts in that condition?"

"Well, that seems to be the fault," I replied. "One is perhaps better than another, but that's where the trouble is, in the fastening of the buckle."

"Look," hollered Pinkham, "nobody is going to get killed if a buckle on a belt tears. Anyway, all the merchandise is sold strictly *as is*. No guarantees. Do you know how much I can buy them for?"

"How much?" I asked.

For the first time in my experience with Pinkham, I heard him whisper, though there was no one in the room with us.

"Twenty cents apiece, and that is the delivered price."

Now he came back in full volume.

"Buy half with me," he boomed. "We'll go in partners. I can

turn these over myself. But why shouldn't I put you into it? That's a lot of belts. You'll make it easier for me. I can have the belts here in less than two months.What do you say?"

"I'll have to let you know," I answered. "Let me sleep on it."

"A fine thing to sleep on," cried Pinkham. "Instead of sleeping on it, why don't you think on it, and let me know today? I have lots of calls to make. I want to know where I stand."

"All right," I said. "I'll let you know later in the afternoon. I'll talk to my associates, maybe make a few calls myself."

Pinkham was disappointed that I had not immediately gone along with him on this fabulous buy from Hong Kong. 400,000 belts from Hong Kong! I saw the impression this image had made on Pinkham's childlike, voracious imagination.

"I'll come to your office later on," I said, but even as I said that, I knew what my answer would be, for in the course of this brief interchange I had already examined all the possibilities.

I surely would not go in with Pinkham on a partnership basis, though I'm sure he didn't mean that in a legal way, and was offering me half the merchandise, leaving the details to be worked out. I was not interested in buying half the deal, because that involved an immediate investment of $40,000, which was plainly more than I wanted to put into the deal.

My immediate reaction, no doubt my instinct, was to stay out of the deal altogether. I could not possibly approach a number of my customers with this type of merchandise. Indeed, if it were anyone but Pinkham involved, I'd have turned the offer down out of hand. Such offers (though not on so grandiose a scale) had been made to me before, and I had never gone along. It was just not my way of doing business. The one-shot deal is indeed just the opposite of my way of doing business, as I've already indicated. I don't do business that way, I don't live that way.

But at the price, all things considered (including the quality of the merchandise) it was a good gamble. Certain of my customers would be interested, others in the trade that I knew by reputation could be approached. Indeed, the conservative way in which I conducted my business would be in my favor, for I had built up a certain reservoir of trust. And I had run down the belts to Pinkham a bit more than they deserved. Indeed they would be sold *as is,* and indeed the possibility of this unexpected profit interested me; it could be a shot in the arm for what looked like a bad year.

But all these considerations would have meant little were it not for my feelings about Pinkham. How disappointed he looked when I told him that I wanted to think the matter over! I want Pinkham to understand that I am not quite the stick-in-the-mud that he takes me for, that I have a bit of the gambler in me.

And I too was fascinated by the 400,000 belts lying in a Hong Kong warehouse. I had once taken a course at the Cooper Union on International Trade. Part of the course dealt with the opening of trade with the East. *The Enchanted Isles.* That fascination revived in me, stirred the speculative element, all so different from my run-of-the-mill business.

All these thoughts and fancies had gone through my mind while I was examining the belts and talking to Pinkham, and before he left my office I had decided to go into the deal for 20,000 belts, 5 percent of the lot. That would disappoint Pinkham in a way, but I was going along with him part of the way, I would now be involved in some of that screaming and carrying on next door, now Pinkham would be hollering for me too.

CHANGE OF HEART

I. MY FRIEND

Do you remember how years ago, and not too many at that, we used to say, in a kind of jocular manner: "my *frand*," not "my *frend*," but "my *fraaand*," carrying the *a* out to inordinate lengths? It was supposed to be funny, but I never could see why. Perhaps it was the trademark of some fogotten radio comic. Nevertheless I'd laugh, even caught myself using the expression and watching others laugh. It was a way of being part of the group; in order to be part of the group, you had to use group expressions (even those used by other groups), that was part of the fun, though the phrase was not particularly funny, not even intelligent. But I am digressing. The fact is that I had a friend, have a friend, and, as the politicians say: *let me say this:* he's an oddball. I mean that he has curious modes of behavior, is full of unexpected turns, has weird interests and surprising categories of information, sometimes knowledge. I cannot be more specific for reasons which will soon appear.

2. THE REASONS APPEAR

As an author, people are my medium. This is a crude way of putting it, but I can't think of a more elegant way of expressing myself. Very well then. People are my medium. Painters, musi-

cians, need people, everyone needs people, but painters and mu-
sicians do not need people the way a novelist needs people. They
are, so to say, the substance of his work, the raw material, the
substratum, the structural, as opposed to the superstructural elements. One takes his people where he finds them, adds understanding, analysis, maybe a dash of humor, or eccentricity, etc.,
and comes up with a brew, a person who fits into a given narrative, and generally gets lost in the shuffle. I have used all sorts of
people that way, sometimes with success, sometimes in a leaden
manner (everything sinks). But that's not the point. The fact is
that I cannot use this particular friend because his oddities are so
unusual. That is a redundancy, but that is the best way I can say
it. What I am saying of this friend is true of all my friends: they
all have unusual oddities, cannot be jelled, so to say, to confor-
mations of a conventional sort. I dare say that most of us have
such friends. It is only necessary to know people well, and we see
how peculiar they are, how they cannot be leveled out in a prose
narrative, and that is what we are considering. Maybe that is not
true of *all* of my friends, it is certainly true of *most* of my friends,
there are always some who are afraid of their oddities, and the
fear becomes the real self, so there is nothing odd about them
except the fear, and that is monotonous. I cannot, therefore, use
my *fraaand* (or any of my friends) because I know them too well.
That wouldn't be fatal (for why not write in a careful, measured,
objective way about your friends—who would complain if the
image is fair, truthful?) except that I am drawn precisely to their
oddities, to their most disagreeable traits, drawn to what is most
odious in them. And there are crudities, malformations which
cannot be disguised. So it is that I have this rich material on
hand, and because of my scruples (I guess they're my scruples)
cannot make use of it.

3. WHAT TO DO?

So I clearly had a problem on my hands, a business problem. I
owned, as it were, a valuable piece of property, but could make
no use of it; it was too individualistic a holding for my use, for, as

the politicians used to say: *let's face the facts,* and the facts are that I cannot make use of those I know who are sharply individuated, for that becomes too delicate a process (and creepy too). These vivid personalities are all too recognizable, so that my problem may not be one of scruples at all, but may boil down to a fear of losing my friends. Auden has pointed out that the Americans are lonely people, much lonelier than the Europeans (what about the Asiatics and Africans?). That may be so as a generalization, but the only thing that's stopped me from being lonely is that I have friends, and the surest way to loneliness is to lose friends (without making new ones) and the surest way to lose friends is to hold them up to unfavorable public scrutiny, for I've already pointed out that I do not find their better qualities particularly interesting. I move toward the weird, even the diabolical. And I definitely do not want to be lonely. Circumstances have on occasion made me lonely, but I should like not to repeat those circumstances, so I cannot ruin my friendships, such as they are, for that way lies loneliness. If only I could write about our Founding Fathers the way Shakespeare wrote about the old British kings, or the Greek dramatists about the old gods and heroes. But I am drawn toward my contemporaries. That's how the billiard balls break. Now I could give up my friend, forget him for purposes of literature, throw him back into the bustling crowd, but that would be most imprudent. I see no reason why this man should not be given his place in the world, if not by me, then by some other author who *could* make proper use of him, that author under no suspicion, being innocent of friendship. But who should I approach with this prize? Ha! I thought of Ned Norris. The very man.

4. NO DICE

Ned Norris was a young man who had tried to bypass the Organization by selling his own poems direct, and then, one thing leading to another, he went into the business of selling plots, ideas, etc.—first his own, and then as a middleman. I had had some contact with him a few years back, when I was desperate for a subject matter, and he was, if not invaluable, of some help to me. What actually happened was that I swapped a few ideas which I couldn't use for the subject matter which I needed so much. There was also a cash consideration on my part, because the ideas I submitted didn't add up to much (otherwise I could have made *some* use of them), rather thin, but Ned thought he could place them. I had never gone to him with a full-bodied character of this sort, you might say a living object, unique, idiosyncratic. I approached the merchant carefully. Norris happens to be an exemplary man of business; he is always dealing in sensitive areas where morality and self-interest join, and his reputation is of the highest, deservedly so (it is not so of all the highest reputations). I approached him carefully, and here it is more a matter of my caution than of his probity. It is like taking a patent to a manufacturer. He is honorable, but you are cautious, because honor has its limits; then, too, there are others in his enterprise, you don't know about them. Also files get lost, papers stolen. There are many reasons for care even in dealing with the purest of individuals. So I told Norris what I had in mind. He listened carefully, then shook his head. "I'm sorry," he said, "but the market seems to be glutted with unique characters at the moment. I've bought three or four of them in the week—a fantastic miser, a lecher beyond belief, a woman of unimaginable purity. I'm really overbought at the moment." I started to be a bit more cagily specific, to prove the unusual quality of what I was offering him, but he waved me off. "I don't doubt you," he said, "I'm just not in a buying position. Maybe in a couple of months." So we chatted for a couple of minutes, and then shook hands before my departure.

5. WHO THEN? I CHOOSE WRONG.

If Norris was out of the picture (and he was out of the picture), who then? I knew of no one else in that line (Ned had a monopoly by default, not by merger or conquest). Why not a writer? We are in a competitive field, but that is no reason why we shouldn't do business together, and we do business together (as well as fight for the available material, and steal from one another). Then it became a question of what kind of novelist I should approach. Naturalist? Realist? Symbolist? Regional? Historical? Picaresque? Hard-boiled? Encyclopedic? In thinking of the categories, I hit on the man. He was a solid-type novelist, who moved freely between the Social and Psychological, who had once sold a novel to the movies and was now either in a decline or not publishing. But I knew that he was flexible, had successfully handled extreme characters (what Sherwood Anderson calls "grotesques")—the fact is that once I had thought of the man, I had no difficulties in thinking of numerous reasons for the aptness of my choice. I phoned him—we mixed in intersecting circles—and he said he was interested, so I went over to his apartment the next day. I had to be even more circumspect with him than I had been with Norris, for the author was more interested than the merchant. Also, since my contacts with the author had been peripheral, for the circles in which we moved intersected at close circumferential quarters, he represented for me—and here I am making an unusually mixed mathematical metaphor—an unknown factor in the moral algebra. I showed my caution by talking with complete candor about the general situation, but holding back on the details. "He is fabulous," I said, and I mentioned the names of two Hollywood stars who would be perfect for the role. "Frankly," he said (and that word heightened my circumspection, for when someone introduces a statement by saying "frankly" or "truthfully" or "honestly," I am on my guard, because it is not for the speaker to characterize what he is about to say, it is rather for the listener to judge what it is that the speaker says)—"frankly," he said, "I am interested in what you have to say, because I can use a strong secondary character." "I have a strong primary character," I replied, for it was clear that he was looking ahead to the price differential. "Whatever he is," said the writer, "I need more information." Now if Norris had said that I'd have given him further information, but I have explained my reasons for my circumspection with this author. So I said nothing about my friend's incredible relations with his wife and children, his attitude toward his parents, but stayed with a certain kind of social behavior. "Well," I said, "he can come into a room, look swiftly at all the books on the shelves, and then amaze the company, particularly the host and hostess, by moving unerringly to the shelf when a given book is mentioned and picking that book out. It is done through the memory of color, shape, and texture. He also knows the maiden name of every president's wife." Now these were not true statements about my friend, but similar in quality to true statements, and when the writer pressed for further information, I gave him more intimate details, not true, but qualitatively analogous. "Come now," he said, "you can do better than that." So I gave a little more information, in the manner I have described. There followed a commercial pause. "Look," he asked, "what do you want for him?" "$2800," I said, though prepared to settle for something in the area of $1500. "You must be quite mad," he said "I'll give you $500." He pulled a checkbook out of the desk drawer. I disregarded that move. "I'm sorry," I said, "but there is no basis for discussion." If I had had papers and a briefcase, I would have put the papers in the briefcase and left. As it was, I just rose and started to leave. He raised the ante to $700. I waved off this amount. "That is not a serious offer," I said, "let's forget it." "I'll go up to $750," he said, "but that's my top." "I'll go down a little," I said, "but first you'll have to come much closer." "No," he said, "that's all I'm prepared to pay," and I believed him, so that was the end of the bargaining.

6. A MORAL QUESTION

I was prepared to leave, but he raised a moral question. "Look," he asked, "how come you're making this sales pitch?" I assumed that he didn't like the style of my business approach, and I started to answer accordingly, to justify that style, but he interrupted me: "Oh, no, I mean what *right* do you have to sell this character to me? You don't own him. He certainly didn't give you permission." He was of course using the word *character* in its psychological setting, as structure, rather than in the invidious sense in which it has come to be used—*what a character*—where a certain admiration mingles with a fairly low estimate of the one so described. I was surprised that he had seen fit to raise this question, because he had lived for years in the world of mass magazines, the big publishing houses, even the movies (not only selling a book to them, but writing scenarios), and no milieu can be so demoralizing as the one which is approached with idealistic sentiments where those sentiments have no place to live and breathe. But man's better nature can somehow, sometimes, survive all manner of horror and degradation. "Why," I said, defensively I admit, "what is this sudden squeamishness on your part?" I wondered suddenly if this weren't a trick, a calculated maneuver to make me lower the price. "After all," I went on, "aren't we all vultures, living on the death of experience, our own and others; do we not circle round, waiting for all signs of life to depart, and not hesitating, when desperate, to attack the living?" I was carried away by my own imagery, saw vultures hovering over far-off deserts where a solitary man stumbles wearily toward his home, his fort, the oasis mirrored in the psyche, but finds no bubbling stream at all, no lovely shade, nature's simplest boon. *Dead souls,*" muttered the novelist, "*dead souls.*" "How wrong you are!" I exclaimed (when I "exclaim" something I always feel like one of the Rover Boys, usually the fun-loving one), "I am *not* selling the dead, I am *not* exploiting the living, I am selling an abstraction, a lifeless structure into which you must breathe a spirit. Call it an idol, even a golem. But who is being hurt, that is my test of morality. Who is being hurt?" "I must say," said my rival, "that your thinking is very shallow, very contradictory, against the canons of both Aristotelian *and* mathematical logic. You're *not* exploiting the living? What do you mean *abstraction?* You are trafficking in human flesh, you are selling a friendship, a living person you cannot make use of. So you peddle him in the marketplace, to any comer. What a concept of friendship! What hypocrisy! What *harm* is being done? You sell a friend to a stranger, who may use him in any way that he sees fit, ridicule or cheapen him, and you set up this absurd, self-annihilating pragmatic test, ask who is being hurt." He paused, for breath and because he had said what he wanted to say. I could not remember the last time I had been spoken to in that way, maybe by an elementary school teacher at whom I had brazenly stared, maybe by my father for breach of some ancient observance. "Well," I asked, "if this behavior of mine is so monstrous, why are you doing business with me? Aren't we in the same boat?" "Oh, of course," he said, "we're certainly in the same boat, but let's understand what it is we're doing; let's not act as though this were a perfectly honorable transaction."

7. MY CHANGE OF HEART

He was right. No question but that he was right and I was wrong. I have always felt that one changes a point of view, a belief, slowly, that the change is part of the proceess, the way a tendency turns into a structure, and have always been doubtful of sudden conversions—to God or to Party. We learn slowly, even painfully, must climb to green pastures rather than be catapulted. So I feel that what happened on the road to Damascus was the end of a process, we not quite aware of what went on before. And when the youth (back in the 1930s) signed the Party card, or was simply swept away by a vision of the City of Justice, it needed more than the act of police brutality or the fiery speech from soapbox or rostrum. So now, feeling that the novelist was right and that I was wrong, I saw that he pointed up for me what I had long been considering, if not explicitly, and that only an exciting cause was necessary to effect a change of heart. I thought of the fuse which (as we learned in high school) set off the powder-keg of Europe. And Lord Grey pointing out, in an image which only visually contradicted the lurid battle flames, that the lights were going out all over Europe. The flames of battle, and the dimming of lights, the diamond points of civilization struggling, the rays sharpened by long labor struggling against the enveloping darkness. But that's off the path. My prospective buyer was right and I was wrong. I was selling what I could not use. I resolved to use it. I resolved to look more honestly at my friend, the one I was selling (they were all for sale); not to focus on his oddities, but to see those oddities in the frame of an ongoing life. Naturally to poke fun at the ludicrous, the irrational, the monomaniacal—consider the debt we owe to Molière—but whatever the emphasis be, the total picture cannot be distorted. Man can become a monster, but the becoming is crucial, as well as the monstrousness. That was the way I changed. "You're right," I said to the novelist, "the deal is off. My friend is not for sale."

THE CALLER

Formerly a sound sleeper, and sleeping regular hours, he began to wake up every morning at 4 A.M. He had tried the experiment, on a few evenings, of setting his alarm for 3:30, then waking and listening for a sound. But there was no sound between 3:30 and 4 A.M., and he was unable to understand what it was that woke him every morning at the same time.

He did not wake with a start; rather he found himself with his eyes open, speedily awake, looking out the window, and with a feeling of lightheadedness which enabled him to see clearly the most indisputable and necessitous facts.

Mainly the death and disappearance of all most intimately connected with him, the inevitable death and disappearance seen clearly and with mounting sense of anxiety.

This early-morning experience was the recurrence of a childhood experience of the same sort, where the sense of extinction involved the whole planet, and incidentally its inhabitants.

But now the planet remained, only certain individuals disappeared from it, off the face of it and under the ground of it. Moreover, where the child, visualizing total extinction, fell asleep shortly afterward, now the young man, with a less apocalyptic, if more intimate view of disaster, was unable to fall asleep, but grew more awake, more and more lightheaded, and more and more anxious.

Out of this state developed his relation to the telephone company. Wide awake and lonely, wide awake and anxious, he dialed for the correct time, and listened for minutes on end to the impersonal rhythms of that announcer.

Or dialed the Weather Exchange, and listened to the impersonal and unchanging pronouncements of that operator. She never varied her announcement, she never varied the tone of her voice, announcing alike storm, calm, and meteorological freaks.

He waited for a break in that voice, never with success, and took to questioning that voice, but never with success; merely the infuriating, evenly timed announcements, and never a break in the voice, come question or demand, or the hoarse shrieking which he sometimes adopted.

If only because the time of the day changes, the voice of *that* announcer seemed more personal; if, from quarter minute to quarter minute, it could change its pronouncements, couldn't it also break out of that ring of time and answer a simple query of his?

It could not, it never did, he was never able to detect a personal rise or fall in that voice, wheedle or scream as he would. Apart from his loneliness and anxiety, he was overcome by a childhood feeling of the personal relation between the subscriber and the operator. "Hello Central Hello." At that time young men were supposed to make dates with the operators.

But here was this impersonal voice, the wax voice, which defied all interruption to continue on its even course, this voice which told over and over the time of the day and the state of the weather.

With a sudden inspiration he dialed the Operator!

That personal voice asked him once, twice, what he wanted, but he was too surprised to answer, and further, wanted nothing but to talk to her.

"Is this the operator? Well, there is something wrong with my phone. Could you, do you think someone could come up to repair it?"

He made up the most fantastic pretexts to converse with that personal voice, and listened with the greatest interest to her technical retorts.

His requests were not unreasonable—neither in conversation with the Operator, nor with Long Distance, nor with Information, nor with the Repair Department (to which, on the above occasion, the operator referred him).

With Information he could carry on long conversations about the numbers of nonexistent people such as dead or removed friends, at existent-enough addresses.

"Well," he'd say, "perhaps it's spelled with an *e*," or "I'm not quite sure what the initial is," and he'd wait for her reply, and then added information, changed spelling in an effort to capture forever that personal voice.

But that could not be. "Sorry, we have no such listing." And the same result with Long Distance, who hung up after giving him the rates to Chicago, San Francisco, and Detroit.

All this was better than the impersonality of the Weather and the Time, but by no means satisfying, for he was never able to depart from the business at hand—the least attempt at a remark apart from the business at hand left him with a dead receiver after a curt "Sorry, sir," or a dead receiver with nothing said at all.

This was far from the "Hello Central Hello" of his childhood, and returning to bed, wide awake, he could only gaze at the night breaking up, and as the gray light spread out, he was able to fall asleep, exhausted, for the few hours before his working day started.

Only to begin again the following A.M., or the one after (for occasionally he slept through like a log, slept past his waking hour) to face that clear recognition of intimate doom. This was unbearable, so he went to the phone.

He was through with the official calls, and dialed a stray number. A sleepy, irritated voice answered. The caller listened and apologized, then listened to the abuse which followed the apology.

Or he dialed and an anxious, pain-stricken, wide-awake voice answered; the caller hung up quietly.

Or a businesslike voice answered, giving the name of the firm, asking him to state his business. He almost became involved in a commercial transaction, though the product was unfamiliar to him.

One morning he dialed a sympathetic voice, a voice almost the echo of his own. Here he detected the same sleeplessness, the same anxiety.

"Yes, yes," said that voice, "I simply cannot sleep. I am filled with foreboding. I see very clearly the end of all my dear ones, there is nothing I can do to stop this. But when I begin working, I transfer this anxiety to my tasks, and am therefore known as the most conscientious worker in my shop.

"But this anxiety, spread over these trivial tasks, takes revenge on me by awakening me every morning and forcing me to face the anxiety. Confronted with this burden, I am lost. I can only stare out and await my release with the beginning of the working day."

And the voice proceeded to disclose in detail tribulations and methods of escape, and to delineate, in the sharpest manner, the mood of anxiety and yearning.

It was only later in the day, and with a sinking feeling, that our friend realized that he did not know the name, or more important, the number of that voice.

Such an oversight! He was planning to communicate nightly with that voice. He tried to remember the number, that was impossible. He scribbled a few numbers down, and that morning he dialed them, unsuccessfully.

One number was no number at all, and another number brought on a little girl's voice, which babbled incoherently and endlessly.

So he lost that sympathetic, echo voice, and was never able to find it again.

But he jumped from his bed a few nights later, tripped all over himself, and reached the ringing telephone on the fourth ring. It was about 3:30 in the morning, the only time he was ever awakened at such an hour by the telephone.

"Dr. Jones, you must come over immediately. Frank has had another attack."

He interrupted the party to tell her that this was the wrong number.

What a let-down, after being sure that this was the sympathetic voice, that the voice had somehow tracked him down, eager to continue the conversation which had started so auspiciously.

Then he began to call acquaintances and friends. This was a risky business. Generally he'd sit there and say nothing, listening to the familiar voice. In this way, distracted as he was, he learned a good deal. Some of his friends grew frantic as they asked for the identity of the caller and got no reply. Others cursed, a few hung up without a word. In general, they behaved no differently than they did in the normal social intercourse.

But on some occasions, simply to draw out conversation, he disguised his voice, gave the effect of having a wrong number, etc, and listened with some interest to the reaction on the other side. At least this was something to do, it kept him away from the bed and from the slowly approaching dawn; when the light began to spread, he felt most uneasy.

One call, however, almost cost him his anonymity—he so far forgot himself as to use a typical expression, and the very use of that expression had the effect of bringing his voice back to its natural tone. There was a short pause, then the friend said:

"Who is that?"

The caller gave a fictitious name.

"Who is that?" asked his friend again. "Is it . . .?" and he mentioned the caller's name.

The latter was panic-sticken and cut off the call immediately afterward. When the two met a few nights later, the friend looked at him with a curious expression, started to ask a question, but decided against it.

One evening, at about seven o'clock, our caller was leaving his little apartment. There was a knock on the door and an elderly man entered.

"I am a representative of the telephone company," he said, and flashed a card with a mounted picture which could have been a representation of the Duke of York, so panic-stricken did our friend become at the sight of this stranger.

"I've tried to get you a couple of times," said the stranger, "but haven't had much luck."

"Is it the bill?" asked our friend, putting on a bold face and making for the door. "I'll take care of that tomorrow.

"I'll walk over to your office during lunch hour," he added.

"It's not the bill," said the stranger.

"Not the bill," repeated our friend, in a tone which indicated the utter impossibility of anyone coming to see him on business unconnected with the paying of an overdue telephone bill.

"It's not the bill," said the stranger, looking around the room (his eyes settled on the telephone). "It's something else."

"In that case," said our friend, foolishly, "I'll be going along."

"Look," said the stranger, "we've been getting some complaints about you, and I'm here to check on them. Are you in the habit of using your phone in the early hours of the morning?"

"What do you mean by the early hours of the morning?" asked our friend, in a question which began on a tone of shrewdness and ended up in a barely suppressed fit of hysterical laughter.

"By early hours of the morning," said the stranger, "I mean the hours between four and six."

"What a crazy thing," said our friend. "The only time I use the phone at those hours is when I'm planning a hike for Sunday morning and might phone Weather in order to find out if the weather conditions are favorable."

"So you're an outdoor man," said the stranger, and his eyes, roaming the room seemed to be looking for some tangible evidence of outdoor life, such as a knapsack or a pair of snowshoes. Obviously disappointed in his search, he went on:

"Just the Weather, eh?"

"Oh, and the Time also," said our friend, "if my watch has stopped and I've got to make a train."

"The Time, the Weather," mused the stranger, and he began to shuffle through some papers. "Well, that part is all right, but how come you make telephone calls to all kinds of strangers at all kinds of hours!"

He said this without looking up from his papers, a kind of lightning thrust which was supposed to unbalance the suspect.

"What do you mean by all kinds of strangers?" asked our friend, too much off-balance to be disturbed by such a thrust.

"By all kinds of strangers," replied the investigator, "I mean all kinds of people that you don't know and that you have no business calling at any time, much less five o'clock in the morning. By all kinds of strangers I mean the following."

And he proceeded to detail, with dates, and sometimes the subjects of conversation, a list of names.

As our friend listened to this long recital, he suddenly remembered that sympathetic voice, and waited for a clue that might enable him to track down that voice.

The investigator came to the end. There was a pause.

"Look," said our friend, somewhat excitedly, "there was one man, I mean he understood this whole business perfectly, he was not the kind of man to complain, but still, it's possible, it was a local call. . . ."

His voice trailed off.

The investigator looked at him coldly.

"Do you think I'm going to act as a spy for you? You have admitted your guilt. You are definitely a nuisance."

(As he said this, he looked exactly the part of a minor field functionary in the Public Nuisance branch of the Psycho-Neurotic division of a giant utility corporation.)

Our friend seized the agent by the arm. "Do you sleep well at night? How do you do it?" he asked.

"From the time that I was eighteen years old," said the investigator, "I have gone to bed every night at eleven o'clock, and woke up every following morning at seven o'clock (that includes Saturdays, Sundays, and holidays) and furthermore, have slept like a log for those eight hours, and woke up refreshed.

"Dreams," he said, "rarely disturb me."

"You mean," inquired our friend, "that you never get up about four in the morning and feel anxious, even a little responsible?"

"Look," said the agent, "my responsibility ends when my day's work is done (*you* must own your own business) and I don't have much time to be anxious, and if I were anxious, I would never get up at four in the morning to prove it.

"My advice to you," went on the agent, "is to go home, forget about it, and then go about your business without losing any sleep over it."

He chuckled at his joke.

"How?" asked our friend, like a fool.

The agent looked irritated.

"I am going to help you gain mastery over yourself," he said.

He moved swiftly to the door and opened it. A lanky repairman entered. He gave the agent a knowing look; the latter nodded.

Without a word, the repairman went over to the telephone, started to unscrew the box from the wall.

"Here," cried our friend, "you can't do that."

He rushed to a spot between the repairman and the box. The repairman shrugged his shoulders and waited.

"Can't I?" inquired the agent, and he flourished a document, waved it about.

"This," he said, "is an order which gives me the right to remove this telephone."

He did not specify whether it was a court order or a company order, but our friend stepped back at this sudden show of authority. The repairman stepped forward to continue his work.

"Don't take it so hard," reasoned the victorious old agent. "This is the best thing that could have happened to you. Now you'll get up at your crazy hour and go back to sleep again, for lack of anything to do."

"Suppose," asked our friend, "I decide to go out to the railroad terminal around the corner and call from there?"

"You won't do that," said the company man, "you won't have the energy. Furthermore, the activity will lose all its charm in a public place.

"But should you try it," he went on severely, "you won't get off so easy. We'll be watching you."

"They'll hound you," said the repairman, casually, going on with his work.

Our friend turned to this possible ally in some excitement.

"You must find this type of work distasteful," he said.

"I'm a technician," replied the repairman. "I disassociate myself from the intent of the job."

This answer was a disappointment to our friend, who nevertheless persisted.

"You are trying to be neutral," he said, "but you don't always succeed. Nor would it be any credit to you if you achieved such a disassociation from your job."

"I keep my ideas to myself," said the repairman, but the tempo of his work increased.

"This is getting very tiresome," said the veteran agent. "It's a peculiar thing," he went on, turning to our friend, "but we get into such a discussion every time we're out on a case of this sort."

Our friend felt humiliated at being included in a *category*.

The telephone rang. The repairman pulled the box from the wall, the ring was cut off.

"What's the idea?" cried our friend. "You cut off a call."

"You are no longer a subscriber," said the agent, rather grimly. "You are no longer entitled to incoming calls."

He shook hands with the ex-subscriber, and then, in a stray gesture, with the repairman. The latter scooped up the telephone directories.

Without a telephone, without telephone directories, without the agent and the repairman, our friend was really cut off.

He walked to the window and vacantly watched the agent and repairman get into a car and drive away.

"Tomorrow I'll move," he decided. "I'll change my name and subscribe again."

THE TOLSTOY MOVIE

Isidore Landorf, a middle-aged dealer in hides and skins, came across and read Tolstoy's story "How Much Land Does a Man Need?" was impressed by it, and thought that it could be made into an excellent moving picture. Indeed, the more he thought of this story, the more he wished to make it into a moving picture. It was somewhat strange that he should think along this line for he had no experience or knowledge in this field whatsoever. He loved the movies and went to them very often. He found something very affecting in Tolstoy's story—the simplicity of it, the moral of it, the drama of the ending.

Landorf had heard that a moving picture could be made at a moderate price (referred to as a low-budget movie) and it seemed to him important that millions of people throughout the land, indeed throughout the world, should see and learn the message of this story, particularly with the immediacy and the vividness provided by a motion picture. He was critical of the rampant consumerism, evidenced in the actual purchasing habits of the well-to-do, and in the psychology, the hoped-for buying habits, of the less well-to-do.

A business associate had once mentioned to Landorf a cousin who was an accountant for a group of filmmakers, a kind of commercial experimental group. Landorf had seen the pictures. They were competently made, and though they did not seem to be important according to his values, Landorf asked to meet the accountant. When they met, Landorf explained his interest, and the accountant set up an appointment with the head of this film-making group, a Mr. Lambert.

The two met. Landorf told the film head of his plans for the picture, and asked him what the cost of such a film would be. Lambert was interested in the idea, and in the fact that here was a ready-made backer, said he would talk with his associates, and they arranged to meet a few days later.

When they met again, Lambert said that he had talked to his colleagues, that it would be difficult to make an estimate without knowing the length of the picture, the number of actors and actresses involved, and where the movie would be made. He had brought with him a young man, Gurfein, whom he introduced as a screen writer. Gurfein asked Landorf to describe the story, and the merchant summarized it in the following manner:

"A land-hungry peasant, Pahóm (incited by the Devil), buys some land, wants more land, works and buys it, and continues to add to his land as his means allow. He forever feels the need to add to his property, and is ready to close a deal for the purchase of many acres when he hears of a great quantity of land for sale in a far corner of Russsia for an incredibly low price. He goes to this far part of Russia, and indeed finds that rich farmland can be bought (from the Bashkirs, a people who lived in tents under the rule of a chief) at a price beyond Pahóm's wildest dreams. For very little money he is offered all the land he can encompass by walking from the rising to the setting of the sun. If he does not return to the starting point by the time the sun sets, he loses both land and his purchase money.

"He starts out at sunrise, walking with great speed, covers a great deal of ground, goes on and on, impelled by land greed. Finally he turns back, walks vigorously, becomes anxious as he sees the decline of the sun, tires, speeds up as the sun begins to set, becomes exhausted, hurries the more, his anxiety mounts, he breathes heavily, the sun is setting, he is desperate, runs, he is breathless, his chest heaves, the sun is falling, he reaches his goal just as the sun sets, and he drops to the ground, dead. He is buried on the spot.

"Six feet from his head to his heels was all he needed."

Gurfein had been listening quite attentively, and when Landorf finished the account, said:

"No doubt an interesting film can be made of this story, and since I make my living as a scenario writer, I will be glad to work on it, but, frankly speaking, the moral of the story is not congenial to me. I don't admire greed in people, but I don't believe in the idea of artificial scarcity either, and it is my view that people should have enough of what they need, even if that is a great deal, to live a good life."

"Then I haven't explained the story properly," said Landorf. "You should read it. The point is that Pahóm wants the land because he wants more land. His driving desire to add to his holdings has become the heart of the way he lives."

"I don't want to be personal," said Gurfein, "but don't you want your business to expand, aren't you pleased when it expands; and anyway, wasn't Tolstoy himself a great landowner?"

"You can read in his books how Tolstoy wrestled with problems of ownership of all sorts," answered the merchant. "As for myself, I of course like my business to prosper, to grow, but if it comes to the stage where the overriding interest in life is the expansion of my business, then I hope that I would see myself in a wrong life position. And I do not claim to be able to live up to my principles or ideals."

"I'll read the story," said Gurfein, "and we can talk about it again."

Lambert suggested a meeting the following week, and that was agreed on.

When the three men met a week later, Lambert said that the firm was definitely interested in making this movie, that he had spoken with his associates, and thought that in view of improved relations with Soviet Union, it would be possible to get permission to shoot the picture there, in the very surroundings that

Tolstoy had described, with perhaps the collaboration of the local inhabitants, though that of course would have to be worked out with the proper authorities.

Landorf was amazed at this suggestion.

"As I've explained," he said, "I want to make this movie on a minimum budget. I am not a very rich man, and to transport actors, actresses, an entire movie crew, to the Soviet Union, to pay their expenses there, is not at all what I had in mind. I think the picture can be made close by, with the aid, perhaps, in the climactic scene, of American Indians. There are the Shinnecock Indians, out on Long Island."

"It seemed to us," said Mr. Lambert, "that to shoot the film on the actual location described by Tolstoy would give the picture a certain authenticity, as well as being a terrific selling point. But if that isn't agreeable with you, we would discuss it further."

"I have now read the story," said Gurfein, "and when the picture is shot (and shooting it in Soviet Russia has, as Mr. Lambert pointed out, a number of decided advantages) the story line would have to be examined closely. My reading has confirmed the doubts I've expressed before. I read the story in the Modern Library edition of Tolstoy's Short Stories, and I agree with Ernest J. Simmons, who in his Introduction, has this to say about 'How Much Land Does a Man Need?' "

Here Gurfein pulled a notebook out of his pocket and read the following:

" 'This uncompromising object lesson in the vanity of human wishes is repudiated by Chekhov in the tale "Gooseberries" where the narrator pointedly declares: "Man needs not six feet of earth, not a farm, but the whole globe, all nature, where he will have room for the full play of all the capacities and peculiarities of his free sprit." ' "

"That," declared Gurfein, "is the spirit in which I think the scenario ought to be written."

"I have read that Introduction," said Landorf. "I have the highest regard for Ernest Simmons. He has done much to bring the great nineteenth-century Russian writers to us, but you will excuse me if I disagree with him here. I believe that Tolstoy would have gone along with this quotation from Chekhov. He is arguing in his story against greed, and not against the expanse, the growth of the free spirit, which is the opposite of greed."

Gurfein started to reply, but Lambert interrupted him, saying: "If we get together on the terms of the picture, there will be time enough to discuss the details of the plot."

"What do you mean *details, plot?*" asked Landorf. "We are talking about the heart of this picture. I am not putting out money to make a picture which would violate the sense, the spirit, of Tolstoy's story."

"Naturally," said Lambert, "as the backer of the film, you must be fully satisfied with it, down to the last details. But you must understand that we are an experimental group whose individual members, such as the writer and the director, have full freedom in their own spheres."

"I am only talking," said Landorf, "about the freedom of Tolstoy's story to remain what it is in any translation to the screen."

"Fair enough," said Lambert. "I'll be out of town for a few days, but I suggest that we meet next Thursday. I will bring along our director, Mr. Sebastian, and perhaps we can together iron out these difficulties."

And that was agreed on.

They met the following Thursday, and after the introductions and some small talk, Mr. Sebastian spoke up:

"I was not acquainted with this story until I read it the other evening, and I'd like to make a few points. The first is about the ending. Pahóm dies as the story ends. But I don't think our American audiences will go along with the instant, on-the-spot burial. I think that they will find the abruptness of the burial comical, and the reaction will be one of laughter, obviously destroying the effect Tolstoy was trying to create. So it is my thought that in the film the burial should be postponed until Pahóm's family arrives."

"I beg to disagree with you," said Landorf. "An interlude of a few days, for a family burial, would precisely *destroy* the effect

Tolstoy was seeking—the tremendous physical endeavor, speed, movement, and then the contrast of the immediate burial, the immediate silence."

"Mr. Landorf has a point there," said Lambert. "What else did you have in mind, Mr. Sebastian?"

"I think," said the director, "that the Devil should be excluded from the film version. It's just too corny and obvious."

"That's not too important," said Landorf, "as long as the greed is convincingly portrayed."

"Exactly," said Sebastian, "and for that portrayal I think I have exactly the right person in mind."

"Yes," said Lambert, in a tone half question and half affirmation.

The director named one of the most famous actors in the world.

"How can you think of it?" cried Landorf. "Why, he will ask five times more money than I can put up for the whole production."

"I am unfamiliar with the financial arrangements," said Sebastian, "but I know that he'll be perfect for the part."

"We'll get to the casting later," said Lambert. "I'm sure that can be worked out to all our satisfactions."

"A famous actor is absolutely unessential," said Landorf.

Gurfein, who had been quiet thus far, entered the conversation.

"I've heard," he said, "that James Joyce considered 'How Much Land Does a Man Need?' to be the finest short story ever written. And I've also heard that this story was a great favorite, if not *the* favorite story of Albert Einstein. Can you imagine the blurbs? I was discussing the matter with our PR man today."

"What is a PR man?" asked Landorf.

"Public Relations," said Gurfein, and Lambert said:

"I suggest that we meet the day after tomorrow and get down to brass tacks," and all agreed, except Landorf, who seemed preoccupied.

(PAST DUE)

We followed the ordinary procedure with this account, took the usual precautions. We received the inquiry, which we answered as a matter of course, enclosing our current price lists, with a covering letter, trusting that the recipient would find the enclosed of interest, and that we would be pleased, etc. A few days later the order arrived, a sizable one, a little over $1000. Although the account had a D2 Rating ($35,000 to $50,000 *Good*), we drew a detailed report, which was satisfactory, from the point of view of Net Worth (disregarding the fixed assets which we naturally depreciated heavily), since they had been doing business at the same location for seventeen years, no fires reported, and because of the overall sense of confidence one gets from the report of a solvent business in steady growth. The business was owned by two partners, both native to the area, both married, both drawing modest sums from the enterprise. They had established satisfactory credit ratings with a number of suppliers (as high as $7000 with their principal supplier) and met their obligations promptly. With some of these suppliers they had been dealing for more than ten years. We had our own rule-of-thumb method in figuring a credit high: we added 25 percent of Current Assets minus Current Liabilities plus 15 percent of Net Worth plus 3 percent of Gross Yearly Sales, and divided the total by three. We were a little more careful with corporations, and there are other elements—years in business,

157

etc. On this basis the firm was entitled to some $3000 credit. We had in fact extended credit in the amount of this initial order to companies with a much less effective report than this one showed, so we shipped out the merchandise without hesitation, according to our usual 10th Prox. terms. This was in fact the kind of account we were looking for—well rated, well established, in an area where we had no representation.

The merchandise was shipped on the last day of March, and the bill was due for payment on April 10. However, when we did not receive a check at that time, I was not surprised. Our new customers had actually received the goods on the third of April (the date of shipment falling on a Friday) and had disregarded, as many customers do under the circumstances, the statement which they received a few days after the merchandise (and a day after the invoice). In looking over the Outstanding toward the middle of April, I noted this omission. It occurred to me that, this being the very first shipment, they could perhaps have gone out of their way to meet the payment on its technical due-date. But I was not very disturbed by their neglect.

When Mr. Magruder, the owner of the firm, paused at the name of this new account in the course of his monthly review of the Outstanding, I explained the circumstances. He shrugged, and went on down the list.

When I went over the Outstanding toward the middle of May, the account was still unpaid. I therefore dictated a letter, of the quiet sort, pointing out that our bill had doubtless been overlooked, and that we would appreciate a prompt remittance.

So, when a few days later, Mr. Magruder asked me, "Say, what about Fowler & Walker?" I was able to say: "I wrote them day before yesterday."

That satisfied Mr. Magruder. I must say that he was an unusual boss. He made no irrational demands on us, was satisfied if we did the proper thing at the right time. He tried, as much as he could, to conduct his enterprise in a civilized way, treated it as a kind of Applied Art. I thought of previous employers of mine who would have raised the roof, certainly at the delay in writing, who would have demanded immediate and drastic steps, and retroactively criticized the unwarranted extension of credit. But Mr. Magruder recognized that the procedure so far was quite in order, and he waited now for the proper time to take the next necessary step. If there was anything to criticize in Mr. Magruder, it was a kind of super-blandness, an excessive bounding of the wild and competitive. Sometimes one forgot that there was money involved. And yet he ran an extraordinarily efficient and profitable business.

After a week's time, having received no answer to my letter, I put through a long-distance call, person to person, for either Mr. Fowler or Mr. Walker. When the operator informed me that neither one was available, I inquired as to who *was* there, was told that Mrs. Walker was in the office, and asked to speak to her. A woman with a strong, but unusually clear southern drawl got on the phone.

"Mrs. Walker," I said, "you've not answered our bill, our statements, nor the letter we sent you last week."

"I'm very sorry," she said, "but my husband is out of town."

"Isn't Mr. Fowler there?"

After a pause, she said: "Well, he's out right now. But we'll try to send you something on account very soon."

"I don't understand, Mrs. Walker, your bill is overdue, you people are well rated."

"We'll have something for you soon," she said, and it was all I could get out of her. She seemed very troubled, and spoke with obvious sincerity.

Two days later, in an airmail envelope, a $50 check arrived. Mr. Magruder was as puzzled by all this as I was, and sent out a letter in which he asked for some kind of explanation before handing the matter over to an attorney. He really did want an explanation, and a reasonable one would have sufficed.

It happened that I was leaving in a couple of days for a trip to Washington, where a niece of mine was being married. This was to be the beginning of a week's vacation. I mentioned to my boss that I'd make it my business to get down to see Fowler & Walker, they being one hundred miles or so further south.

"Fine," said Mr. Magruder. "It would obviously be better for you to see them before turning the matter over to an attorney for collection."

An old German proverb says: "The air of the city makes free." Although mystified by the origins of this proverb (for the German state has not been backward in surrendering to the centralizing and tyrannical tendencies to which all states are prone), I go along with it. In its remarkable diversity, in its built-in snooping character, "the air of the city makes free," and I rarely have a particular need to leave it, except to go to another great city and breathe there another *kind* of freedom. Small towns depress me, they can be taken in too easily, are too easy to unify; there is no mystery, no dark alley, no arcade, no way of losing yourself in a crowd which, generally speaking, lets you be, without contempt or suspicion, with a kind of natural indifference.

These, at any rate, were the thoughts I had in leaving for this short vacation; no doubt they are related in some way to my disinclination to travel, which is related in turn to a somewhat insanely purist notion that the time to travel arrives when your work and experience at home are absolutely exhausted. But that time never arrives, and so you find yourself criticizing other areas, other kinds of life; you discover that only the city is free, because you are disinclined to leave, and make a fetish of freedom on the base of an inexplicable fear.

As soon as I drove past the outskirts of the city, I felt very thin, very attenuated, as though my blood had suddenly cooled; the unfamiliar landscape had so little meaning to me, I could not get close to it, and the continual disappearance of objects with which I had only the most tenuous connection dispirited and continued to dispirit me. I turned on the radio, sought some warmth in the familiarity of "The Masterwork Hour," in the incessant jabber of the disc jockey, in the latest that Tin Pan Alley had to offer. That all helped, but the sounds seemed so far off, and I headed south in hardly a vacation mood.

I came into Washington Saturday afternoon, checked in at a hotel (which had been previously recommended to me by one of the salesmen in the firm—this created for me an air of familiarity), and headed for my sister's house. The wedding was scheduled for Sunday afternoon, and I was naturally caught up in all the preceding social activities. I am very fond of my niece, and in the presence of her imminent marriage I was quite absorbed, emotionally taken up. I had little opportunity to see and to taste the city; it did not strike me as particularly Southern, it was stony and impersonal. Of course the government bureaus were closed over the weekend, and I was seeing the city out of a dense sociability; the best way to experience a city is to experience it alone, or alone with another. But even that kind of experience can be pretty superficial, betraying at best a yearning for experience. By Sunday afternoon—before the wedding—I had decided that I would leave the next morning, drive down to Fowler & Walker, probably come back the same night, and spend the rest of the week in Washington, in my sister's apartment. It was a small apartment, but since Isabel was going off on her honeymoon, there would be no room problem—I mean to say that my sister and brother-in-law would be no more crowded than they had ever been.

I felt all the usual emotions at the wedding; it is the sign of my irreversible conventionality that I share on these occasions all the emotions that all the others are sharing with me—in this case the sadness and hopefulness before this curious legalizing of the wildest feelings. Watching Isabel, in all her beauty, in all her girlish yielding, as Joyce wrote, "Begin thou softly to unzone/ Thy girlish bosom unto him"—I forgot my own miserable marriage, which had ended three years ago after five miserable years, years of monstrous quarrels and inconclusive reconciliations, years buried beyond cause or blame; it no longer mattered who had left whom, or who had tried to give the effect of making whom the prime mover, in order to create what sense of who not being left? This was how I forgot my marriage as I looked on at my niece's wedding, and I was amazed at how surprised I was that I could feel this sense of hope, this confidence; for the idea of a marriage, the continual marrying everywhere, was a sign of humanity's stubborn belief in itself, in the value of its own continuance.

If the institution was not destroyed by the continuing failures of the individual marriages (looking around at the married couples, I wondered if perhaps the institution was not held up by these failures), why then the institution is needed; it is answering some deep and ancient need, a need which will ultimately be answered, if not by this institution, then by another institution which will spring from this one, or from the need which this one does not altogether answer. I was rather confused by my own optimism, even a little ashamed of it, but enjoyed the wedding, and was able to absorb the sense of uneasiness which the prospect of my next day's trip south was causing me.

Riding south the next morning, I tried to understand what was so difficult, so unpleasant, about riding in this direction. It was connected with an early fear of disease which was in turn equated with the jungle. I remembered the apprehension with which I had read *Arrowsmith* as a boy, how I was scared by the vividness of the living germ. For me the jungle was disease-ridden; out of its dense vegetation swarmed the dangerous flies and menacing mosquitoes. The South was therefore for me a taboo area, and here I was, riding toward that early danger. I turned on the radio; the voice was familiar, but in dense static, and I turned it off.

I sought for a sexual explanation of these rather strong emotions. Certain words in my own formulation led that way. The forbidden area. The geographical direction. The dense vegetation. What clearer symbols were needed? And the disease, the equation of disease with prostitution. We had gone together to the whorehouse, and my friend had picked up a little dose. Then the awesome possibilities of syphilis were brought home to me— the eating away, the softening of the brain, the whole miserable process from chancre to paresis. My attitude was obviously lacking in objectivity, my unconscious equations were founded on faulty premises. But fears are not refuted by recognition of illogicalities. I gripped the steering wheel more firmly, looked blankly out at the unfamiliar landscape.

Would this blundering analysis account for other feelings I had about the South? About its literature, for example? I have a distaste for much of Southern writing, I find unpleasant the nostalgia over an order forever gone; the attitude is quite unAmerican, in the sense that it conflicts with the American movement forward, our dynamic building, as opposed to the reconstruction of what can obviously not be put together again. I except Edgar Allan Poe. His cry was above sectionalism, a universal shriek; it is still sounding.

Let me now describe what happened in the Fowler–Walker matter. Their concern is located in a small southern city; for all I know it may be a large southern town—I am not expert enough to say. I would not plainly call it a city: it does not have the approaches of a city; one suddenly falls on it. But it is a county seat, and that seems to mean a great deal. It has a bank, a library, a movie; people are said to come in on Saturday to shop, and on Saturday night to enjoy themselves. I discovered that Mr. Walker had skipped town on the very weekend when our merchandise was being shipped, though there was no connection between the two matters; merely another illustration of how business goes on, if not as usual. He had skipped with the wife of his partner, Mr. Fowler. This departure marked the latest stage in an affair which had been going on for a number of years. There was a rumor that they were in Europe. Mrs. Walker now seemed to be in charge of the enterprise; it was with Mrs. Walker that I fell in love. Fowler was either more upset than Mrs. Walker or he showed it in a different way, because he rarely came into the place of business, leaving the burden on Mrs. Walker. Mr. Walker had apparently taken a fair share of the cash assets with him and his wife was faced with a formidable indebtedness, which she was doing her best to work off. The local suppliers, knowing the situation, were going along with her. She was a woman with an extraordinary winning manner, I gathered that she had had no connection with the business up to now; nevertheless she handled affairs with a sure touch. Why would a man have left a woman of such an obviously superior nature? But this is an idiotic question—judgments by strangers cannot get close to the mystery of withdrawals and attractions.

We spoke at length, not because we had so much to talk about but because personal interest (in this case *my* personal interest) gives conversation drama and extension; also I was making every effort to keep the conversation from dying, because I was formally bound by the time limits of a business call. When I had first introduced myself, she did not act surprised; she had a dead-pan expression, really a kind of fixed, hurt look which I found most interesting. But no doubt I would have found another kind of expression on her just as interesting. She was running an impressive General Store, specializing in high-tag items—home appliances, farm equipment, and the like. She explained, rather quaintly, that Mr. Fowler was very depressed by what had happened, and was not now very active in the enterprise. Nevertheless, sales were holding up, and she thought that she'd be able to make a sizable payment to my firm in a few months. Meanwhile she gave me a check for $75. The news on the business side was definitely favorable. I could just see the surprise and acceptance on Mr. Magruder's face when he read the letter which I was planning to write to him later that day.

After a while I recognized that I was outstaying my time, lingering beyond the call of business. Every now and then she'd excuse herself and take care of some business detail out front. When I suggested that we dine together, she accepted my invitation. I do not know whether I was amazed more by my boldness than by her acceptance.

I returned early in the evening. She got into the car with me. The compromising nature of the situation was somewhat obscured by the flight of her husband. Still, I was a stranger (would it have been any easier for her if I were a local man?) and she was a married woman, mother of a seventeen-year-old girl.

She seemed more fragile, close in the car, than she had in the place of business. She directed me to a restaurant on a road off the main highway, some ten miles off. The evening began to move with an extraordinary swiftness. I could not quite catch up with the strangeness of the situation; I only knew that I should not like to move from her side. Our conversation was intimate and impersonal, our relation was basically absurd. I was not so spellbound that I couldn't observe how wounded she was, and how I represented, by my constant interest and unflagging attention, a healing force, comfort from a stranger. But it was a situation without a past or a future: she had no plans, no desire to leave this town, and was prepared to accept the transiency of whatever was happening between us. I tried to create a past by mentioning the telephone call I had made months ago, from the city, but she smiled, refusing to be drawn into this factitious area. I then tried the method of recapitulation.

"Look," I said, "I came down from Washington to collect a bill, find out the reasons for the lengthy indebtedness. . . ." But my details trailed off. Now it seemed that I could not break through the business barrier. That was it, our connection was a business one, I was trapped in some monstrous, impoverished world, attempting, vainly, to break out into the open, to approach this woman freely. That was truly impossible. Never before had I understood so clearly how far apart people can be, how the desire to be close is not enough to bring you close, how there is an illusion of closeness, worse than distance, how we must come to one another from a long distance, being able to move slowly and surely through the cold space. At the other end was the awful familiarity which suffocated spirit, life's incredible stratagem to show people at their worst, to dirty one another by an unloving closeness. Wasn't that what we were both trying to avoid?

I had called my sister before my dinner engagement with Mrs. Walker, telling her that I would not be back in Washington until the next day, being kept over by business necessities. However, I now decided that I would not stay over, but head straight north, and not for Washington, but for New York. Somehow the idea of spending the rest of my week's vacation with my sister and brother-in-law in their small apartment, as a kind of stand-in for their honeymooning daughter, did not appeal to me. So I started to drive through the night. After some hours of driving along the mostly deserted highway through darkened towns and lost-looking villages (looking as though they had strayed off from some big friendly town), past houses buried in fields, being rather tired, I began to have a phantom feeling, afloat in an ever-present lightness, weightlessness. The lit-up pumps of a gas station bring your body back to you, and then you are off again into the desolate darkness. It became perfectly obvious that I could not make New York without a stopover, and I headed for Baltimore. In the immaculate hotel room, with its inevitable furnishings, which struck me, on entering, as the props for some long-abandoned play, I had a feeling similar to the weightlessness which I had felt on my auto ride. I felt denuded of experience, as though nothing had really ever happened to me, as though it was not possible for anything ever to happen to me.

I realized suddenly that this was Poe's city. The poet of desperate experience, the fighter for a lost personal cause, who struggled to create a harmony out of the undifferentiated chaos of everyday living—"None sings so well/ As the angel Israfel."

"Ha," I thought, "so this is the meaning of natural immortality, for a shade to hover over a living man?"

And my empty soul began to fill with bits of matter—room objects, wall shadows, remembered events, and with streamings of experience.

Then I fell asleep and dreamt a wedding ceremony. Mr. Magruder and Mrs. Walker were the groom and bride. They walked slowly over a Civil War battlefield. Now and then the air was filled with the boom of guns, with clouds of smoke; the newlyweds walked imperturbably through scenes of carnage. I saw myself, incredulously, as the best man, and when it came to sign the papers, I handed over to Mr. Magruder a check for $879.23.

Then I woke up and headed for New York City.

NOT QUITE ALONE
ON THE TELEPHONE

I picked up my telephone receiver, cradled in the slightly curved arms of the solid mother base, and I heard not the familiar dial tone, that serene hum which tells us that all is electronically well, and by extension, well in general, or in the words of Juliana (also known as Julian) of Norwich, that "all shall be well," I heard not the familiar dial tone but silence, not a golden silence, but the silence of a far-off emptiness, growing more and more ominous as the time passed. The phone went dead into an extraordinary deep silence, a silence with bells on, then suddenly came to life again, celebrating its resurrection with a piercing whistle, a kind of clear-the-track whistle.

I picked up the phone, dialed a long-distance number, and instead of a voice I expected to hear, found myself in the midst of a conversation between a bank official and a man who was trying to borrow $12,000 to modernize a superette. I quietly hung up the receiver.

I picked up the phone, heard a series of staccato noises, like that of a generator crying for help, hundreds and hundreds of these noises, part of an apparently endless wave of sound, then quiet, this side of dead.

I picked up the phone. There was a click, as though two small objects had come together—perhaps in a magnetic field? (the surmise of an electronic cretin)—then the familiar reassuring dial tone, that marvelous golden hum we used to take so much for granted.

I picked up the phone and heard a shriek, the sound echoing as from the wall of a cave, and then slowly dying away, and after maybe thirty seconds, the pure tones of a string quartet.

I decided that my phone was tapped, but tapped for no specific reason, on a random basis, part of an overall selective process, the way you might be chosen as a participant in a Neilson rating or in the *Daily News* straw poll. It is, I analyzed, part of the selective policy of the FBI, the CIA, or some intelligence-gathering service that I had not yet heard of. But in our country the most secret agencies become well known; we even hear of splits in the CIA between liberal and conservative factions.

Having decided that my phone was tapped, I called my Business Representative on the advice of the Operator, and that was the beginning of a series of conversations with individuals of various ranks, of letters received and answered, of calls following up unanswered letters, and I finally wound up in the hands, rather the voice, of a young woman, who, I understood, was in a kind of Public Relations Security branch of the company, and after a number of cable checks, electronic checks, and investigations, she, without firmly saying that my phone was *not* tapped, said that she was very sorry about the spectrum of noises, silences, and interruptions, that it was all part of the problems created by the unprecedented growth of the phone company, that the company was in the process of catching up with that growth by the special training and employment of old and new personnel, by the installation of new, very sophisticated equipment, that once this newly trained personnel was on the job and once this new equipment was in full use, she was confident that these clicks, interruptions, whizzing sounds, thunderous noises, hums whistles, clangings, whirrings, buzzes, indeed all the varieties of noise and silence, would disappear. Added to this was a promise to check further, all said in a sweet, agreeable tone, understanding, sincere, and reassuring; she made me quite ashamed of my complaints and my suspicious nature.

Then, when I came home that evening (I had spoken to the

telephone representative from my office where I am employed) and picked up the phone to dial a number, all trustingly, in remembrance of the reassuring sonorities of the woman at the company, I heard, far from the dial tone I was prepared to hear, hoping and expecting to hear, a policeman's whistle, piercing, as though he had sighted a thief, followed by a silence not quite long enough to be ominous, but close to it, and that followed by a familiar click, and then a voice of a woman asking me what number I wanted. When I said that I was calling Weather in New York City, she explained (more slowly and patiently than I thought necessary) that I had reached a number in Sacramento, California, that she would connect me with the operator. The wire went dead; there came the sounds of a kind of electronic music, and then, what used to be the most reassuringly *domestic* (all that electronic chaos out there tamed) of all telephone sounds, the equable, unwavering, steady, warm, and welcoming Dial Tone.

I have always had mixed feelings about the telephone in my house, all that coiled power, and sometimes, when it rings at odd hours of the night or when I am in an absentminded or bemused state, it is as though a wild beast has leapt into the room. The roach surprises, the mouse frightens, the rat scares, the telephone terrifies. And when I heard that a phone could be bugged in such a way that it will record what is said in a room even when the receiver is *on the hook,* that reinforced my sense of its silent and forbidding animosity, its treacherous and inhuman nature.

(And yet—what pleasure this same phone has given me over the years—the long, cozy converstations, the telephonic pleasantries, confidences, ideas, jokes, gossip, while the wind rattled the window panes, the rain covered these panes with crooked streams, and the phone always there, an obedient, helpful, accurate transmitter of your words, the sounds beneath the words, and the spirit beneath the sounds.)

Once I was convinced that the phone was tapped, my attitude toward it moved dramatically in the direction of suspicion, hostility, indeed to the limits of suspicion and hostility. Let me say this: it is possible to have strong personal feelings about a telephone.

I moved toward the negative pole first, in a kind of respectful, cautious way, the way you deal with a mysteriously powerful enemy, and used the phone as little as possible. My next month's bill was the lowest I can remember, because of the absence of the Message Units so inexorably used up in those long cozy conversations (like watching logs burn in a fireplace) which take the place of a visit, or a night at the theater, or just out.

Yes, my phone was quite abandoned for a spell, though it was on my mind. It is curious, by the way, how we remember, far back, our own old phone numbers, like the rock strata which geologists make so much of. I remember very old numbers when the Exchange was a name, like "Circle" or "Butterfield." When you stopped *saying* the name and started to dial it, you of course dialed only the first two letters, then the first two letters and a number (CI–2 is quite different from Circle, though if you *know* the name of the exchange, you are always aware of it). And then came the takeover by the numbers.

My feeling of trepidation in front of a mysterious power, particularly uncanny to one who is electronically backward, soon faded and was replaced by an amalgam of feelings, a many-sided thronging, not too easy to sort out—anger, scorn, sense of outrage—which brought me closer to this instrument, to an involvement, an engagement, a kind of confrontation.

The way I said it to myself was "If this phone is going to bug me, two can play at that game."

Let me say right off that the fact of a government agency's going to the trouble and expense of tapping my phone indicated to me (forget the random sampling) that I was a person of more importance than I had ever imagined myself (since the daydreams of childhood) to be. Indeed this situation reactivated those daydreams of childhood. I imagined, for example, I was called before an investigating committee of the Congress, asked my name and occupation, which I gave under oath. The committee members then proceeded to launch a barrage of questions at me, regarding dozens of trips I was supposed to have taken abroad, about contact with individuals I had never heard of, all of which made it as clear as the most perfect sentence ever written that I was being confused with another person with my name and occupation. I quietly answered "no" to hundreds of detailed questions about trips to Havana, Buenos Aires, Hanoi, East Berlin, Hong Kong, small towns in Cambodia, and cities of which I had never heard in countries which I could not locate nor identify.

"You are telling this committee, sir, on your sworn word, that you were not on the premises of the Swedish Embassy in Jakarta on January 9, 1967?"

"I am telling you just that."

"And you are telling us, sir, that on the afternoon of June 17, 1967, you did not meet a certain representative of the government of Albania in a tavern on O'Connell Street in the city of Dublin, and that certain documents were not exchanged on that occasion?"

"Sir, I am telling you just that."

After some three hours of questions—direct, involuted, oblique, sometimes coming at you, sometimes bouncing off the ceilings or walls—a man moves quickly into the room carrying a sealed envelope which he hands to the chairman after a short whispered interchange. The chairman halts the proceedings, opens the envelope, reads the letter, shakes his head in a kind of weary puzzlement, calls a recess, confers with the committee members, raps his gavel, and calls the meeting to order. He has a rather strained, awkward look. So do the other committee members.

"I have a statement to make," says the chairman. "We sincerely regret that a serious error in identification has been made. There are apparently two gentlemen with similar names and occupations, approximately of the same age, height, and appearance, one of whom lived at an address which, with the transposition of two numbers, would be precisely the number of the house on the avenue at which the gentleman on the stand resides.

It is the *other* gentleman we are seeking to interrogate. Again, we sincerely regret any inconvenience we have caused due to this unfortunate case of mistaken identities. . . ."

These fantasies helped to break down the tentative reserve I had adopted toward my telephone. It was one of the factors that emboldened me in my dealings with that instrument.

In the formulation of Leon Trotsky (perhaps I shouldn't mention his name) I have skipped a stage in my description of this process, for after minimal use, and before anger, emboldenment, etc., I went through a kind of intermediate stage, one of easy, impersonal contact.

During that period I called Weather, Time, Dial-a-Poem— made the most neutral calls possible. I made calls to strangers which involved a minimum of conversation (those calls to strangers I regret, for they can be suspect on the theory that they are coded), calls to the supermarket about deliveries, to the dry-cleaner to find out if my jacket was ready, that kind of thing. It was a warm-up, where calling had a specific, circumscribed purpose, giving me the old feel of the phone, after a period of disengagement.

Actually, the phone *did* ring, the way it does in the normal course of events. My deduction—for it was nothing more—that the phone was tapped (curious how *tapped* is a technical word, and *bugged* a word from the natural world) naturally had no effect on the telephone habits of my friends and associates, and to my amazement, for I had not set myself on such a course, I found myself reducing all the conversation to the blandest possible level; I found myself taking the sting out of all potentially partisan or politically controversial subjects.

It is a rare conversation which does not include at one time or another mention of the day's news, or yesterday's news, so it would not be unusual for a friend to mention the Conspiracy Trial (though I noticed some shied away from touchy subjects out of a vague sense of discomfort, imagined maybe that their own phones were tapped), but when I responded by paraphrasing his words or by calling attention to some totally insignificant element and did not push ahead to meaningful dialogue on the merits, or when I sometimes blandly changed the subject—"How do you like the way the Knicks are going?" (though had I thought the matter through, I would have seen that this kind of trivialization was more suspicious than the routine give-and-take of conversation)—well, the manner of my response had a way of taking my friend's subject off its track. It is surprising most people accept these conversational shifts, as if it doesn't matter what is the topic of conversation as long as the time passes agreeably. If a friend was to mention the latest development of the war, and I would respond by asking when he planned to take his vacation, he'd accept that conversational shift, seeing it maybe as a kind of impressionistic way of keeping the ball rolling, of filling the void which had initiated the call.

It is amazing how many subjects are potentially touchy, even controversial, so complex and interlocked is the world, I mean touchy from the point of view of telephone surveillance, though that is a visual word, and the tap or bug is an auditory intervention, but now we are approaching that era in the communications world where we will *see* the ones with whom we are conversing.

It is easy to turn away from the difficult, to reduce the thrust of the controversial, by a process of homogenization (that recently popular word from the dairy world), so easy to take the sting out of the thorny. You can do it by tone, by inflection, by showing no interest, so if a political assassination is mentioned, you swing it easily to the airplane crash (then it turns out *that* could have been sabotage, politically motivated). As I've pointed out, this kind of blanding (to coin a word) this obvious change of subject from the potentially controversial to the ordinary— "What do you think of our chances in the Olympics?" (but this can lead to a discussion of the killed and jailed students in Mexico City)—is, to any kind of trained listener, a most obvious indication of apprehension, and further, conversation becomes extraordinarily boring if you cannot discuss a subject in depth but must leap, like a gazelle on a mountaintop, from one conversational ridge to another in an effort to throw off your trail some unknown listener telephonically stalking you.

Now, though in many respects, and likely deep down in my character structure, previously called human nature, I am a prudent, cautionary man, carefully weighing the next step, considering as best I can the distant possibilities, the hazards flowing out of present behavior, I am also, thank God, a rather fun-loving person, who recognizes that *all* contingencies cannot be taken into account, that we have all been blessed with pleasure possibilities, that joy attends us, that we scorn volatility, ebullience, at peril to our bodies, to our very lives. And living as we do in a society full of all sorts of freedoms, we'd have to be pretty retarded not to take advantage of some of the pleasure possibilities that inhere in the bureaucratic madnesses of the repressive elements.

So I decided that I'd have a bit of sport with my unknown tappers. The way to do it, obviously, was to present to these unknown listeners as *wide* a spectrum of views as I could possibly manage. Indeed I sat down to my desk and wrote a list of views, ranging from the fascist right to the terrorist left. On second thought I excluded the extremes, for what would stop them from using *only* the extreme statements? My revised spectrum therefore ranged from reactionary to the limits of the constitutional left. Who has the patience to reenumerate such a list? And then I threw in religious musing (omitting none of the great religions of the world), antipolitical statements, all kinds of philosophical analyses on the nature of the state, the moralities of political behavior, threw in quotations from thinkers famous and unknown, copied quotations and passages from books, encyclopedias, magazines, newspapers. Working from this list, and from the free-associational, spontaneous working of mind and imagination, I went to play.

Never had my friends, relatives, associates, even random callers and neighborhood shopkeepers been subjected, from me anyway, to such a farrago of thoughts, opinions, views, analyses, doctrines, probes, questions, descriptions, commentaries, on so wide a variety of subjects bearing in any way on the political scene. Plato's *Republic*, the *New Republic*, Tolstoy's views on nonviolence, editorials from the *Manchester Guardian*, quotations from Hobbes, Aristotle on politics, passages from Fourier, Kautsky, Eugene Debs, remarks on the Brook Farm experiment, Burke on the American colonies, comments from the *National Review,* Sukhanov (Carmichael's translation) on the concept of the power lying in the streets, critiques of nihilism, sections of the kabbalah, *Daily News* editorials, thoughts out of Thoureau, Harold Lasswell, Myrdal, *Le Monde,* the *St. Louis Post Despatch,* Mahatma Gandhi, A. J. Muste, Thomas Jefferson, reasoned critiques of all sorts of revolutionary thinkers, opinions from Reston, Buchwald, Mark Sullivan, Walter Lippman, Westbrook Pegler, Heywood Broun, Wechslor, A. H. Raskin, Hentoff, Roger Baldwin (special emphasis on the great libertarians), passages from Léon Blum, Kierkegaard, Bosanquet, Yeats's airman, Freud and Einstein on war, Goodman, Mailer, Nelson, Feuer, Macdonald, Dorothy Day, Oswald Garrison Villard, Morris Hillquit, Barry Goldwater, the *New York Review of Books,* William Buckley, the *Louisville Courier-Journal,* Henry Clay, R. H. Tawney—a motley of names, views, magazines, books, pamphlets, dissertations, theories, manifestoes, for, against, neutral, a mélange of all political positions and doctrines, revolutionary too (let *them* make head or tail of it). Anyway, for one week I made tapes of all my conversations which I carefully dated and filed.

A week of it and that was all. A frenetic, chaotic week, and then one might, as I entered the apartment, the phone rang and I had an ordinary chat with a friend. I said just what I felt, the madness was over, my tapes were carefully dated and filed for any future legal confrontation. I was back to my old telephone, accepted the weird noises, silences, electronic beeps as part of the growing confusion, the growing complexities, the growing struggle for a better America. Only now and then, when I think of it, I talk into the phone with the sense of that third party by dramatizing the subject at hand, going into an extra bit of song and dance, pouring it on, making it memorable for the unknown listener:

I heard myself explaining to an old woman who spoke little English that she had a wrong number, that she was dialing the letter *o* instead of the number *0,* the zero, and *for that reason* she was getting the wrong number, but the old woman kept getting my number and I kept explaining about the small *o* and the large *0,* and she kept not understanding, and the phone continued to ring, and I continued to explain about the big *0,* the Operator *0,* mentioned *Oscar* Robertson, said something about the *Marquis of O.* She couldn't understand hardly anything I was saying, and I started to holler: "Call the big *0,* call the Operator, not the little *o* with the *M,N,* and *6,* but the big *0,*" and I hollered so loud that I woke myself up and stared at the familiar phone on the desk and it was just as quiet as it could be.

One evening, talking to my Uncle Max on the phone, I explained the kabbalistic notion of *Tsimtsum,* about which I had read in Gershom G. Scholem's work *Major Trends in Jewish Mysticism:*

"This is what it is, in an oversimplified summary. God decided (think of it! God deciding) to make room for the world. He took up the whole of space, and in order to make room for the world, he contracted, and that made the space. It is the *Tsimtsum.*"

My uncle is a *misnagid,* in the rabbinical tradition, and somewhat cool to the kabbalistic doctrine, but he was naturally fascinated by this notion.

"How is it called again?"

"The *Tsimtsum.*"

"*Tsimtsum.* A curious word."

"Isn't it? And a curious notion too."

Then we discussed further, I forgetting after a while the Third Ear, but then recalling it as I imagined this interchange as part of a variegated spectrum which the unknown listener would have to work on.

The noises continued intermittently—in the middle of a conversation, the entrance of a whizzing sound, as though a wind, a hurricane, is roaring over some distant prairie; and the one that bugged me the most, the busy signal which starts up as you are halfway through the dialing. That is somehow insulting. Well, I wasn't going to give up the phone and I wasn't going to change to an unlisted number.

In our country, with its vast reservoir of freedom, one likes to think that these inquisitorial tendencies, these inquisitorial actualities, will sink to the bottom of the clear waters and there dissolve.

MR. MINTZ RETIRES

(For Paul Goodman, who brought Leviathan into the Hudson)

At the insistence of age, under the pressure of a son and a son-in-law, both in the flush of an ever-expanding standard of living, Mr. Mintz retired. Though his blood pressure was high, and his sight of a dimness, his mind was as clear as ever, only afflicted with the fanatical regard for minutiae so characteristic of the obsessed and the aged.

But at the insistence of age, under the pressure of the two young men (who weren't as young as all that) and of Mrs. Mintz, who wanted justice done to both her children, and who knew (from 1907, from 1929) that standards of living could stop expanding,

He retired.

From a material point of view, Mr. Mintz was cushioned. There was cash money (medium five figures), insurance, bonds, a modest income from a Florida boomlet.

From a spiritual point of view, Mr. Mintz

From a spiritual point of view

Mr. Mintz?

In the consciousness of a rough rectitude, maintaining a comparative purity in the fleshpots of Egypt, lusting too for the whore of Babylon.

178

That trade convention in Louisville—a lollapallooza.

A rough rectitude, a comparative impurity, a shuffling of the good and the evil, a wary eye on the Lord, who is jealous.

But He is not jealous of man's good fortune, or sideline fornifications, lust for the stranger far from home.

For He is a jealous Lord, rides the whirlwind and metes out a rough justice.

Jealous of the ideal incorruptibility, haltingly approached by the lusty rectitude, buried in the Word buried in the Book buried in the Ark protected by lions, guardians of the law?

For He is a jealous Lord, but does not consign His sinners to the burning pit, to the slime, but to the narrow grave, the *Sheol.* It is a narrow place.

Mr. Mintz retired.

THE DIFFICULTIES OF RETIREMENT

Because you have retired, when you retire, it is not easy to retire. "He'd die if he had to retire." How many times had Mr. Mintz heard that, and then of the ones who retired and did indeed die. Man-of-War was retired to stud, but with men it is different. The alternative to busyness is idling, and that was not for Mr. Mintz, being restless. The substitute for busyness is play, and that was not for Mr. Mintz, who could indeed play as a distraction from busyness, but not as a busyness.

Consider the case of Mr. Kronk, a friend. He too, under the impetus of age, illness, and son-in-law, had retired. He too had vainly faced the substitutes and the alternatives, and then quietly almost surreptitiously, the way you enter on forbidden ground, had gone back to the shop, and slowly, like a fine rain, which puzzles without soaking, he began to make his presence felt. Then he was able to roar out: "I have retired from retirement." Particularly if he was asked.

But Mr. Mintz was too proud to return. His busyness used to be extreme. One day the Lord had tapped gently on the window of his soul, and he swooned. Then he recovered, and did not die, for the Lord was compassionate to him. And the Lord said unto him:

"Thou hast labored these many years. It is enough."

Then Mr. Mintz recovered, and that day shone exceedingly.

And since the Lord had spoken to him, Mr. Mintz was too proud to return. Nor was he unafraid.

It was difficult for him not to retire from this retirement, the way it is with any man who has long been taken up with the world's work. So he grumbled, and complained, and took some inventory around the house, and the time was heavy. The hours of the day smelled different.

A LESSON IN PURCHASING

He slowly became the Purchasing Agent.

The Mintzes had lived in the neighborhood for twenty-seven years. In that time one makes connections with storekeepers, establishes preferences and loyalties. At first Mr. Mintz ran the errands blindly, the way a child does. He dutifully made the purchases, paid or charged. Then he began to be interested in the price, in the labels, in the quality. It was in the period before the supermarket, before the cutrate drugstore.

Things were deceptively simple. You did not necessarily buy where it was cheaper.

"So what if the meat is a few pennies cheaper?" asked Mrs. Mintz. "It's a better piece of meat."

What could he say?

"Suppose the eggs are a little less?" asked Mrs. Mintz. "I've been dealing with the Gordons for twenty-three years. She's a friend."

What could he say?

Still, there were so many stores, so much buying, and Mr. Mintz began to have some influence on the purchasing side.

It was a personal blow not to buy at the necessarily cheapest price, contravened the business habits of a lifetime. It was neither money nor principle, but the bony habit of a merchant constantly fighting competition and expense.

"But I am buying for consumption," thought Mr. Mintz, "not to resell."

"Ha," he said to Mrs. Mintz, "in the domestic economy there is no profit in the buying."

This was a good lesson he learned here, mellowing, smoothed off the fangy greed. With good grace he paid the extra three cents for the dozen eggs.

"But the Gordons must look to the price," he thought, with some satisfaction.

"If I hired this kind of myself for a Purchasing Agent," he said, "I'd fire myself very fast."

So his activity was not very businesslike, oh no it was the chastening buy, the introduction of the human factor.

"In business," said Mr. Mintz, "all things being equal, you deal with the nicer person. But here all things are not equal, and you deal with the nicer person."

HE DREAMS OF TRAVEL

"Let us travel," said Mrs. Mintz, in a dream. He heard it in a dream, in a trembling of the night.

And he answered her from on high, the plain being populous, not as the Lord, but as an emissary of the Lord:

"The Lord is compassionate, and he creates a shadow into which the body may slip, and warning for the soul to heed.

"He weans the child from the breast, and that is a warning, that the good and the warm and the copious will not last forever.

"He creates institutions for the child to grow out of, and that is a warning, a foreboding, the sadness of the graduation, the last day of camp, the human sundering.

"He makes a family, for the child to leave, a warning, a premonition, the transparency of the flesh.

"He creates an ocean, for discovery of far lands, and that it may be crossed, as a warning, a hint of the soul's journey."

Mr. Mintz dreamed of Sarah, and he laughed in his dream, for they were old, and it was not between them as between man and woman. The sound of geriatrics was heard in the land.

On the plateau between the plains and the mountains.
He dreamed the dark journey of birth, travail of the matriarch.
The Lord spoke unto him, and he answered:
"*My Lord.*"
"A child shall be born unto you, *a hostage to fortune.*"
Mr. Mintz snickered.
"My Lord. A child? What are you saying?"
He was enveloped in lightning.
"All right, all right, my Lord, who created Man-of-War."
"As a warning," thundered the Lord.
Mr. Mintz awoke.

HIS PHILOSOPHICAL DISQUISITION

Mr. Mintz stayed retired. He was of an age. He had an exact figure, a firm walk, a bright eye.

I came to know him at this period, when he had decided to stay retired. We met in the neighborhood cafeteria, where citizens and other refugees brought their own teaballs and asked for cups of hot water. After a while the cafeteria closed. That was on account of the refills.

One afternoon the shadows lengthened. Mr. Mintz spoke out:

"How wrong can I be?" he asked, "I thought that with age and retirement one developed a broader view, a perspective! Gestalt! That could be a reason for retirement, if not a justification for age. But that is not how it is. On the contrary: you become crabbed, brood, grow impatient over unexpected details and singularities. Absurdities assume significance, life's minutiae become life.

"Because you cannot achieve the total view (where you face the danger of seeing nothing) that view becomes refracted, breaks up, you are left to gather the pieces of the fabulous vase, the one you have never seen.

"No cure for pettiness here.

"I have been sitting here for a half hour, looking out the window, and what have I accomplished?"

He waved a piece of paper.

"I have written down the following occupations. These are culled in part from the identifications on the trucks that passed by."

He read the list:

"Pie-maker, tagger, truck-rent, carloader, freeloader, 'consistently superior' baker, air-freighter, three-dimensional packager, Blue Crosser, jaywalker, jaycaller, jailbird, sponge examiner, sponge shrinker, sponger, slipcoverer, suspend-o-folder, dye-worker, set-mover, emergency repairer, handicap-hirer, handicapper, handy copper, handyman, piper, pipedreamer, shorer, shnorrer, feuilletonist, two-toner, towel-supplier, solderer and dodderer, premises-protector, false-premise detector, rare postager, oxygen supplier, carnation-wrapper, desmogger, farmtruster, overstocker, mattress-tufter, Barbary coaster, Burberry boaster, cinnamon toaster, fur storer, self-servicer, self-server, handknitter, timer and chimer, rat-renter, five percenter, torsion-leveler, contortioner.

"I ask you, is that the long view, the wisdom of age, or is it pettifoggery, schematism, and garrulousness?"

But he was old, and not altogether displeased with his list.

HE IS NOT LIKE ADAM

Mr. Mintz retired. Between Mr. Mintz and the original Adam there were a number of significant differences:

#In the landscape, in the situation.

#Mr. Mintz had more to remember, more to forget.

#Between good and evil Mr. Mintz maybe knew the difference.

Still, it was a kind of setting forth, a beginning.

But he could not make it to be a new world, being a worn world.

"Lord, it is an old and worn-out world."

He was enveloped in lightning.

"*My Lord.*"

But spring did not flower easily, it did not flower softly in his old heart, though he strove for spring to flower, and spring did not flower easily in his heart.

For he was enveloped in the miasmas of age, where the sun could hardly penetrate. His skin was tough and leathery, and a touch would hardly penetrate. His mind was like a box full of compartments, and *the sacred river* did not flow.

HE DREAMS AGAIN

One morning he fell out of his bed and woke up laughing, tears were in his eyes. His laughter was so genuine that Mrs. Mintz joined in. Then she asked:

"Why?"

"I have just finished a dream," he said, "broken by this fall. I dreamed a sea-monster, gliding slowly up the Hudson, its mouth wide open, creating a vacuum into which were swept the fish, the debris. On top of this monster was a familiar fellow— sure enough it was me. Crowds were cheering on both sides of the river. It was a kind of truimphal procession, a welcome home. I rose to acknowledge the cheers, and then fell into the water."

"So get off the floor," said Mrs. Mintz.

"There was another part of the dream," he said, "it was more serious. 'Thou shalt judge the land' saith the Lord, and I walked into the street and cried out:

'The fall of Hackensack'

but it sounded kind of silly, for there was depravity abroad, without pleasure, and a joyless materialism, and much decency midst the terror, and the mantle of the prophet did not fit me, a little large, that was all clear in the dream. I do not see evil clearly enough, but under the spell of causality. I never fail to see the mixture of the good and the bad, of the will and the circumstance."

"You don't have to be a prophet," said Mrs. Mintz. "Do you *have* to be a prophet?"

SOME QUESTIONS?

Mr. Mintz retired. Was the world his oyster? Was he like the figure in the Sunday magazine section, sprawled at his ease on a modest three-year-old lawn in front of a modest dwelling? Did he watch, without tension, without a worry in the world, as the great procession went by—the powerful, the lame, the visionaries and the blind, the motley crew, raw material of the human comedy? Did he loll at his ease, thinking on time past, golden childhood, adolescent dream, the struggles of manhood, all cast in the peculiar glow of retirement? Did he spend many a pleasant afternoon (fading into twilight) with an old crony, in the sexless badinage of the aged? Did he sit over a glass of tea with Mrs. Mintz, enjoying the retrospective view, the joy and trials of the children, the rise and fall of friends, the family wars? Did he softly swing in the hammock (at the northeast corner of the house) glancing idly at the verses of the Psalmist? Is this the way he retired, leaving the scene of action, avoiding the responsibility, washing his hands of duty, his soul of desire, gazing at the world the way one gazes at the passing clouds, admiring this one's configuration, that one's disappearance? Did he walk slowly to the corner of some country road, and turn back from the road leading to town? Did he loaf at his ease? Was the world his oyster? Did he? Was it?

HIS POEM

One day, much to his surprise, Mr. Mintz wrote a poem:

> *The prose writer is ashamed of a poem*
> *The way a poet is ashamed of money*
> *And a merchant of love.*
>
> *A child shows shame*
> *Because of her name,*
> *Reddens in shame*
> *At sight of her name.*
>
> *I knew a man ashamed of the world's beauty,*
> *Ashamed of desire, ashamed of duty,*
> *Ashamed of women,*

Ashamed of men,
Ashamed of Halevi, ashamed of Blake
And of the dream for love's sake.

For love's sake.

ANOTHER POINT OF VIEW

"Who is that little fellow? He looks familiar."

"That's Mintz. Don't you know Mintz?"

"Of course, Mintz. Why is he walking around that way? He looks different."

"Oh, you didn't hear? He's retired. He never goes to the place. He walks around like a kid. Also he's a little bit a Talmudist."

"What do you mean 'a little bit a Talmudist'?"

"Well, you know the joke about the suitcase in the trolley aisle. A little Jew, not a big Jew, sits next to the suitcase and he hums *deedle deedle dee* when he's asked to move it. Finally the stranger in the aisle gets mad, throws the suitcase through the window and the little Jew says: *deedle deedle dee, it's not my suitcase.* Well, Mintz wrote a regular Talmudical piece about it, how it means that the Jew doesn't protest his innocence because he'll be punished anyway. And how the suitcase represents the Torah, how it is being protected, and being defiled, and so on. Then Mintz showed the writing to the rabbi, who told other members of the congregation (in private) that Mintz was plainly *meshugge.*"

"Is that right? So he never goes to the place?"

"I'm telling you. He's retired."

CHAPTER XII

Pushed by a son and a son-in-law, representing the *hungry generations,* by the dictates of age, by the blandishments of reason and of his wife, Mr. Mintz retired. Neither a Talmudist nor a traveler. He fell into the sea and swam to the land. It was a sandy place, and he cursed that place. He was enveloped in lightning.

My Lord.

Mr. Mintz bowed, being most alone, in the most unfamiliar place, feeling himself separated from himself, a nonhuman sundering, an unusual intervention.

Then the air thronged with familiarity, the warm, the palpable. He cried in his loneliness and created a music.

MINKIN COPYING

(The story of another madman.
Another story of a madman.)

In our free and easy American speech, we use the word *mad* quite loosely. It can be curved on a graph, a spectrum of mental instability, ranging from "odd," a bit "batty," all the way over on the right of the paper to a description of a person who is a certifiable lunatic, mad in the original and irreducible sense, one who is indeed "certified" (though not all these judgements are correct, out of error, out of collusion) and is indeed in an institution for the medically insane, the looney bin (curious how we sane ones get pleasure out of the various names for lunatic asylums, the bug houses, and for the varied descriptions of lunatics, "off his rocker," "around the bend," "turned the corner," "bats in his belfry" . . . but any dictionary of slang will give you the current references).

It is in the medium range, with a word like "nutty," or "*meshugge,*" that Minkin would be best described, but for literary effect I use the word *madman* in the subtitle of this story (Beware of a story which is titled before it is written!). Furthermore, as the story progresses (it is all clearly planned and worked out) you will note that Minkin moves, if not to the extreme of the spectrum, then, in these hieroglyphs of mental disturbance, certainly toward the center. I have already—and with so few words written!—pointed that out. In the close and far ranges of the spectrum (isn't that a terrific word?) of mental disequilibrium (it is important not to repeat the same word all the time) let us then characterize Minkin as a Centrist.

Although Minkin is a New Yorker, a true child of the teeming metropolis, formerly the Melting Pot, he is also a throwback, a clerk out of the great nineteenth-century Russian novelists, who spawned these figures out of the bureaucratic interstices with a facility that never fails to astonish.

Beginning is difficult. Our night-school teacher in his course on Composition (it was before the word *creative* came into such vogue) emphasized the notion—it was almost a stricture—of Edgar Allen Poe that in a well-constructed story (and he saw no sense in any other kind) every word should have the conclusion in mind, should bear on the end. That anyway is my remembrance of how our teacher quoted Poe. It happened quite a while back. I have a strong impulse at this point to describe our night-school teacher. Landau was his name, but whatever it was that Landau quoted Poe as saying, in that clear and pleasant voice of his—I mean Landau's voice; I never heard Poe's voice—this I know: that for me now to write about Landau, to characterize him, analyze this personality, his mannerisms—I am sure *that* would violate whatever it was that he quoted Poe as saying about the construction of a story. So, with respect for both Poe and Landau, I must return to Minkin.

It is really one aspect of Minkin's life that I want to describe. Everything I write should bear on that (That must be what Poe meant!). And the aspect is his preoccupation, later on a stronger word will be needed, with copying, the phenomenon and the act of copying. Now I remember Landau telling us never to start with a general proposition, but always to start with the specific, the actual. Too late for that now.

Copying is as old as the hills. That's an exaggeration, for no mechanical process is as old as any aspect of nature. I am not thinking of copying from others, cheating or gypping, the way kids do on tests and older students on examinations, but of making copies, facsimiles, of what you have written (that is not the same as copying from yourself) or of what someone else has written. Say you write a letter. Then you realize that for one reason or another you want a copy of that letter. The memory of the contents is not enough. So you make a copy of it. The same with a bill or some other one-of-a-kind document. You decide to copy it, to keep it "for your records." There's nothing unusual about this. After a while you buy carbon paper, and if you think of it, slip the carbon paper between the pages, if you are writing something for the first time. After a while Minkin bought some carbon paper. Nothing unusual about that, indeed this description of the obvious is an insult to the reader, though of course I am leading to something. For, the way it often is, Minkin wrote a letter and *then* decided he wanted to make a copy, so he didn't use the carbon after all. It is kind of unpleasant to copy mechanically what you have written with interest or attention, but that's what you must do if you haven't used carbon.

The middle is difficult. But let's try to stay with Minkin. His situation as to copying was pretty normal at first, but slowly, for reasons which I cannot explain, or do not wish to explain (for an excessive, even lengthy analysis of motivation *can* get you very far from Poe's directive, and from Landau's emphasis on that directive—Landau, how well I remember you, in those late-hour classes on 23rd Street, your eagerness, your interest, the lively cafeteria conversations after class, but enough: away from Landau and Poe, back to Minkin), slowly then, Minkin entered on a period of preoccupation with copying, carbons, reproductions, that led to the behavior which is somewhat exaggeratedly described in the subtitle of this story.

But Minkin's behavior on this score, though it undoubtedly developed for inner reasons, the word *dynamics* should be used here, out of obscure needs which made necessary the physical retention of materials which he was sending out, was also the result of the development and then the widespread commercial use of the Copying Machine, sophisticated child, geared for single copies, of the Mimeograph, the Multigraph. As this copying machine (Xerox, the best known, even becoming a verb in the language) came into use, available in stationery stores and in enterprises which did only copying work, Minkin, like many others, began to see the need for copies, duplicates (sometimes multiplicates) where he and they had never seen that need before. Amazing, is it not, how so many had lived all their lives without missing or needing the copying machine, now suddenly making extensive use of it, to the extent of sometimes waiting on lines for a considerable length of time to have mechanically copied a letter or document which, before the time of the copying machine, they never would have bothered to copy? Is it possible that advances in Technology bring into being needs and yearnings which never before had the necessary outlets?

Slowly, slowly, Minkin saw the necessity of making copies of more and more materials. For example, as he made out an important check one day, it struck him: suppose this check is lost, it happens now and then, so why not copy it? So he went downstairs and had a copy made. And some companies, in asking for payment on bills, want the bill back. Why not a copy of such a bill, for the records?

The slowly developing situation now and then picked up speed. A voluminous letter writer Minkin was not, but it became apparent to him that copies should be held of *all* letters written. Say the response to a letter is based on a misunderstanding of what is in that letter. You must quote your own letter to make clear the basis of the misunderstanding. If you don't have the letter, you must quote from memory. Isn't it better to have the letter in your possession, so that the quotation would be 100 percent accurate? For the kind of people who create misunderstandings would probably not accept your memoried version against what they had in writing. They could even send you a copy of your own letter to prove that your memory was not absolutely accurate. It was on the basis of this kind of thinking that Minkin decided to xerox *all* the letters he mailed.

Minkin's Income Tax was not very complicated. Wages, Interest on money in a savings bank, Dividends on three stocks he owned (two on the advice of a broker cousin), Medical & Drug Deduction (a chronic ulcer situation), Charitable Deductions (admiring the fortitude of blind people, he gave to Institutions for the Blind), a few expenses related to his work—these pretty much made up his tax. For years and years he had mailed off his tax form and check without further ado. But now he thought: my copy of the return is not enough. Suppose the original is lost in the mail? Suppose the return is questioned? For forty cents he xeroxed all the supporting documents, the check itself.

One day Minkin had to leave a note for the laundryman, giving instructions about the cleaning and repair of some garments and upholstery covers. He thought: you often have troubles in these matters, instructions not properly carried out. Didn't it make sense, for a dime, to have a copy of such a note, so that if the slipcovers were washed, and not dry-cleaned, and shrank, he could triumphantly point to his note, the *exact* wording (that is very important), and refuse to pay the bill, demand payment of damages?

Why couldn't Minkin copy such a note by hand, as well as the other documents he forgot to use carbons on? He thought of that, and decided that a hand-copy is not the same as a mechanically perfect facsimile, for, in copying by hand, you could easily, unconsciously, make little, or even significant changes here and there. Now the reader will begin to see why this story is subtitled the way it is.

And not only current letters, documents, forms. Why not old material too? Looking through boxes of such material, he came across a number of papers, yellow with age, ready to fall apart. A xeroxing job, specifying the use of strong paper, would preserve the life of these papers. And in some cases, where the papers were in fairly good shape, why not a copy nevertheless, so that if one copy were lost, as in a fire, there would still be one left. So he put the new copies in *another* box, in *another* part of the apartment. Fires were often put under control.

Among the papers in his possession which Minkin had xeroxed were the notes of his course with Landau. He had taken these notes more than thirty years back, he *sometimes* looked at them. Age was curling them at the edges. But even if the papers had been in superb condition, on rag paper, he would have reproduced them, for the reproduction gave a sense of novelty. Looking at the newly xeroxed notes, the features of Landau came to mind, those exciting nights of discussion and argument. He glanced at the notes. A reference to Edgar Allen Poe, that nothing in what one writes should be inessential, everything should bear on the heart of the matter, lead to an inescapable conclusion. What did that mean now, practically speaking, to Minkin, who wrote an occasional letter? But these notes were dear to him. He asked the Xerox man to copy them onto especially strong paper. Yes, he understood there would be an extra charge for that.

And the love letters he came across! From his fellow-student in Landau's course. Now, in the time of Xerox, he looked again at these letters, he read them, extravagant declarations, effuse and flowery. They made Minkin angry. "Bah," said Minkin, "What nonsense." He had followed the fortunes of the letter writer, knew that she had just married, for the fourth time, knew who it was she had married, where she lived (all this information from a crony at the office, a man who kept up with everything about everybody). Minkin went to the Phone Book, found the exact address, wrote it on an envelope, put the letters in that envelope, pasted on an extra stamp, went downstairs, it was quite late at night, there was a pale and wandering moon (what does this have to do with anything, you too should remember the dictum of Poe) and dropped the envelope into the corner mailbox.

Then pangs of guilt assailed him. Unchivalrous. Mean. And the husband wondering about such a thick envelope, obviously from an individual, not from some organization. Bah! thought Minkin. What nonsense. Insincere. Four husbands. And suppose the husband reads the letters, or she shows him the letters. The thirty-year-old effusions (Minkin liked that word, the way he liked the word *spectrum*) of a girl. Minkin held back a few tears. Maybe he should have xeroxed the letters. Maybe xeroxed them and not mailed them.

Ending is difficult. Minkin now has his own Copying Machine, a secondhand one, but serviceable enough. Copying has become second nature with him. Surrounded by the copies of what goes out to the alien, even menacing world, he feels a kind of security, for all misunderstanding, all lies and slanders can be effectively rebutted. Landau and his class begin to fade.

FRIMMELL'S SUCCESSOR

I suppose if I were a little keener I should have been able to see that new things were in the air, that new combinations, so to speak, were forming and reforming. I came into the office and sat down at my desk—the little ceremonials, the minute little actions that one picks up on the way, and is really not aware of until he sees somebody else at work, I will not mention. I forbear. Everything was as usual, things were quite in order, and I picked up where I had left off yesterday.

The most characteristic thing about work of this sort is that you are never finished with it and can never hope to be finished with it as long as you live. It is a fact that when you die, the work is unfinished, there are bills to be sent out, books are not balanced, and it is for this reason that when I see a young man come into the office and begin to work like mad so as to finish this bit of work by the end of the week or by the end of the month, I cannot help thinking that this young man does not see it all clearly enough; when he comes to realize that the work will at any rate be unfinished when he dies, perhaps he will not be so eager about it. Of course there is the question of advancement, and you will see in a moment why I have raised this problem. My immediate superior had as yet not arrived. There is no point in making a melodrama out of this either—in fact he was never to arrive; at this moment, when I was sitting at my desk, he was dead at home. However, I did not know this; I am generally one of the earliest to arrive, he generally came a little later, and by that time the six people in his department were all busy at work.

I was caught up in my work in a little while, or better, my work caught me up in it, and I hardly heard when my name was called out. There is a simple reason for this: in the office there were only a certain number of noises that I had come to recognize, only a certain number of people had occasion to call me and it was not so much my name that I recognized as the particular inflections, the intonations of the people who were calling me. The boss himself was calling me. He had actually come into the office where I worked, or more precisely, he was standing at the door, and he had already called out my name two or three times before I became aware of the fact that I was being addressed.

"What is the matter with you?" he asked. "Are you deaf?"

I admit that I was astonished at this question—I thought it very unbusinesslike, he looked like a drugstore lounger there, leaning against the door, and hardly like the president of such a large business organization.

"Come into my office," he said to me, "I have something to tell you."

I followed him into his office. This was the first time in years that I had stepped foot into it; there was simply no reason for me to be there. You can imagine that I was a little surprised at this request. I could not understand what it was that he wanted from me, it was somehow outside the sphere of normal relations. Yet I was not at all thrilled—if anything I was a little perturbed. I will not say that I thought myself to be in any danger from the point of view of tenure, my conscience in this respect was clear, I felt that nobody would be able to perform my tasks any better than I was able to perform them—and yet there is no question but that somewhere at the bottom of my mind there was a very uncomfortable stirring, there was surely some submerged fear at work.

He did not bother to ask me to take a seat.

"You know," he said, "that Frimmell is dead."

This last word galvanized me—it sounded so out of place, it shook me up a little. I began to see that I was in an unusual situation.

"Dead," I repeated. "How is that possible? He was here, at work, only yesterday."

As soon as I spoke this sentence, I saw the folly of it, and I sensed immediately the content and the tone of the answer that the boss gave me. What in the world made me say such a stupid thing, I asked myself; I hurt myself in asking it, I suffered for my recognized stupidity.

"Yes," answered the boss, "he was here yesterday, but he is dead today. Is there anything so strange about that?"

To a T. Just the answer I had expected.

I admit that it all sounds heartless—here my immediate superior was dead, by no means an old man, a man with whom I had had the most intimate contact over a period of eighteen years, and I could only think that I had said the wrong thing, the stupid thing, that I had opened myself up for this curt response. I thought not one bit of Frimmell, I thought only of my humiliation, and I cursed myself for having uttered this perfectly ridiculous cliché.

"You will step into his place," he went on, "you will take over all his responsibilities, and naturally your salary will be increased accordingly."

I was about to answer him, accepting his offer with thanks, telling him that I was ready to step into poor Frimmell's shoes, but just then the telephone rang and he waved away the beginning of my sentence. Then he seemed to forget all about me as he engaged in a heated telephone conversation; it was just as though Frimmell had not died and as though I was not in the room at all.

I was grateful for the opportunity to collect myself—the rudeness no longer disturbed me actively, I had long grown used to the fact that there is an automatic rudeness toward the person in the inferior position, that when a more important person enters the scene you are automatically relegated to the periphery of the world, you have entered the further sphere of the boss's consciousness. I say I no longer *actively* resented this rudeness; how can you continue to grow angry over an inevitable part of your daily routine? One doesn't have the courage, the strength, for this.

Do you know that I felt much closer to my employer at this instant, with the rudeness and all? It was a simple matter of gradation of rank: I had risen in the ranks, I was one step nearer to the top of the organization. I really did feel a slight swelling of self-importance, it was a feeling that I had not felt in years, ever since my childhood, perhaps. There was an occasion that I now recalled, however vaguely: it was the first time that I had ever thought of it. It was in elementary school, some classroom, an election, I was suddenly made a member of a committee (say, could it have been a practical joke?). I only got the effect of how it lifted me, how I suddenly felt myself wrenched from the class-room community, somehow set above it, a little superior even. I was closer somehow to the president of the class, to the vice-president, to the teacher. It had been a very pleasant feeling, I do not remember how it turned out, how long this feeling of plea-sure had lasted. At that time I even thought that utter strangers looked at me with more regard; it was as though the news of my election to the classroom committee had gotten into the streets.

"My dear man, you are dreaming," my employer said to me. He had finished his telephone conversation. I believe it was the first noncommercial remark he had ever addressed to me.

"Poor Frimmell," I said.

"Do you know," my employer said to me, leaning forward in his chair, "do you know that he was a fine fellow, we will all miss him a great deal."

He then gave me some instructions, which I listened to with great care, but which, when you come down to it were quite beside the point—what he was telling me I already knew; the instructions covered the general duties of the deceased. What I had to know my employer was really in no position to tell me. The special ways of doing the job which one only learns by doing the job. It was all very businesslike—a new job, new duties had to be learned. Life goes on, I thought to myself. I indulged in this bit of philosophy.

As soon as I left the boss's office (that was a funny handshake he gave me, as though I were going off on a long journey) my mood changed again—really I have never spent such a confusing day, everything changing from one minute to the next. I am sure you already have an inkling as to why this day has exhausted me so much. Nothing is so tiring as to experience too many different emotions in the course of a day.

As soon as I left the office, the practical aspects of the affair began to present completely unforeseen problems. It was a great surprise. All my life, all my working life I mean, I had trained myself, I had been trained, to do the job in front of me, if there was a slight variation in the job, to adjust myself as quickly as possible to the variation. It did not work out that way at all here. I did not simply sit down and take over my new duties. If it had all been so simple, the whole day would not possess the extraordinary vividness which it does possess; it would hardly have lingered in my mind past the office hours.

What exactly was the difficulty? Now that I am able to see things from a slight vantage point—not much of a vantage point it is true, a few hours and a new location—I think I see what the difficulty was. I was really a split man—while officially, legally, so to say, I was in a new position, comparatively speaking, in a position of authority, in fact, psychologically, I was still in my old post. Is it not perfectly evident that it should have worked out this way? Would it not happen to almost anybody under the same circumstances? Of course it would, it is all a matter of habit: you change your patterns of habit, and then you are on a spot for a while: you can't adjust yourself, you continue with the old ways in the new position. Consider a child who is learning to walk; doesn't that child often succumb to the temptation of crawling? Of course, why talk about it?

In fact, what gives point to today's experiences, what makes them, I mean, so memorable (such a recent occurrence, and already memorable?) is not their unusualness, but rather the degree of intensity with which these experiences struck me, that is what the whole thing is all about.

Furthermore, I have begun to see that there is something very cowardly in assuming that such and such an experience is not so remarkable for the reason that so many people have shared it. This strikes me somehow as an attempt to share the guilt: you bring into the picture a whole crowd of people who do not belong there at all, you somehow lose yourself in this crowd you have summoned, it is the way that people are relieved at the prospect of death—if they are—when they reflect that this is a fate shared by all humanity.

At any rate, when I left my employer's office I really began to have my troubles, there is no question of it.

I had to take instructions from people I had never taken instructions from before, I had to give instructions to people I had never given instructions to before. Do you know that the latter was the more difficult for me, that I find it very trying to give instructions to the people with whom I have worked together, on the same plane, for so many years?

"Here," I said to an old fellow clerk, "do so and so."

How easy it sounds! And yet it cost me an effort to get these words out. I somehow did not want to feel more important than these others; in fact I think I was a little afraid to give them orders. Isn't it a peculiar thing, though? Like most people, I believe that I want power, that I want to be in the position to rule, to control others, and here, when I was given this opportunity to some extent, I shied away from it, I suddenly became very tender, very squeamish.

What in the world were you afraid of? I see the perfect reasonableness of such a question. After all, you may say, you were not sending these people on any dangerous errands, it is not as though you were risking their lives through foolhardiness of your own. No, not at all, you were simply telling them to do what they had been told to do for years, what they expected to be told to do.

That is all very well, I understand that, and yet there is no question in my mind but that I feared for my life. I really felt somehow that I would be physically annihilated for daring to assume the robes of power, for playing this commanding role.

It was all very shocking to me, but please do not think that there was no element of pleasure in this new role that I found myself playing, please do not think that I got no sense of power in watching people carry out the instructions that I gave to them, please do not think that I am so inhuman. Of course there was pleasure in it for me. After all were they not forced to do what I had been forced to do for so many years? Do you think people have no need to inflict on others the humiliations that have been inflicted on them?

It was precisely this combination of fear and pleasure that drove me frantic; the combination of feelings was really a little too much for me, I must confess that.

When it came to the taking of orders from a new superior, there were further difficulties. I'm used to taking orders, but do you know that the fear element in my new commanding role somehow reinforced my own rebelliousness, so that I adopted an attitude toward my new superior that I had never dared adopt toward the unfortunate Mr. Frimmell.

Really, this new superior of mine, this Mr. Rankin, infuriated me with the manner in which he gave his orders, with his curtness and his air of self-importance. He treated me in a way that Mr. Frimmell had never treated me. He made my subordinate relation to him very keenly felt; it seemed as though this is just what he wanted to do. I am sure that he asked me to carry out orders not because it was essential that they be carried out, but rather because he wanted to show his power over me.

Do you want to know what I thought? I thought that this Mr. Rankin had divined my fears in regard to my own powers, and was purposely bringing these fears out, underlining these weaknesses of mine by emphasizing his own sense of power, his own ability to *use* that power.

He must have noticed some rebelliousness on my part, because at one point during the day he said:

"My dear man, what seems to trouble you? You seem not at all anxious to carry out your new tasks."

He said this in an insufferable way. I did not have the courage to respond to him in kind, but merely took out my resentment on him inwardly for hours afterward. You would think that I would descend on my own subordinates with fury, but I did not. I really feared to do such a thing.

There is no question in my mind but that my subordinates have nothing but the greatest contempt for me: I could see it all day in their eyes, I could see them comparing me to Mr. Frimmell, he was a much more confident person, even more aggresive.

Even when I attempted to act a little more brusquely, with a little more authority, even then, though they carried out my in-structions, they did these tasks with a certain air of slyness, as though they were saying: "We must do what he says, but we can see right through him."

And this Mr. Rankin—don't think that he wasn't always around just at the moment when one of my orders was carried out in this really contemptuous way. He was always situated most advantageously at these moments, and he seemed to have an understanding with these subordinates of mine. It was an under-standing which excluded me; they all of them were laughing at me, there is no question of it.

I will never allow this anymore—I will act with becoming dig-nity henceforth to this Mr. Rankin, I will go about my business with him in a very . . . businesslike way, I will show him my true feelings, but I will have control over them. He is nothing but a boor at any rate; as for his wife's unfaithfulness to him, it is a matter of common gossip. And I will show a stronger hand to my subordinates; one day's nonsense of this sort is really enough for any man—it is ridiculous to believe that they will do me any harm. Who are they anyway? Most ordinary kind of people, they don't have the courage for an act of violence; they fear the law as much as I do.

But enough of such thoughts—they are of no earthly use; they only have the effect of inflaming me, of filling me with desires for revenge, and I know how miserable, how cowardly it makes me feel when these vaguely thought feelings of revenge are not put into practice, when I only hope to put them into practice, but do not really decide to do so. Yes, I am a great coward, I know that. The fact that I am always thinking in terms of revenge, that I cannot stop myself from thinking in such terms, proves that; it is simply that my thinking takes the place of acts, and with so little satisfaction.

Yes, it was my cowardice which was the cause of all my troubles today, thank God I have something to blame it on—and I do not know yet how I succeeded in getting out of that office without collapsing altogether.

Do you know that for as long as half an hour I sat and did nothing but regret the death of Mr. Rankin, that is, Mr. Frimmell, nothing but regret that I was not back at my old work, that work the monotony of which seemed at some times the most unendurable thing in the world, but to which one gets used in the same way that one's body gets used to an increasing dose of some poison.

In the evening, I went out to dine in one of the two or three restaurants I frequented. As I sat there it was very clear that I could not act as though this were the end of an ordinary working day, that I simply could not go through the usual pattern once again. But what to do?

When you come to think of it, there is really very little to do when you have the feeling that you ought to do something special. I decided to visit a friend; he lived with his wife in a downtown apartment. I do not think I had ever visited him before this way, in the middle of the week, without making an appointment. What was it that motivated me? Simply the desire to explain myself, to get a little sympathy perhaps, in a way the most reasonable thought I had had all day.

On the way from the subway to my friend's apartment, it was necessary to pass along a narrow, poorly lit street, quite a phenomenon of a street in our city. A most acute and unpleasant feeling now came over me—yes, it was as sudden as that, though I admit that the groundwork for such an acute unpleasant feeling had been nicely laid by the events of the day (and why not, while I am at it, of my whole life?). In fine, I fancied myself the murderer of Frimmell. Just like that—his murderer, nothing else, mind you. I was responsible for his no longer being in the office. I had put him out of the way.

Naturally I did all in my power to push such a tormenting thought out of my mind, but it refused to go—really, I have never had such a stubborn thought—it was as though this thought felt, on its own hook, that it belonged just where it was, and resisted any attempts at being ousted.

This is what the devil said to me:

"You see, you have done it. You have somehow done away with this innocent man, and now that you are in his position, you are quite naturally afraid of your subordinates, afraid that they will do away with you in just the way that you did away with him."

Can you imagine anything sillier, more idiotic, than such a thought? Ridiculous, I said to myself, there is no foundation to such nonsense, you are making it up out of your own head. But the thought and the guilty feeling attached to it lingered on; I could not shake them off by any amount of counterthinking or counterfeeling. I went over almost every minute of time I had spent on the day of his death—it was quite clear that I could have had nothing to do with it, that I was not even in any physical proximity to him.

But then what upset me most was when I turned on myself for even attempting this kind of justification, for even attempting to exculpate myself when I was actually guilty of nothing. This infuriated me; it made me turn on myself with savagery, demanding what I meant by such thinking and that I put such imaginings out of my mind immediately.

Up came the office scene, and the attitudes of the subordinates—so this is why they grin at me in such a peculiar way; this is what they are thinking of, that I have done away with Rankin; so this is why they walk around and gloat at me. What are they not capable of, these smiling men?

You will believe me when I say that pursued by such thoughts, I ran with the utmost speed to the house where my friend lived— a policeman looked at me, with some suspicion, naturally—and when I finally rang the apartment bell, I was exhausted, terrified, and waiting anxiously for some nice warm living room, where I might sit for a while and chatter the Lord alone knows what.

Pratt seemed to notice nothing strange in my behavior. I am sure he was a little surprised at seeing me, but even this was hard to detect.

"Why, come right in," he said to me, "this is an unexpected visit."

Before I realized what I was about, I had blurted out that Rankin was dead, and that I was in his place. Oh, perhaps there were a few introductory remarks, formal questions about health and so on, I hardly recall. But I know that I wanted sympathy, I wanted to have my fears dispelled. I told about my feelings—oh, you can be sure that I said nothing of my suspicions about my own part in the death, I could not get myself to talk about that— but the very fact that I was talking about the subject at all was enough to relieve me somewhat. I did not express everything I was thinking.

What a fool I was! I should have just sat there and exchanged general information, said that I had been in the neighborhood and thought I would drop in for a call. Then we could have discussed general matters of interest—our mutual friends, the political situation, a thousand and one things.

I think Pratt was sympathetic enough, but that terrible wife of his! Do you know what she thought? She thought that I had burst in so unexpectedly merely to show off my new position, with its greater position and greater salary, to gloat over her husband, who was little more than a breadwinner.

Though she said nothing directly, her whole attitude was a challenge to me, her whole tone was very belligerent.

Her husband, my friend Pratt, tried to smooth things over. He tried to sympathize with my feelings; he said that I would get used to my new post soon enough, it was only a matter of habit, of adjustment. He congratulated me—I could have had a fine sympathetic time if only that wife had gone off somewhere.

But as things stood, it was I that had to go. It was impossible to stay any longer, really too trying.

He took me to the door and shook hands warmly with me— God knows what he said about me after I left.

I got home as quickly as I could from that visit.

THE PHARMACIST

Monroe Hyman grew up in the secure knowledge that his means of livelihood had been laid out for him; like an ancestrally chosen bride, his occupation was waiting.

This occupation, or profession, was that of a pharmacist, and Monroe accepted it with a sense of inevitability which was the next best thing to choice, though actually the furthest removed from it.

The knowledge was double-edged, for though it brought closer, within limits, the distant and mysterious future (so that Monroe was never at a loss when asked about his plans, but would solemnly say, "I am going to be a pharmacist"), it had the effect also of destroying the elements of doubt, openness, and thus it helped make of Monroe a rather solemn, not altogether pleasing boy. He was not very open to adventure, the impulse of the moment.

Still, as he grew older this purposeful sobriety kept him on his destined road while his boyhood friends were tossed in all directions, ending up as millionaires, struggling merchants (independent), gangsters, and professional men.

He became a pharmacist, and found a job, through a relative's friend, in a drugstore on the Upper West Side.

Here he found the security in which he had grown up was shattered, and that he was at the mercy of his employer, an impatient old man who by no means controlled his temper because of his friendship for the friend of Monroe's relative.

Monroe labored in his cubbyhole in the back of the store, compounding his prescriptions with the conscientiousness which had always characterized him.

The old man, Krakauer, shuttled between the front and the back of the store; as the years went by, his heart was more and more in the over-the-counter sales.

One day, after Monroe had been in this place a little less than a year, there was a dramatic occurrence which shook him profoundly, creating an unusual disturbance, a terror.

Monroe was working on a prescription; Krakauer was at his side, sorting out some drugs. The front was empty. A customer entered.

"Go ahead," said Krakauer peevishly, "take care of the front."

Monroe obeyed his employer and went forth to meet the customer. This gentleman was looking to buy a vaporizer, or at least he was looking to investigate the possibilities of buying a vaporizer. His questioning and close observation of the various models, his comments and comparisons, all without the slightest indications of purchase, unnerved the old man, who rushed to the front of the store, waving Monroe to the rear.

This pleased Monroe, who disliked selling and was happiest in his cubby compounding the prescriptions. He worked slowly and finished the prescription just as Krakauer stormed back, no more successful than Monroe in completing the sale, and blaming his assistant for starting the transaction *on the wrong foot.*

"You spoiled the sale," he said. "You confused him by showing him everything he asked for."

Monroe did not understand this remark.

"Here," called Krakauer to one of the kids who hung around waiting to run prescriptions, "deliver this."

He wrapped the prescription which Monroe had just finished and gave it to Zeck, one of the speediest of the messenger boys.

Zeck took off as though he had been given the stick as the anchor man in a close relay race.

The store got a little busy, and Krakauer stayed up front. When things slowed down, he came back and continued his work. At this point Zeck came back and delivered the money.

"My God," cried Krakauer, "where is the mercury?" Monroe looked up, astonished.

The old man, in his rushing back and forth, had somehow got his hand into Monroe's prescription—at any rate, the mercury was missing: there was a good chance that this lethal dose had landed in the prescription made up for Mrs. Gordon.

The old man bolted, with Monroe in close pursuit.

"Watch the store," shouted Krakauer to Zeck. The redoubtable child found himself in charge of the establishment.

In spite of the marked difference in age, the proprietor of the drugstore ran well ahead of his assistant, for the reason that he knew the Gordon address, so that the younger and presumably faster man had to lag behind. The pair made a rather unusual picture as they ran through the streets. The old man had probably not run so fast in forty years. He could not regain the gait of his youth, and the awkwardness of his stride doubled the amount of exertion; his anxiety prevented him from calling out the address to Monroe, whose own anxiety prevented him from asking. The Gordons lived only a block away, on the fourth floor of an apartment house. The old man rushed up the stairs and burst into the apartment, followed by Monroe. They ran past the amazed Mr. Gordon and into the open bedroom where Mrs. Gordon was lying.

Mrs. Gordon was about seventy; she had run a grocery store with her husband for forty years and was not ignorant of the ways of the world.

Krakauer seized the little hinged box which stood on the bureau next to Mrs. Gordon's bed. He swiftly counted the pills. This accomplished, he closed his eyes in blissful weariness, his body relaxed to the point of limpness, and he opened his eyes, facing the company as an absolutely reborn person, with a new and unexpected outlook.

"What's the matter, Mrs. Gordon, you don't take your medicine, you don't trust the doctor?"

Monroe too had counted the eight pills and retreated to the corner of the room, experiencing active relief. The old man, Mr. Gordon, was somewhat dazed by the swiftness of the storm which had risen and then of the calm which had followed.

The old lady was very suspicious of this unaccountable behavior, and could not be mollified.

"What do you want?" she asked. "Why did you break into my house this way, without even ringing the bell? What is happening here?"

Krakauer laughed hysterically, with the laugh of the saved, with the laugh of one who knows that the worst has passed, that what follows can be snarled, a little unpleasant, but the dread outcome has been avoided.

"You are right," he said. "Of course I owe you an explanation. You see, these pills are not for you."

"Not for me?" repeated Mrs. Gordon. "What do you mean they're not for me? What are they doing here?"

"They *are* for you," said Mr. Krakauer. In the middle of saying that two prescriptions had been switched, he realized that this was the last possible thing to admit (next to the truth itself) and switched his story, on the wings of a brilliant idea.

"You see," he said, "Dr. Kornbluth called and said to add a little something, a sedative, to the prescription. But it was already made, so we came to get it back."

"Why a little sedative?" she asked.

"To make you sleep better," said the druggist, who was becoming more and more exhilarated by this tissue of lies which he was making up as he went along.

"I have no trouble sleeping," said the old lady, and she reached for the pills.

"No, no," cried Krakauer, as he and Monroe leaped desperately for the box, which was captured by the proprietor.

Mrs. Gordon settled back in her bed.

"What is it, poison in that box?" asked the old lady.

Krakauer laughed and looked meaningfully at the sober Monroe, who somehow joined in the laughter.

"You both had to come?" she asked. "To get the pills, to add the sedative?"

"It was such a nice day," said Krakauer, "I asked Monroe to take a walk with me."

"And who's taking care of the store?" she asked.

"Zeck," answered Krakauer, and a cloud crossed his face as he thought of what was going on down there.

"And if you were taking a walk on such a nice day," she continued, "why did you rush in like a pair of wild men?"

Krakauer was nonplussed, but Monroe said quite idiotically: "We weren't sure it was the right apartment."

Mr. and Mrs. Grodon looked at each other helplessly.

"*A por mishugena,*" said Mr. Gordon.

"Well, thank you," said Mr. Krakauer. "I will take this prescription and send over the new one in a few minutes."

"Maybe this time," said Mrs. Gordon, "you will close up the store altogether."

"Ah, Mrs. Gordon,' said Krakauer, "such a tongue, like a sweet-and-sour pickle."

On this note Krakauer and Monroe left, the old druggist clutching the prescription box.

After this experience, which, in spite of its happy ending, its deliriously happy ending, had a most sobering effect on Monroe, if it were at all possible for anything to have a sobering effect on a young man already steeped in sobriety to the point of stupefaction—after this experience Monroe was forced to consider again the basis of his security, and found it sadly wanting. On top of the perpetual menace of Krakauer, there was the ever-present possibility of accidental poisoning of the customers. His conscientiousness, always extreme, now passed well beyond the bounds of normal caution. He insisted on a fixed space, a *cordon sanitaire,* where no one could penetrate, and especially not Krakauer. He dreamt idly of going into business for himself, but found it difficult even to leave the corner where he labored, carefully compounding, for good or for bad, the medicine prescribed.

So there he sat, there he sits, a man more willed against than willing, quite incapable of movement. Of course he recognizes dimly that Krakauer will die some day, and then he will be faced with the problem of taking over the business, of leaving his narrow professional cubicle and moving onto the rough, the unpredictable economic seas. Or, of course, he can hire himself out again.

But meanwhile Krakauer is alive. He rushes from front to back, but the shuttle has slowed down; he spends most of his time in the beloved front of the store, where he can both sell and *shmooze*, leaving the rear, for the most part, to his associate, whose youth is gracelessly fading. All that predestination, all that early serenity gone to waste!

"Here, Monroe," says Krakauer, sliding a prescription slip through the cage where the younger man now works, "this must be ready in half an hour."

Monroe barely nods, moves the slip to the side, and continues, as meticulously as ever, on the tasks so early chosen for him.

THE PERILS OF TRADE

In my type of business, the buying and selling of General Merchandise, domestically and internationally, one becomes accustomed to all sorts of curiosities, takes for granted happenings before which a more sensitive (or less desensitized) individual might recoil.

We have a saying for this: *It is all in the Day's Business.*

This means: If it can be bought, and if it can be sold, there is nothing so remarkable about it.

For example: In one of the many circulars which comes to my desk detailing War Surplus Commodities open for bid, there was a line which caught my attention.

"*Secondhand Dwarfs*—located at such-and-such an island in the Pacific—excellent condition, etc."

This line caught my attention because I had recently been the agent in the purchase of a Czechoslovakian castle for a retired grain speculator, who, just before he set sail, asked me to be on the lookout for any accessories which I thought might be fitting or useful in this type of home.

Now it is well known that no castle can be considered fully appointed unless there is available a dwarf whose chief duty is to sleep each night outside his mistress's door.

I checked the line and handed the circular to my secretary, noting what I thought would be a fair price for an item of this sort. She handled the transaction in the routine way.

(Back of my mind was an image of a small Pacific island, uprooted in some diversionary tactic of the war, these little people milling around, until some exasperated bureaucrat filed them under the head of Surplus Commodities and so they found their way to my desk.)

Three weeks later, under the errata listings, was the notation: "*Secondhand Dwarfs*—should read *Secondhand Wharfs*—such-and-such a port in the Pacific—excellent condition, etc."

My secretary brought this erratum to my attention.

"What would a secondhand wharf be?" she inquired, exasperated.

This is the girl who fainted the following week under circumstances which prove that no matter how one accommodates himself to the unlikely and weird (by a cowardly self-preserving process which turns every unlikely happening into a likely happening) there is sure to be some trivial occurrence in the course of the day's business which takes on the proportions of a disaster.

Returning from lunch I found my secretary out cold on the floor. It took me some time to revive her, and the only words she spoke during this period sounded like: "King Kong." She held a letter tightly gripped; it was impossible to take this letter from her without tearing it away. I decided to wait.

When she revived, she was dazed, shook her head in bewilderment at the questions I asked her. I asked about the letter. She did not seem to understand, gazed blankly at the sheet, moaned, and then opened her hand in a kind of resigned despairing gesture. I picked up the letter.

The letterhead was of a Hong Kong firm, one unfamiliar to me. After my trade name and address, both correctly written, and salutation "Gentlemen:" there was nothing, a blank page.

I admit to a certain tremor of fear at the sight of this blank page. Precisely the point of a business letter to give and ask for *information,* and here nothing. This is surprising; there is certainly no business to be transacted here.

My common sense came to my aid. I saw exactly what had happened. The man (for it was a man's handwriting) had just started on the letter when he was called away, somehow distracted. Then, having thought the letter through, it was as though he had written it. Having written it, he mailed it. This blank page was rather funny—I determined to write a humorous reply. Something like:

"Dear Sir:

"Have received yours of the 12th instant, and lack of contents noted,"

A glance at my secretary quickly dissuaded me from this course. She was pale, trembling, gazed vacantly out the window. I sent her home for the day.

(A woman is absentminded—this means that the repressed material is in a state of activity. At this moment there is a blow from the outside—a slip of the eye revives a primal fantasy—overwhelmed by a primate. The repressed material, in a state of activity, is galvanized. Defenses are overthrown. The woman faints.)

I spent the remainder of the afternoon clearing up some work, also writing a few letters which had to be mailed that day. The work went slowly—I was quite absentminded, my thoughts reverted to old scenes, memories I thought were buried forever, people long dead or long out of my life. It grew late, the room darkened, my gloom deepened. I shook my head vigorously, to shake out the unpleasant thoughts.

"Back to work," I said, "before you too are hurled to the floor."

What I meant was: Back to this acceptable madness which protects you from the hidden self. Let this self appear, then you will first appreciate this madness. As mad as you become, you will never exceed this madness which you have lived under the guise of sanity, this madness which protects you from nothing but love, truth, and reality.

What I should have meant was: What a providential blow! to cleave the armored soul, make way for the despised love, truth, and reality.

UNCLE BENNY

Years ago while considering my future I took to reading manuals of salesmanship. While my friends were busy studying the Greeks and the Germans, I was looking into such matters as: *Six Ways of Cornering a Prospect,* or *Introductory Approaches to Clinching a Sale;* or *Self-Mastery & Masterly Selling,* or *Psychology of the First Call;* or *The Use of Set Jokes in Moments of Crisis,* or *The Mystery of the Bottom Price;* or *The Personality Approach: Apparel and Appearance.*

How much time I wasted! What a fool I was! What I was trying to learn so laboriously, I could have learned at close quarters from my Uncle Benny, who was not only a remarkable salesman but a theoretician as well, and he did not hesitate to describe the rationale of his selling technique. This was in itself unusual, in a world full of trade secrets, of cost prices, of mysterious credit ratings, but Uncle Benny did not hold back:

Never Let a Customer Out of the Store!

That was his cardinal principle, the be-all and end-all of his selling, and what he meant was:

*Never Let a Customer Out of the Store
Without His Buying Something!*

215

I have seen him carry out this policy—at the very moment that I was reading the manuals of salesmanship!—live it out, I should say, for he was a consummate actor, ran the emotions ragged, ranged from bellicosity and dire prophecies to pleadings and cajolings, to say nothing of the Ulyssean stratagems in between.

When a customer shook his head, signifying the beginnings of doubt about the price or quality of the merchandise, or worse, when the customer took the first steps toward the door, the door leading out, then Uncle Benny, hurt in the pride, sprang into action. His tactics were variable and unpredictable: he might pull out other merchandise, for purposes of contrast or as a delaying tactic; he might start a political discussion or probe weak points in his enemy's character, make fabulous self-confessions, rundown the competition, ask the customer's opinion on matters profound or trifling, discover friends in common, confess to curious errors of price, recall recent shipments of merchandise which absolutely fit the bill. Everything, in fact, but card tricks and phantasmagorias on a wall suddenly darkened.

I have seen Uncle Benny hurl himself in the way of a departing customer, creating a human roadblock which had to be pushed aside, or hurdled, or else made for the desirable state of standstill, the point from which the situation could be revived.

"It isn't only losing the sale," he once explained to me, "it is also losing the customer, for once a man goes out of your place empty-handed, the chances are you'll never see him again. Buying from you, he makes a connection: you become a part of his life. When he doesn't buy, you are a nothing, and nobody will return to a nothing."

(Yet I have seen Uncle Benny call a customer's bluff, let him walk to the threshold and watch him return. Another step and Uncle Benny would have leaped after him.)

But it was even more than losing the customer: Uncle Benny had a personal stake in the matter. A sale was a kind of challenge, the customer was an enemy until he bought; *then* he became a friend. But more than that, buyer, seller, and merchandise were mere chaos, mere turmoil before the sale; the sale brought harmony, and the failure of the sale was monstrous, an unbearable void.

When things looked darkest, Uncle Benny lowered the price. For, as a second principle, really as a corollary to the first, he felt that:

Sometimes You Make, Sometimes You Lose.

Working on this principle, he did not hesitate to make the most fantastic reductions in price, past reasonable levels of profit to the dangerous area of cost, and to go under cost. He preferred a sale at a loss to the lost sale.

"So what," he'd expostulate, "he'll come back, we'll have another chance. You can't expect to make money on every sale. *Sometimes you make, sometimes you lose.*"

We had to go along with that, suffering the loss, knowing full well the incredible profits he made on other transactions, profits which made a mockery of "the just price." Yes, a customer could certainly win or lose with Uncle Benny, could carry off bargains beyond the dreams of avarice, or be scalped beyond the seller's dream of gain. The customer was a pawn, in the grip of forces more powerful than he had a right to expect; he comes to make a purchase and finds himself in an Extreme Situation.

It was sad to see how changing circumstances undercut Uncle Benny. There were controls, there was Fair Trade. The price was hemmed in on all sides. The price was a captive. For Uncle Benny the price had been free, above individuals, above government, above business itself. It had been the raw material of art, which he could mold to his heart's desire. Then came the agencies, the bureaucracies, laying their leaden administrative hands on the price. . . .

Also, the nature of our enterprise changed. More and more our business was done through the mails. A sale became an impersonal thing; it was no longer a struggle between individuals, or rather, the struggle was disguised: it became less an act and more an "operation." The desk took the place of the counter; new machines appeared which did most amazing feats of calculation and reproduction.

He was lost. He could not adapt. A young man was stationed at his side. When Uncle Benny soared above the price, the youth tugged at his sleeve and whispered the fixed price into his ear. When the customer shook his head, meaning *no,* or made that preparatory (and serious) step toward the door and Uncle Benny dropped the price, hurled it deep into the abyss of no-profit, Abner tugged at his sleeve and whispered the fixed price into his ear.

It was sad to see, very sad.

Uncle Benny waited around. Customers appeared less frequently. The business was done behind him and around him, over the wires, in the mails, it was transcribed on the noiseless machines, was electronically posted. And there was no money in evidence! Behind and around Uncle Benny flowed checks, notes, trade acceptances, letters of credit! They flowed silently, as blood in a body.

Then after a while the merchandise itself disappeared. It was off somewhere in a warehouse: all he had were the samples, the soiled samples from which the customer made his choice.

"Wait," cried Uncle Benny, "I'll show you what you're getting." But there was only the soiled sample, not the thing itself, and he withdrew more and more from the world. . . .

But I am going beyond the bounds of this remembrance. It started as a matter of self-criticism: there I was, a pedant, looking into these manuals of salesmanship, where the obvious was tortured beyond recognition, while in front of me the truth was being lived.

"Say," cried Uncle Benny, in that desperate voice which signaled that the sale was being lost. I raised my eyes from the book.

"Say, did you ever hear this story? A small boy falls off an ocean liner. An elderly man dives into the water right after him. A lifeboat is lowered, the old man and the child are pulled in, then onto the deck. The father of the child rushes over to the old man and embraces him. 'You've saved my son. How can I thank you?' he cries. 'I'll give you anything, anything you want.' He pulls out a checkbook and begins to write. 'Here, how much should I make it out for? I'm a rich man.' 'That's all right,' said the old man, 'I happen to be well-to-do myself. I own a small chain of stores, a little real estate in Florida.' 'Anything you want,' cried the father, 'just tell me what you want, and if it is humanly possible . . .' 'Well,' said the old man, 'there *is* one thing you can do for me.' 'What, what is it?' *'Find the bastard who pushed me in,'*

The lantern-jawed customer who was the object of Uncle Benny's attention slowed up for a minute, either in appreciation or surprise. Then the rigid lineaments of his face seemed to thaw into the confirmations of a smile.

"Ha," cried Uncle Benny, "and do you know the man who was looking to buy the most expensive burial casket for himself? Finally he found one, very fancy, with golden handles, for $4500. He goes to his old friend and tells him the news, triumphantly. '$4500?' asks his friend reprovingly, *'For another $500 you could be buried in a Cadillac!'* "

The process of thaw continued, there followed a smile, a true smile, and Uncle Benny moved into the situation newly opened.

BRENNER'S DREAM

Not having dreamed, as he thought, for a considerable length of time, or having dreamed and disremembered the dreams, than unable to recall them, Brenner was very pleased, even relieved, one morning not so long ago when he woke and there in his mind, clear as the sight of the bureau across the room, was a dream.

This was his dream, as he now told it to himself:

I climbed a fiery path, to the top of a mountain, and on that mountaintop was a cabin, which I entered. Inside was a grave, handsome man, with rather thick wavy black hair, seated near a window, out of which he was looking, in a way I considered pensive. The walls were empty, except for two pieces of pinewood, with the following inscriptions:

A physician for the cure of moral diseases.

NATHANIEL HAWTHORNE

and:

A dim capacity for wings
Degrades the dress I wear.

EMILY DICKINSON

"Yes?" asked the man at the window, turning to me.

"You are the physician for the cure of moral diseases," I said, "and I should like to tell you my symptoms."

"Please," he said.

"In the first place," I said, "I fear love."

"One moment, please," said the doctor, though there was nothing in the room, nothing in his appearance, or manner (except maybe for the way he said: "Please," and the way he said: "One moment, please") to indicate that he was a doctor, "Are these your symptoms?"

He handed me a slip of paper, in appearance halfway between a prescription blank and a page out of a notebook, on which was written, in an elegant hand, with a great deal of space between the letters and between the words, the following:

1. Fear love.
2. Life not important—in general, or in particulars.
3. Do not make people happy.
4. Don't have respect of people (and rarely *for* people).
5. Lack a sense of value of people.
6. Death not real.

These were exactly the symptoms, to a word (except in symptom 4 I had written *do not,* not *don't*), which I had written down and started to read to him.

"That's just what I was going to tell you," I said.

Neither one of us seemed surprised.

"These are common complaints," he said, "for certain kinds of people."

There was a rather long pause, which he was not disposed to break, and I said:

"Well then, what is to be done?"

He shrugged his shoulders.

"I am not exactly a doctor of moral diseases," he said. "How should I answer you?"

I looked at the words on the wall:

> *A physician for the cure of moral diseases.*
> NATHANIEL HAWTHORNE

"Oh," he said, "that was an idea for a story by Hawthorne, one of his famous jottings.

"It is my feeling," he went on, "that if these symptoms you describe are real to you, the way a grocery list is real in the sense that you go to the store and buy what is on the list, putting an end to the list, if it is real to you that way, not merely a list to look at, then you can do something about these symptoms, relieve your suffering."

"But what?" I asked.

"I don't know," he said. "Maybe you haven't suffered enough."

He returned to silence.

I got up to go, and looked again at the words of Emily Dickinson:

> *A dim capacity for wings*
> *Degrades the dress I wear.*

"These lines," I said. "Why . . . ?"

I was going to ask him why these lines were on the wall, but my voice trailed off, though the question was just about asked.

"Sir," he said, rising, "if these lines have not brought tears to your eyes, your symptoms are surely superficial, you have not suffered enough."

His eyes were moist.

Then I went out the door, and down the trail.

That was the dream as Brenner remembered it, as full and clear as his own image in the mirror, as the automobiles in the street, at the two great headlights on the subway train that took him down to work.

SUSPENSION POINTS . . .

As I passed my money to the stationer for the newspaper, it flashed across my mind (with the speed of a meteor, though less dramatically) that I could, if I so wished, spend a good part of the rest of my life describing this act, in its immediacy (I could add information about the money I gave, the change I received, in which hand I held the money, and how I folded and held the paper), its historical antecedents, all its ramifications, both foreground and background, to say nothing of tributary and peripheral elements.

There is the act itself, now in its more abstract quality, of exchanging money for a commodity. What belonged to him now belonged to me. He profited materially (must be a 40 or 50 percent markup, or why should he bother with it?), I gained possession of an object of which I could make various uses—read it, use under the kindling in a fireplace, roll up and swat people or flies with, spread on the floor after washing same, work into airplane or other interesting shapes, use in collages the way the cubists used to do (but that's not my line of activity), clip out interesting items for own future use or to send to interested friends, make confetti with, line garbage cans with, could even (though I've never done this) save the paper, day after day, and then sell to a scrap-paper man, thus retrieving some part, however infinitesmal, of the original purchase price.

This buying of a paper is an act expressive of the history of the exchange of objects, an act old as mankind and whose analysis is no doubt almost as old (in the sense that it would probably have to be done before being thought about), moving through history down to the times of Adam Smith, Ricardo, Marx, Weber. . . . Can you imagine the time I'd have to spend learning and relearning the history and the analyses of theories of exchange in the spheres of economics, sociology, political science? And then summarizing all that material?

And then there is my partner in the transaction I started with. We are not friends, but I know him quite well, in the way that you get to know quite well people whom you have been dealing with steadily over many years. I know how long he's been in this spot, what he did before he was here (he was a car dealer, and before that a salesman for a hardware company in the Southwest), and I know his wife, who sometimes helps in the store. I've followed the history of their children as they've grown, and as much as I know about him he knows about me. Over the course of years these exchanges of nonintimate confidences—another kind of exchange—can add up to a good deal of information, knowledge, even insight.

And his physical description, and that of his wife, and of their children (from the few glimpses I've had of them over the years). And the character analyses, and behavior patterns, and the description of the store itself—its size, layout, decor, and how all that has changed over the years.

The fact is that I knew this store before the stationer moved in, know something of the history of its previous occupants, their businesses and families, and the history too of the building in which the store is located, for it so happens that I once, at a social gathering, met the real estate agent who handled that building, a man with a strong memory as well as a keen historical interest and imagination, who told me what he knew about the building going back decades—who had built it, some of its better known occupants, who had occupied the various storefronts, a veritable treasure-trove of information about the building, and naturally, about the neighborhood too in which he had grown up, and about which he knew a great deal, combining interest with daily experience and reading. All this I remember, and could set down pretty much as he told it to me, for I am blessed, or cursed, with a photographic memory, and the flow of associations, particularly when I am in a certain kind of reflective, even slightly gloomy mood, leads me to a recall approximately total. And there is a good deal to be said about the agent himself—I heard about him from others, the complex deals he'd been involved in, but I won't even go into a summary of all that.

And I could describe in detail (only space, time, and disinclination forbid it) the individuals who were in the store at the time I bought the newspaper—not the clerks whom I've already mentioned as part of those I could describe, but the other customers. There were five such customers, three of them strangers, one of them an acquaintance, and the fifth a man I knew by sight, a well-known publisher who lived in the neighborhood, and who had in his hand some half-dozen magazines, to make himself *au courant,* no doubt, with the newest developments in the business and literary worlds, which have so many points of intersection. (Or maybe he was going on a long journey.) Yes, I could describe this publisher, what I knew of his life, his firm, the nature of his publishing activities, the authors he's published, his successes and failures. I could describe the three strangers, one a lanky, perfectly groomed man who seemed to be waiting to speak to the proprietor; another a child trying to decide what candy bar to choose among all the candy bars—and I could describe too all those candy bars, their shapes and tastes, the history of their prices and wrappers and so on; the third a young woman of great beauty, with the imperiousness that sometimes comes with such beauty (it showed in the movements of her head), and an abiding sadness (yes, it is possible to tell in a glimpse what abides), perhaps bitterness, which did not flaw that beauty but cast a kind of shadow over it, and I could speculate on the causes of this sadness or bitterness, in the way of family upbringing, problems of character, of love and marriage, a veritable panorama of possibilities thronged my imagination as I glimpsed this young woman, who was browsing among the paperbacks. And I could describe those paperbacks—I have browsed among them myself—to give an idea of what people are reading, to analyze popular taste, to explain how it is that among the mediocre and trashy books there are always a few works of genuine merit, to examine the prices, to write indeed a history of paperback publishing on the basis of the selection in this store, in front of which books stood the young woman I've already mentioned, the third of the strangers in the store at the moment that I picked up my newspaper.

And the acquaintance! I haven't forgotten him. He lives in the neighborhood; we had once met in the apartment of a mutual friend, and though neither one of us was seeing much of that mutual friend, we never failed to ask one another about him, what he was doing and so on. This mutual friend is a man who made a pile of money in corporate law, gave up the law, and spent a good deal of his time traveling the world in search of coins, the possession of which was for him a passion bordering on mania. No wonder neither my acquaintance nor myself hardly ever saw him. He was always in the suburbs of Rome, or on the isle of Crete, and indeed one of the invariable subjects of discussion between my acquaintance and myself was the whereabouts of our friend. "I got a postcard the other day from Ankara." "I heard he was in Labrador." I don't think either one of us *ever* saw this mutual friend anymore, but he was responsible for the continuance of this acquaintanceship, that and other things, for we discovered that we had other interests in common—horse racing and local politics, for instance—and these are subjects of inexhaustible interest. The history of racehorses and horse racing! The psychology of gambling! The complexities of big-city life! That's just for starters (you have to be careful, by the way, in the use of exclamation points: too many of them create a factitious interest, and that is one step away from boredom).

I don't believe I mentioned where I was coming from and where I was going. I'm sure I haven't mentioned it. I was coming from home and was on my way downtown, by subway, on matters of business. My stop at the stationer's was a way stop. Most stops between home and a destination are way stops. No? Home is not a way stop. To flesh out this account (to spirit it out too) I'd have to tell about home and family and about my business life, means of livelihood and so on. Well, this is obviously not material for a page. You perhaps now more clearly see what I mean when I say that I could spend a good part (*good* meaning *long* here) of the rest of my life to give the full story, foreground, background, and middle ground, of my purchase of the newspaper (and the subway ride! The experiences down there! The history of urban mass transportation!) and I don't plan to do that. I plan, and am in the process of carrying out the task, to show how it is possible that the description of this simple act of exchange, if elaborated in all directions, could easily lead to so ample an expenditure of time.

Included in so comprehensive a survey and analysis would be a picture, in words of course, of my mood at that moment of exchange, my situation, place in the world, whatever it is that we have come to mean by the word *existential,* the meaning and bearing of a life as regards one's hopes and anxieties, as regards its importance, value, fulfillment, and in relation to other lives, to society, nature. . . . Just imagine the complexity, intricate variety, of all these relationships (and so many others!), all these ways of explaining (curious how a single word, *explain,* is not sufficient to cover the meaning) just how it is and where it is that one has a place in the world—how he stands, falls, leans, and inclines, the various tensions, yearnings, advances, and withdrawals (this the incompletest list of all) which make up one's life at a given time. Why, you could use up dozens and dozens of pages just listing these existential stances, adding so many words after *tensions, yearnings, advances,* and *withdrawals.* . . . Those four dots tell it all.

Exclusion has its place in the scheme of things, and catalogues are forms of exclusion, just because they are incomplete.

I've neglected to mention the time and weather. It was a cold, blustery November morning—that's as exact as I'm going to be in these matters (I'm not going to say a word, except to state that I'm not going to say a word, about Time and Weather as concepts)—but I do want to say a few incomplete exclusionary words about the newspaper I bought.

Indeed, finally (how do you like that for an arbitrary exclusion?) the newspaper itself. I don't mean its physical dimensions and weight, though why shouldn't those characteristics be described any less than one describes the lineaments of a person or the appearance of a room? But its content, the total reading of which, unless you've learned one of those new methods of Speed Reading, would surely take a number of hours, and the summary of which, if you wish to include necessary and proper historical, grammatical, psychological, sociological, anthropological . . . (praise these suspension points, which make unnecessary the completion of all those lists, catalogues, itemizations, collections, numerations, etc. Though couldn't the *etc.* take the place of the suspension points?) would take up more space than time permits. I don't know how many words that particular issue of the *New York Times* (there, you see, I am not hiding anything) contained, but to give you an example of what would be involved in an adequate survey, let me just state that in this particular edition of the paper the name of a person was mentioned (two words, mark you, out of perhaps hundreds of thousands) who happens to be a man I know extremely well, we have had business dealings together, some of them of a quite fantastic, even profitable, nature, involving the purchase of mineral rights in certain countries (I cannot be more specific because some of these operations are still in progress, of a certain delicate international and diplomatic import), a man, as I've said, and I repeat myself for reasons of sentence clarity, that I know very well, to the fibers of his being (how more apt an expression that would be if we were engaged in the textile business), know him not only through our commercial connections but also on his own, as an individual, as a family man, as a political participant, as a man of the world, know his fraternal connections, his peccadilloes, his childhood and growing up, know a great deal about his parents, his lineage, the genealogy of the man, know him at home with his intimates, as a watcher of television, know his interests, his hobbies, his passions, his eccentricities, know his temperament, his character, the details of his psychoanalysis (he is in some ways an extraordinarily frank man but oh, with such reservoirs of secrecy), know his qualities good and bad, know the clothes he favors, the books and women he prefers, know what he thinks of his friends, of himself, know the nuances of his behavior, as well as the grosser outlines of it (what stops you from going on with such a list?) and he represents (I haven't gotten away from my subject at all) just two words—first and second name—in this newspaper of how many hundreds of thousands of words (lucky it's not a Sunday paper), the one I bought as an exchange commodity and about which I've said so little, when you consider its makeup, from news in its various categories, local to national to international to extraterrestrial (soon the moon correspondent will have more glamor than the foreign correspondent), not forgetting business, sports, finance, real estate. . . . (what *is* the proper number of suspension points?), its various departments, with their analyses of literature, politics, theater. . . . (the suspension points have it all over *etc.* because of the physicality, the ideographical extension), its advertisements, from the minutest classified to the full-page spread for products, causes. . . . , its prophecies in the way of weather, the outcome of horseraces and other sporting as well as political events. . . . , but I really haven't had a chance to read it, just glanced at it. . . . (the suspense in these suspension points).

THE TOLSTOY QUOTATION

*I often want to die. I cannot
get caught up in my work.*

TOLSTOY

Henry North looked carefully at Tolstoy's sentences. Before noting his reactions, I'll say something about his name. Henry is the first name of my old friend, Henry Malin, who died in 1966 when he was fifty-six. It was to Henry I addressed these words:

Dear Henry:

Getting along in years, we carry more and more of the dead with us. It is not a burden, it is perhaps less a burden than carrying the living within us. We struggle with the living, and our struggles with the dead are ended.

(But we struggle with the dead too, and our struggles with the living also come to an end.)

I carry lightly, pleasantly, and sadly, the memory of Henry Malin.

He was my friend, the friend of our family, the only one of our friends who called my father by his first name.

"Hello, Joe," he said, and we smiled at this real, though transitory, closing of the generation gap.

An incredibly popular math teacher at City College, he once, in the middle of an examination, threw a piece of chalk at a student, saying:

230

"Stop gypping, Silverman!" (or whatever the name).

I can't think of anyone with less pretense than he had. Can such absence of pretense be a fault?

He once told me that he had powerful ambitions in his field, but when he recognized that he was not in the ranks of the supreme mathematicians, he took that in stride, gifted mathematician though he was.

Most of us in the arts and sciences do not so plainly (won't say easily) give up a sense of our ultimate supremacy. Most of us are wrong. Was it wrong of Henry to recognize his limitations? Should he have judged himself against the supremely outstanding? Might he not have been wrong in his judgment? Shouldn't one delude himself with the possibility of supreme achievement?

Henry said that in his field you knew pretty well at a fairly young age whether the dreams of early youth had a real possibility of being realized.

To dream, then to admit to oneself the impossibility of that dream's being realized—it is a powerful blow to the ego, makes for a sadness, a poignancy, to live honestly with the dissolution of a dream.

On Saturday afternoons we'd take our children (Henry and the boys, myself and the girls) to the playground at Fort Tryon Park. Keeping an eye on the kids, we discussed all the situations. He had a marvelous combination of interest, wonder, skepticism, and admiration. He had a curious way (one conversation out of a thousand) of discussing the longevity of reputations. "So you think Balzac is a five-hundred-year man?" "Newton is easily good for a thousand." Off in the distance the kids were on the swings and slides. How is it possible not to grow with growing children? The stimulation, excitement, and marvel of it.

He said:

"If so and so were famous, he'd be considered a charming fellow."

Listening to City College–Bradley, City College–Kentucky. The great basketball tournament games after the war. We created a whole audience for these games being broadcast on radio.

We indeed carry lightly the memories of dead friends, a cargo precious and light—the appearance, the character, the movements and gestures, the mannerisms. Words tend to disapear. The spirit abides. Of loves, friendships, whatever gives meaning, joy, and wonder to existence.

North is the last name of a character of F. Scott Fizgerald in *Tender is the Night,* who is thought to be based on Ring Lardner, a writer to whom I am strongly drawn, in the personal way one is drawn to favorite writers. He died in East Hampton, Long Island, when he was forty-eight. North is also a name for the Hudson River (in its upper regions). Hudson it the last name of the character in Ernest Hemingway's novel *Islands in the Stream,* about which I wrote the following:

HEMINGWAY AT HOME

When reading Ernest Hemingway's book *Islands in the Stream,* I was struck by his writing: ". . . it is much less lonely sleeping when you hear children breathing when you wake in the night."

I jotted it down. Because it is an accurate and touching thought or sentiment.

Reading, in the *New American Review,* the elegaic thoughts of Reynolds Price, entitled "For Ernest Hemingway," I was therefore taken aback by his example of writing that is "simple-minded, dangerously vapid":

"The boys slept on cots on the screened porch and it is much less lonely sleeping when you can hear children breathing when you wake in the night."

What I found "accurate and touching," Reynolds Price found "simple-minded, dangerously vapid."

Two men, two readings.

But if there is a marked disagreement here, I find myself very much in agreement with Reynolds Price when he points out the importance for Hemingway of his family life (mostly neglected in his writing). The stories of Hemingway almost invariably take place outside the home, in public places, such as bars, battlefields, railroad terminals, rarely at home.

And *Islands in the Stream,* on whose merits I fully agree with Reynolds Price, is, in large part, a kind of family, domestic work, and I thought that the quotation about waking to the breathing of sleeping children illustrated so well the quality of Hemingway's presence in this world that he so much avoided in his writing, and which, from the evidence of this book, meant so much to him.

The Hudson is also the river associated with my old friend Paul Goodman, who died a little over a year ago, not quite sixty-one. He lived as a boy and young man in Washington Heights, loved to walk along the river. "The Lordly Hudson" is undoubtedly the most popular of his poems:

The Lordly Hudson

"Driver, what stream is it?" I asked, well knowing
it was our lordly Hudson hardly flowing,
"It is our lordly Hudson hardly flowing,"
he said, "under the green-grown cliffs."

Be still, heart! no one needs your passionate
suffrage to select this glory,
this is our lordly Hudson hardly flowing
under the green-grown cliffs.

"Driver! has this a peer in Europe or the East?"
"No, no!" he said. Home! home!
be quiet, heart! this is our lordly Hudson
and has no peer in Europe or the East,

this is our lordly Hudson hardly flowing
under the green-grown cliffs
and has no peer in Europe or the East.
Be quiet, heart! home! home!

I "happened" to be in the Heights recently, in Fort Tryon Park, above the Hudson, and walking the familiar terrain, I remembered what Paul had written to me a little less than a year before he died: "I certainly don't give out any joy to anybody," and I contrasted the sadness of his last years with the incredible joy-giving of his youth and manhood, the streams of his complaint and discontent feeding into the majestic river, and I recovered too the sense of Paul's dazzling movement of thought (when he was on), akin to that of the great City College basketball teams of our time, the driving power of his imagination and being in the world, here along the river of his growing up, his neighborhood, his longing, as he wrote in a poem on our first space landing,

> . . . we have come
> into the great hall as a man comes home.

Looking at Tolstoy's sentences, Henry North thought:

He writes, "I often want to die." It means that he does not always want to die, but more than sometimes. And he says nothing about putting an end to his life, but that he often wants its cessation. And the reason that he "cannot get caught up" in his work. Not that he cannot work, but that he can't "get caught up" in the work. It is his complaint that his work has lost meaning for him, that he cannot get caught up in it the way it is with meaningful work, where you become part of the work, in a way indistinguishable from it. And by the word "work" he means imaginative work, that is my guess.

He writes "often," not "always," not "sometimes," nor does he omit the limiting word, nor does he write "I want to be dead." He uses a kind of future tense and qualifies the universality of the feeling. Nor does he write *desire,* but *want.* He cannot get "caught up" in pleasurable toils, his "way of being in the world," to use a favorite formulation of Paul Goodman, has been disturbed, and creature of habit that he is, he is at a loss, not being caught up in the pleasurable and meaningful toils of his work. His dear world suffers a blow of emptiness: it is not the world in which he was used to function with such expressiveness, such imaginative and moral energy. His way of being in the world is more and more disturbed, he is not at home in the world, he wants to die, often wants to die, does not want to be dead, at the instant of writing, but to die, at a future time, the way he did, at eighty-two and not to kill himself, to take himself out of the world, the way Hemingway did, the competitive man, who measured himself against the best writers of all time (including Tolstoy) and the best of himself, and finding that he was not up to the best of himself (who can really tell about the others, or has to?), that his way of being in the world was disrupted, but irreversibly (so he must have felt), that his powers of creativity, in the wide-ranging spectrum, were gone forever, gone that old blessed and familiar surge (so he must have felt, else why, at age sixty-two, blow his head off, even in the manner of his father?). It is the absence of the meaningful passing of time, sometimes called boredom; power meant for creation, for love, it is the same thing, is stilled, or misdirected, that familiar powerful surge for making, for loving, it is the same thing, will not return, he cannot get caught up in his work, he often wants to die, or feels the loss of power is irreversible, he kills himself or dies later, because his way of being in the world is violated, death fills the emptiness.

So thought Henry North, in looking at Tolstoy's words, and, as a character in a fiction, a world being made, there crossed his mind these sentences from Hemingway:

"The only writing that was any good was what you made up, what you imagined. That made everything come true."

Is that the case? Henry North thought, still looking at the sentences from Tolstoy, but the Russian (thought Henry North) didn't exactly imagine these sentences, they are more the truth of his thoughts at a particular time, the truth that he didn't make up, but did express, the truth of a real person in a real place in a real situation, thought Henry North, who, in a story being written, is reading the Tolstoy quotation in a book, and then, putting the book aside, Henry North was off on paths of his own, in accord with the demands, the desires, of the actual imagined moment.

THE INTERMEDIARY

Saul picked up the phone a little before the office closed, while he was clearing his desk. "Hy," he said to the familiar voice. "Look," said Larry (his name wasn't *Hy* at all), "I've got to see you right off. Can I meet you for a drink in about fifteen minutes?" Saul was not astonished, merely surprised, because Larry knew his habits, and among these habits was that of going home right after work. Saul disliked drinking before dinner, said it created an artificial hunger, once characterized the activity as a "synthetic climax." He had fairly strong, if not altogether explicable feelings about this custom. "Can't it wait?" he asked. "I can see you later on. Why don't you come down to the apartment?" "No," insisted his friend, "it's just a question of a few minutes. I'd rather not discuss it over the phone, and you won't be late for dinner." So they arranged to meet. Saul wasn't at all sure about the dinner, know-ing the tricks that time played over a drink or two, so he called his wife, said that he was meeting Larry for a drink and might be a bit late for dinner. "I should be back on time," he said, "but just in case I'm late." He meant to complete the sentence by saying "then start without me" but he didn't say that, and the sentence had a fairly complete ring about it anyway. "Can't it wait?" asked Ma-thilda, "I've got to get Stan over to the Cub Scout meeting by seven." "That's just what I asked Larry," said Saul, " 'Can't it wait?' but he said it couldn't. I think I'll be home on time, but if I'm not, just start without me."

236

He finished clearing his desk, which meant putting a few things in the drawers, and then had a few minutes to wait. He was a junior partner in a fair-sized law firm, one which specialized, so to say, in a general practice, though of late years, because of a sensational settlement, they had been attracting divorce work. He had no work to catch up on (lots of people don't) so he looked out the window. The office, in a high building in the upper 50s, commanded an excellent view of Central Park, and as he looked at this greensward so miraculously saved from the encroachment of land-maddened realtors, he wondered why Larry was so anxious about meeting him.

They met, as prearranged, in a bar around the corner from Saul's office. It was one of those bars very masculine virile in its decor—hunting scenes and one of those antler heads never changing the direction of its stare—which lived on its five to seven crowd (time, not age). Pretty empty all day—maybe a small steady lunch crowd—it filled when the offices let out, and then you had to fight your way to the bar to get a drink. That is just what Saul and Larry did, and then they fought their way out of the crowd again, seeking, if not absolute privacy, at least a corner where they could talk. Actually the din was so great that it was difficult to make out what your companion was saying, no less to understand the talk of neighbors. The privacy was in the noise. After a minimum amount of small talk (they hadn't seen one another for over a month, so they inquired about one another's families) Larry got to the point. "Look," he said, "I'd like you to take messages for me on your phone." While Saul was looking puzzled, Larry continued: "There's a girl that sometimes calls me, and you know what my set-up is." His set-up was that he worked for a small organization where the phone calls went through a switchboard. "That girl at the switchboard," said Larry, "is something special. She is very preoccupied with the private life of everyone." "Why does your friend have to call at all?" asked Saul, "Why don't you do the calling?" He was being ironically naïve. "Cut it out," said Larry, "if it were as simple as that, would I bother you? There happen to be complications. The fact is that you wouldn't be getting many calls." Now Saul had a private phone in his office, and the office was private. He and two other junior partners shared a secretary, who had an office of her own. Most of Saul's work was inside, though of course he sometimes had to go out on business matters. He did very little courtroom work, worked up briefs and other necessary material for the trial lawyers. "Your set-up," said Larry, "is much better." Although Larry had used the word *set-up* only twice, Saul was tired of hearing the word, though he realized that his set-up, certainly from Larry's point of view, *was* better. The fact is that the projected arrangement displeased Saul; it was sneaky and he was very fond of Larry's wife. "Look," said Larry, "try it for a while, and if it doesn't work out, I'll figure something else out." Saul expected Larry to say that he'd figure out another "angle" and he was glad that word hadn't been used. Saul continued to be disturbed, and said so, but how could he turn down so old a friend? and the arrangement on a temporary basis? So he reluctantly agreed (and felt the more disturbed on his agreement) and then Larry went ahead, explaining that when the woman called, she would use the name "Miss Fanshawe," and the message would invariably be that Larry was to call her at a given time and number. "What happens if I'm not in when she calls?" asked Saul, "You know, when I'm out, my secretary takes over the calls." He thought of saying "that's part of my set-up," and then he said it. "When that happens," said Larry, "she'll leave word that she called, she'll mention the name of some organization she's connected with, give it an official air, she's clever that way." "How many organizations can Miss Fanshawe be working for?' asked Saul. Larry grinned. "Well," he said, "I see what you mean, and if you don't answer the phone, she'll switch the name, but there'll always be a *Shaw* in it somewhere—Bradshaw, or Shawnee, or something like that. You'll know who it is. I'll tell her not to call during lunchtime, and you're not out of the office much at any other time." That was true enough, but Saul, though he had agreed, continued to dislike the arrangement, so much so that he waved off the idea of a second drink and left his friend in the bar as a sign of his displeasure. Larry first thanked him, added that he'd appreciate Saul's keeping the matter to himself, not even mentioning it to Mathilda. Saul nodded and went off to the subway.

Saul and Larry were friends of old standing; growing up in a city at a time when families used to move every few years in order to avoid the discomforts of an apartment painting (plus the rent "concession" at the new apartment), these two lads nevertheless went through public and high school together, and then were classmates at one of the municipal colleges (for the purposes of this story, it does not matter which of the municipal colleges it was). The fact is that their families didn't move so much—what they did was to move from one house to another on the same street, even from one apartment to another in the same house, and so avoiding the discomfort and winning the "concession." It was also an accident (though far from miraculous) that the two families, in the course of their wider emigrations, somehow landed pretty close to one another. At any rate, the boys were friends from childhood, stayed friends after college, and even (a more far-out accident) met during the war, they both in the army, spent two weeks together in San Franciso before they were shipped to different islands at pretty much the same time. It is the kind of thing that happens to old friends. Now the war was over, now they were both married, both with young children; the families saw one another maybe eight, nine times a year, occasionally went out for dinner without children. Larry and Saul had lunch every now and then. The families were in touch, though the wives were not *too* close—but fond of one another. The wives of close friends (and the husbands of close friends) are generally not too close: they resist close ties, one doesn't know exactly why, a kind of resentment perhaps, or maybe not wanting to have too much of a good thing.

Saul was home in time for dinner—the one drink had not befuddled his time sense—but the dinner was kind of rushed because Mathilda (as she had explained over the telephone) had to take Stan over to the Cub Scouts (he was eight) and Saul put their younger son Carl to bed. Carl was six, and not always eager to go to bed. Once in bed, he was not eager to go to sleep. He had a number of tricks, dodges, dissimulations, procrastinations, and plain phony business, which he used each night, as though for the first time, to put off these inevitabilities. Knowledge of these dodges made Saul's problem no easier, so that Carl was awake when Stan returned with his mother. That created further difficulties, and it was close to nine (and the next day a school day) before the kids were quiet, if not asleep. Keen judges of parents' patience, they knew when to stop, the moment short of fury. "What did Larry want?" asked Mathilda. Husband and wife were now in the living room, seated comfortably, after the day's labor. "He needed some money," said Saul, "He lost $350 in a poker game last night, and is a little short, or maybe he's worried that Maura might notice the withdrawal and ask about it." Unhappy at having to tell this lie, Saul, to his amazement, found himself embroidering the story he had determined to tell. "You know," he went on, "he plays with a pretty fast crowd, they must play a dollar and two." "I don't know what that means," said Mathilda. "It means a dollar on the opening, and then up to—" Saul started to explain, but Mathilda interupted him. "I'm not interested in the details of the game," she said, "I think the money has nothing to do with poker at all, but has to do with a woman." Saul was not too surprised that his wife had come close to the truth, for she had a clear mind and an unclouded imagination, but he was pleased that she had accepted the story about the money as far as she did. "I suppose," said Mathilda, "that you happened to have the $350 in your pocket." "No," said Saul, "Larry said that he'd drop by at the office tomorrow. I'll draw the money against my office account." He thought of this at the very last moment, realizing that otherwise he'd have to write out a check on *their* joint account, and that would have meant a lot of juggling and confusion. "Old friends come in handy, don't they?" asked Mathilda. She liked Larry, but resented his easy manner, what she called his irresponsible behavior (it *was* irresponsible behavior) and thought that Saul had a tendency to be an easy mark, to be taken advantage of. "He wouldn't hesitate to do the same for me," said Saul, and that was true, both in the sense of the lie of the matter and the truth of the matter, for Larry loved intrigue, loved to be in the midst of social complexities, to hover on the verge of disclosures and blowups. "That's true," said Mathilda, "but if he can't afford to lose that kind of money, he shouldn't play those stakes." "I guess," said Saul, "that he's not the prudent type, like you and I." They both laughed, for this was not a crucial matter, not at this point.

A few days afterward, on returning late from lunch (there was a long conversation with a client about a case that was coming up, an involved marital case where the line betweeen fact and opinion was pretty hard to draw) Saul was handed a message by his secretary. A Mrs. Bradshaw had called, from the New York Democratic Committee, and the number was written down. Saul looked puzzled to show that the woman was a stranger, but the secretary, Miss Knowles, did not seem interested, and apparently did not see his puzzled look, for she certainly did not react to it. Saul was annoyed that the woman had mentioned a prominent political organization that way; he wasn't sure why he was annoyed, thought that she perhaps should have mentioned one of the department stores, though that was fairly senseless too. Once in his office, he called the number and a woman answered. Suppose it were a man, thought Saul, but it was a woman, and he asked: "Is this Mrs. Bradshaw?" realizing that he did not know the woman's real name. "Yes, it is," she replied, and she kind of laughed to show that she appreciated the oddity of the situation. "Would you tell Larry to call me at this number, I'll be here until five." "I'll call his office," said Saul, "and try to get the message to him." He made it clear that he was guaranteeing nothing. "Thanks very much," said the woman, and that was the end of the conversation. Then Saul called Larry, who was in his office, and gave him the message. (Larry was employed by a public relations firm which specialized in publicizing organizations which were attempting to eradicate major diseases in the United States.) "Thanks," said Larry, "she's at her sister's house." But Saul didn't really care whose house Mrs. Bradshaw was in; he felt pretty contemptible, angry at himself for having agreed to transmit these messages. Two days later the woman called again, this time when Saul was at his desk, and gave him a message, which he immediately phoned in to Larry. Then Saul went out for coffee, and when he got back, Miss Knowles, who was quite attractive, said that a Miss Shaw had called from Sears and Roebuck, and left a number. That's too big an organization, thought Saul; it's very likely that Miss Knowles would know that this number isn't the Sears number. Then he called the woman, and she said that she was sorry to bother him, but that her plans had changed, and would Saul tell Larry that she wouldn't be free until ten o'clock that night, which message he dutifully transmitted to Larry, though he wasn't in when Saul called him, so he had to leave a message, and then Larry called back and received the new message. "I'm sorry," said Larry, "that you had to call me again." "Oh, that's all right," said Saul, but it really wasn't all right. Not that the calls took up much time, but since they were annoying, they took up energy, therefore real time, and Saul was angry, not so much at Larry (though he was angry at Larry) but at himself for being used in this unpleasant way. Then the next week he came down with a heavy cold, and took to bed. Mathilda came in and said that Miss Knowles had called, and left a few messages, one of which was from Mrs. Shaughnessy, connected with the League for Women Voters, so he had to call her at the given number (she was usually at one of four of five numbers, she was apparently not the kind of woman who sat at home all day curled up around a good book). He called her, got the message, called Larry, and passed the information in the course of some gossip, all of which pleased Larry no end. Indeed, he not only thanked Saul, but congratulated him on the clever way in which he had worked in the message. So in the days that followed the calls continued to come in—from Mrs. Burnshaw, Mrs. Kashawsky, etc., until Saul had to advise Larry that the subterfuge was wearing thin, and that instead of the Shaw gambit, Larry's friend ought to use the name of English or Irish authors, after making sure that she was acquainted with the Anglo-Irish literary tradition. "But tell her not to use the name of Shaw, or Crashaw," said Saul, and he didn't join in with Larry's chuckle. So for the next few weeks he was hearing from, or getting messages from, Mrs. Lawrence, Miss Swift, Miss Bennett, Mrs. Conrad, Mrs. Wells, all from fairly well-known organizations. Miss

Knowles by now had a kind of knowing look about it all—in keeping with the character of her name—and handed him the messages with a look which said: "You're a pretty keen one, aren't you?" But that didn't bother Saul so much.

What really bothered Saul was that he was helping to deceive Maura, Larry's wife, a girl half-Irish, half-Jewish (though this admixture was not the bother, nor is it particularly to the point) who, for Saul's money, was pretty unusual. He knew that if he were not being used as the go-between, that Larry would have thought of some other scheme to keep the lines open, because he was very clever about such matters, even enjoyed this elaborate rigamarole. He has a kind of spy mentality, thought Saul, a need for deception, a special pleasure in it. But the fact that Larry would have surely managed without him was no justification, that was a cheap bypassing of honesty in behavior. And his liking for Maura had no logical pertinence, his behavior would have been just as noxious—he was sort of being used as a patsy—if he had no feeling at all for Maura, even if he actively disliked her. But the fact that he did like her made the behavior *more* unpleasant: matters of preference play a curious role in the moral scheme. It is easier to act in the interest of those you admire, and against the interest of those you dislike. Yet, from a material point of view, it was difficult for him to beg off, because the amount of time he actually spent in these calls was no more than ten of fifteen minutes a week. That was because he made the conversations very businesslike, took the messages and transmitted them in a very mechanical way, almost as though he were being paid for the work. But Saul detected a kind of interest on the part of Larry's friend—sometimes her voice was soft, had a personal inflection, was moving away from the routine aspects of their conversation. At one point it crossed Saul's mind that he could get to see her, to go along with the nuances of her approach, and he saw this as a blow in Maura's defense, an act of revenge against Larry. But this was only a passing thought. Perhaps he misunderstood her tone, and even if he didn't—were these sufficient, were they honorable motives? Laws, taboos, and difficult moralities stood in the way of his average sensuality. He wondered what the trouble in their household could be, for as friendly as Larry and he were, they never discussed their family matters in a serious or confidential way. That is, they talked about their children, but rarely about their wives, and if they did, in a rather superficial manner. "Look," he said to Larry one day over the phone, "I don't like this business at all, can't you figure out another angle?" He was always angry at himself for using these crude formulations. "Sure," said Larry, "give me a little time and I'll figure something out, just give me some time." And Saul agreed (it was only costing him ten or fifteen minutes a week). Then a couple of days later Mathilda dropped into his office, and naturally Larry's friend called while she was there. Mathilda picked up the phone and told Saul that Miss Fanshawe wanted to talk to him. Saul picked up the phone and spoke in a rather dry, noncommittal manner. "Certainly," he said, "I think we can handle that." Mathilda asked, rather idly, who it was, and he proceeded, just as he had when describing Larry's poker game, to elaborate on the fabrication. "She's from the Legal Aid Society," he said, and then he told a story about a case that was coming up, creating absolutely unnecessary details. But he was angry at Larry's friend, who had apparently forgotten the new arrangement, or run out of Anglo-Irish literary names. As he walked Mathilda to the elevator, he was aware of the knowing glance of his secretary, who recognized the voice of this woman who came up each time with another name, another organization, but often the same number. Miss Knowles looked with interest at Mathilda and that angered Saul. But I can't blame her, he thought, and he was determined to put real pressure on Larry to change this absurd arrangement. But then the woman didn't call for a couple of days, and Saul thought that maybe the affair, or whatever it was, would die of its own steam, so he let the thing slide.

It was just about this time that Saul and Mathilda were dinner guests at their friends' apartment, as part of the home-and-home series which had been going on for years. There was another couple present, Frank and Audrey Pitt. Frank was a sports reporter on one of the city dailies, and a member of Larry's poker group. The men were fairly heavy drinkers, so that dinner wasn't served until about 9:30. They were a pretty congenial crowd, conversed amiably, with a minimum of hostility, and the free-associational routes, loosened by alcohol, never reached the outer limits of hysteria. Saul was not in the *very best* mood, felt guilty in the presence of Maura, and particularly so since Larry was in such a jovial and tempestuous mood, roaring at the puns, witticisms, and all-out oddities which began to appear between the second and third drinks. But all this is not to the point. Maura was her usual quiet and modest self, a modesty charming rather than colorless. She was not self-effacing. On the contrary, she made her presence felt. Though she had come to America from Ireland at the age of ten, she retained a delightful edge of the Irish accent. Saul and Mathilda were both very fond of her, but neither was close to her, Mathilda for reasons already described and Saul for reasons partly explained. Seeing her now, Saul examined, though not seriously, the idea of telling Maura about her husband's activities. But it was not for him (he immediately thought) to confess to other people's wrongdoings, and anyway he didn't know a thing about the circumstances. For all he knew, Maura might know perfectly well what was going on, so by telling her he would only be violating a confidence of his old friend, as well as embarrassing Maura by showing himself aware of her husband's behavior. And who knows, he thought, there may be compelling reasons for his behavior, maybe (unbelievable as it was) she had another man, maybe their sexual difficulties were profound and this was their way of keeping the marriage going. They did not seem to get along badly here in company— they smiled and spoke to one another, reacted to one another's remarks and presence, there was none of that grim divisiveness or acerbity which is sometime apparent in unhappily married couples. But perhaps it was not for Larry that he wanted to confess, but for himself, for his cowardly and monstrous behavior. But such a confession must implicate Larry, a notion which he had already dismissed. So Saul returned to his determination (although the woman had not called for a while) to talk to Larry in the next day or two and definitely break off from this degrading role. The conversation (after dinner, over fresh drinks) wandered erratically, and then somehow got onto the recent college basketball scandals. Frank was on top of the situation as a reporter, Saul and Larry were emotionally involved as City College men (that was the municipal college previously hinted at), and the wives were carried along by the interest of their husbands or by the wider issues invoved. "Think of it," said Saul, talking of the CCNY Cinderella team which had won *both* the national invitational tournaments, "we went way to the top, it was a kind of swift mass psychoanalysis for tens of thousands of our students and graduates, giving them a place in the great society; it really made Americans of us, even more than the success of Frankfurter, Senator Wagner, Goethals, Upton Sinclair. Such immigrant pride, so classic a success story, and then that monstrous fall, only for money." "You say only for money," said Mathilda, "but that is part of the horror of the times, this inflationary madness, this gambling everywhere, easy money being made. Why should those boys be stigmatized this way? And they weren't even throwing games, they were just winning by a given number of points. I'm not justifying it, because one thing can lead to another, but. . . ." Then they discussed the metaphysics of shaving points as against throwing games. "The worst of it," said Larry, "is the deception, all this trust and idolization, all this terrific psychic involvement, and these kids trifled with it, fooled those who lavished all that love on them." Hearing these words, Saul was astounded, but they were spoken with the utmost seriousness. He looked at Maura, trying to understand what her feelings were. She listened gravely to her husband's remarks.

Saul's decision was not so easily carried out. On the morning after this dinner party he was late in getting down to his office. He was about to leave his house when the phone rang. It was Miss Knowles, apparently in a great hurry, for she gave the message to Mathilda to transmit to her husband. "It was Miss Knowles," said Mathilda. "She said that a Miss Crashaw, connected with some kind of Childrens' League, wants you to call, and she left this number." She gave the slip of paper to Saul. "When I was in the office," she said, "it was Miss Fanshawe;

when you were home with a cold, it was Mrs. Shaughnessy; now it's Miss Crashaw." Saul could have said that there was nothing impossible about businesslike dealing with three women whose names sounded somewhat alike, that he dealt with hundreds, even thousands, of people, and that drawing any deductions from this coincidence was just a way of looking for trouble. But he didn't say it. He suddenly realized that the woman had probably used some kind of biographical dictionary, and idly picked the name of the English poet Crashaw, forgetting the injuction not to use any more "Shaw" sounds in her messages. And he had specifically mentioned the name "Crashaw," at which Larry had laughed, so he had obviously not mentioned it to her. Or he had mentioned it to her, but she forgot, and then the name came right out to her on the page, the way a familiar name does. Had she used another name, Mathilda would not have been suspicious, for she had seen no connection between *Fanshawe* and *Shaughnessy*. But this third name rang the bell. So Saul decided to tell his wife the true story, and he did tell her the true story, and she said that she didn't believe a word of it, so that led to an unpleasant quarrel, and Saul was more than an hour late to his office. "Why did you have to call that message to my home?" he asked Miss Knowles, "and having called my home, why didn't you speak to me?" "Miss Crashaw said it was urgent," said Miss Knowles, "and I was very busy here." In this sentence she answered both his questions. But he didn't think that she was telling the truth; it even crossed his mind that she was making trouble between himself and Mathilda because she (Miss Knowles) was interested in him, but that didn't make any sense at all. As he reached his office, the phone rang and a familiar voice said "This is Miss Banshawe calling," and of course it was Mathilda and she hung up without another word. So he called Larry, told him what had happened, said he wanted out, and Larry said that he was sorry for Saul's difficulties, but he was also interested in the message and asked for the number. Saul, in his upset and anger, had forgotten to take the slip which Mathilda had given him, and said that he would call home and get the number. But then, after some immature reflection he called

Larry again and told *him* to call Mathilda. So Larry did, and then he called Saul and told him that Mathilda had asked whether he (Larry) thought that she couldn't see through this little game, and that if Saul wanted Miss Inshaw's number, he'd pretty well call Mathilda himself. "I'm really sorry," said Larry, "I didn't think she'd be *that* steamed up." "Would it have been all right," asked Saul, "if she were a little *less* steamed up?" Then, after some further reflection, Saul called home and asked for the number to give to Larry, but Mathilda said it was all too disgusting for words, and that anyway she couldn't find the slip. "I daresay," she said, "that you'll somehow be able to get in touch with her." So Saul called Larry and said that Mathilda wouldn't give him the number, and Larry suggested that he go home and get it, but Saul demurred, saying in fact that he would like hell, and that anyway Mathilda had surely torn up the message. Then he hung up, and the phone rang. It was a familiar voice, saying: "This is Miss Clare," and it wasn't Mathilda at all, but Larry's friend, and she wanted to know whether Saul received her message, because she hadn't heard from Larry, and she had a very urgent matter to take up with him. So Saul said that he had received the message but had left it at home, and that his wife had refused to give him the number, because his wife thought that he had some connection with the woman who was calling, of a nonbusiness nature, and Miss Fanshawe said that his wife was preposterously jealous, and Saul told Miss Bradshaw that he didn't think she ought to be making snap analytic judgments about a woman she didn't know. So the caller said she was sorry, and could Saul call Larry immediately, and she gave her number again, which Saul automatically jotted down. But then he said he thought that she ought to call Larry herself, and gave her his number. She said that she had Larry's number, but that he forbade her from calling there, and then she started to cry. Meanwhile Miss Knowles came in and told Saul that his wife was on the phone, had been waiting for five minutes, so he told Miss Knowles to tell his wife that he'd call her right back. Then he told Miss Fanshawe that there was no point to her tears, that she'd just better call Larry up, hung up on her, and called Mathilda, who wanted to know whether he had been talking to Mrs. Shakespeare on the phone. He said that he *had* been talking to her on the phone, that she had called and checked on her earlier message, since she hadn't heard from Larry, and now she wanted Saul to call Larry again. "But I refused" said Saul. "Is there anything special you're calling about?" She said there was, but that he could take it up with her lawyer. Then Saul called Larry and gave him the woman's message, and Larry said that she had called him, crying, and said that he (Saul) had insulted her, and he (Larry) didn't see why Saul had behaved that way to her. So Saul said that he hadn't insulted her, just told her the truth. Larry said that the truth could be insulting, and Saul said that he wasn't interested in these deep problems, and that he was out of the Answering Service business, and Larry said: "Look, let's have a drink after work, and we'll puzzle the whole thing out." So Saul silently hung up the phone and decided to go out for a long walk. "Look," he said to Miss Knowles, "I'll be in Central Park, at Sheep's Meadow, for a couple of hours. If a woman calls, just give her my wife's number." "I'll do that," said Miss Knowles, "I'll certainly do that." So that was the situation when he left the office.

NO SALE 1

Danzig's store was quiet. In the morning the store was empty, and then, early in the afternoon, a man came in and said that he needed a pair of gloves.

"You are looking in the right place," said Danzig in an affable manner, thinking as he looked at the stranger that this was the approach that was called for, and also pleased, relieved, that a customer had come in. Gloves were what Danzig sold. Only gloves.

The customer did not react to Danzig's show of affability. Not that he was glum or unpleasant or saturnine. Not at all. He was plain, straightforward, level, even-handed, like that.

"My old pair wore out," said the customer. "Show me a good, serviceable pair of gloves."

"Of course," said Danzig. "Would you like wool or leather?"

"It doesn't much matter," said the customer. "Show me what you have."

So Danzig brought out a few pairs of gloves.

"Let's try a couple for size," he said.

The customer put on some of the gloves, and the size was decided on. Then Danzig brought out various pairs of gloves in this proper size, though in different materials and styles, and the customer tried them on.

Some of the gloves, though they were the correct size, didn't fit. One pair, according to the buyer, was too tight, one a bit loose. "Too much play in the fingers" was the way he described it. In some cases one hand was a perfect fit and the other far from it.

Danzig then tried gloves a half size smaller or a size larger, but it wasn't only a matter of fit. The customer complained of the roughness of the texture, of the quality of the material, of the appearance of the gloves, of the nature of the stitching, of the color—it was quite amazing how many kinds of complaints he could make about these pairs of gloves he was trying on. One pair of gloves, he said, was perfect, but they didn't come quite high enough up on the wrist.

And these were not so much complaints as plain straightforward, level, even-handed comments, no sense of irritation nor even of fussiness. Sometimes he didn't like the price.

On an ordinary day, Danzig couldn't have paid as much attention to his customer, for there would have been a number of prospective buyers in the place and he'd be moving from one to the other, with each customer at a different stage of the purchase process, or the nonpurchase process.

But on this day nobody else came into the store, and the time moved steadily ahead. The customer did not act as though he were taking up too much of Danzig's time, never excused himself, followed negative comments with further suggestions. And he often praised the gloves which, for one reason or another, he found unsatisfactory. By now he had been in the store for close to three hours, and what could Danzig say? There was neither a body nor soul in the store (though a soul is invisible, so you can't be sure about that). The phone didn't even ring. Danzig could have put some boxes which had arrived yesterday onto the shelves if he had wanted to act busy, to give a broad hint to the customer that there was no point in continuing on the road of this transaction, but somehow he wanted to pursue this sale, to consummate it. Not that the customer showed any anxiety. He was altogether unruffled as the time went on, and the gloves continued not to be satisfactory for one reason or another. At one point he praised Danzig's stock.

"You have a nice variety of gloves here," he said. "There is a great deal to choose from."

"Certainly," said Danzig, "I deal with a number of suppliers, some from abroad. I have been in this business for many years, and on this location."

"Do you have silk gloves?" asked the customer.

"I do," said Dunzig. "They're not the most *serviceable*," and brought some out. But the customer was displeased with one pair because it was too "snug" and with another pair because it was a bit more than he wanted to pay.

"You're better off with a leather glove," said Danzig.

"Of course," said the customer, and he tried on a pair, with which he was not exactly displeased, but he expressed in his plain-spoken manner the reason for the rejection.

"These gloves are fine," he said. "They look good, and every finger-fit is fine, but the pinky is not right, feels rough."

He moved his pinky back and forth, first the whole finger, and then from the joint.

The customer continued to act as though this was not an un- usual transaction, as though no *inordinate* amount of time was being spent on it. He was just buying a pair of gloves though he had been in the store now for five hours. And Danzig had some- how fallen in with the customer's attitude; he did not complain about the passing of time, though it was now dark and coming to closing time.

"Maybe this pair of woolen gloves," said the storekeeper. "It's a kind of old-fashioned style."

"Old-fashioned is all right," said the customer, and he put on the pair of gloves, the way he had put on every pair that Danzig had brought out, put them on carefully, smoothed and stroked the gloves, flexed his fingers, held the gloves away from him under the light, just the way you would expect from a customer who was choosing a pair of gloves, with a more than usual amount of care. He now made fists, spreading his fingers as far apart as they would go.

"The right hand is fine," he said, "but on the left hand there is a kind of bunching between the thumb and forefinger."

He took the gloves off and laid them on the counter.

Never in all his years of selling gloves had Danzig been made

so aware of the various fingers and joints of the hand, the softness of the palm, the rougher aspect of the back of the hand, the
quiddity of the thumb, the various relationships of the fingers,
how one finger differs from another, to say nothing of the quality
of the nails, and how the hand moves slowly, but irresistibly, into
the wrist.

"Here is another material," said Danzig. "It is a special
leather, an import."

A clock in the distance started to strike, a clock which Danzig,
in the usual hubbub of closing, had never heard, or never paid
any attention to, but now he heard the strokes very clearly. "It is
seven o'clock," said the customer, "is that your closing time?"

"I usually close about seven," said Danzig, "except when it's
busy."

It was not busy now, but Danzig was tired, as though he had
put in a full day.

"I'll come back another day," said the stranger. "I can't make
it tomorrow, but another day, another time."

And he walked out. There were dozens and dozens of pairs of
gloves on the counter, on the tables, spread around the store,
and Danzig put them back into the boxes and then back on the
shelves, while it was all fresh in his mind, for by tomorrow he
might forget the exact places from which he had taken the gloves.
So he put the gloves away now and closed the store.

(NO SALE 2)

"Hey, hey" cried the candy-store man, "put that back, put it back, you little crook, you."

With a speed which belied his fifty-seven years, Weiner rushed from behind the counter and seized the offending ten-year-old boy.

"Give me that," said Weiner, and he opened the boy's fist. There dropped a chocolate sponge, boxed, formerly selling for one cent.

Weiner picked up the box and squeezed it, creasing and bending the box.

"Who stole anything?" asked Ronnie, as he coolly put two pennies on the counter and took another chocolate sponge.

Weiner seized him by the shoulders and shook.

"Kids like you belong in reform school. What kind of home do you come from anyway?"

"My father's got more money than you," said Ronnie, and Weiner knew it well enough, for the child's father often came in and bought a fistful of Corona Belvederes.

It was this knowledge, in fact, which kept Weiner this side of insane hysteria, and it was knowledge of this knowledge which burned the insides of Weiner with a dull and smoky flame.

He coughed.

"You and your gang have been stealing from me for years. Where is that green tricycle?"

254

Ronnie looked at him blankly, and Weiner, like a man who has a good case but cannot prove it, shook in fury, for though the wheel had surely been stolen, this theft dated back eight years, when Ronnie was two years old.

"Let's see what's in your pockets," and though he knew he was liable to arrest for this unlawful search and seizure (which accounted for the speed with which he put the objects back), Weiner pulled out a yo-yo, picture postcards of Admiral Sims, Whitey Witt, and Tom Mix, a stringless top, and a pulpy mass of white stuff which could at one time have been a taffy bar.

"Taffy was a thief," said Ronnie, but Mr. Weiner, a large part of whose trade was with children, did not catch the allusion.

"*Who's* a thief?" he asked. "What are you saying?"

Ronnie grinned and said:

"I've seen you shortchange little kids."

This was a lie. Ronnie knew it was a lie, the other kids knew it was a lie, Weiner knew it was a lie. It happened to be true of the old lady three blocks away. She shortchanged kids who came into her store without the exact change. But it was not true of Mr. Weiner, it had never been true of Mr. Weiner, who had to listen to this charge, in front of a few interested adult customers, from the lips of a kid he had just caught stealing from him.

It was too much for Weiner. Some thirty-five years behind the counter of a candy store had not given him the strength to withstand this blow.

He fumed, he stuttered, he started to say something and stopped, his face grew red, he shook. Then he slumped down on the counter, his head buried in his hands, to the dismay of Ronnie and the other kids, who fled, for they enjoyed his fury (knowing he was powerless) but were frightened at his collapse.

"My God," cried Mr. Weiner, raising his hands toward the ceiling of the store, "my God, what am I doing, fighting with a kid about two cents worth of candy? Was it for this I was created in Your image, to earn a living with the sweat of my brow?"

And before the astonished gaze of more and more of his customers, he picked up the two pennies which the child had laid on the counter and hurled them blindly away.

A NOTE ON CHIVALRY

I. INTRODUCTION, WITH JOKES

Jokes. Ha! Ha! I am among those willing to become a captive audience (or whatever the singular of the word "audience" is), if only the joke is funny (not unfunny) and is told well, either in the elegant *or* the embroidered style. A joke is a bit of folk art. Why scorn it? And the joke cycles—fascinating, are they not? Traffic jokes, psychoanalysis jokes. . . . Have you heard the mother-in-law joke?

> A mother-in-law gives her daughter's husband (son-in-law) two ties for Father's Day. Daughter, son-in-law, and children come to visit Grandma on this occasion, all properly dressed. Dad is wearing one of mother-in-law's ties. She opens the door and says to him straight off: *"What's the matter, you didn't like the other tie?"*

Curiously enough (why curiously enough?) I have recently heard a number of other jokes in what I call the mother–mother-in-law–grandma complex. It is a recurrent trend. I have a sociological friend, he is in fact a sociologist, and I plan to ask him to explain this trend to me, in its urban-rural sociometrics and all the rest of it. If I remember to, I will tell him the following joke:

> A woman is running along the ocean beach, and she cries: *"Help, help, my son the doctor is drowning."*

trusting that he (the sociologist) will be cognizant of the Jewish middle-class prestige propulsions involved here and not be unaware of the tragic status-destiny dichotomy which provides the atmosphere for this fine current joke.

Then there was that party a while back at a friend's house, and an elegant girl came in. I don't mean that she was elegantly dressed, but there was something fine and real about her, one of those absolute strangers you feel you have known forever and will continue to know forever. What a lovely, warm, and reassuring smile! And she brought into the room romance, I mean, the coming into existence of so many possibilities, beauty to be sought and never reached, all those forgotten streaks of glory. It was something that the room needed very much.

You know how even the prettiest girl gets lost in a room full of noise and drinking, and then suddenly you are standing together, in all that noise, all that (suddenly) lovely confusion, and she tells you, what? A joke:

> A grandma is wheeling her grandson; an acquaintance looks into the carriage and says:
> "My, what a pretty baby."
> Says Grandma: *"You should see his picture."*

We discussed the formal problems raised by the last line of this elegant joke. There are possible variants: *"You should see the picture,"* or *"But you should see his picture."* and we discussed these variants, seriously weighed them. Her smile was warm, reassuring: I felt very much at home, not so much in the house of this friend, this stranger, but at home in the world, once more at home in the world, this cold and bitter world, this monster of a world. I was home in a world suddenly made warm and reassuring, a glorious world, full of infinite promise, round and golden, a world in which it was no longer possible to fall off.

2. THE MIDDLE GROUND

Let us by no means forget the great middle ground of experience— the American Midwest, the Victorian novelists, Wednesday at three o'clock in the afternoon, the land lying between woman's breasts, all the forgotten working hours—and through the confusion of friends and strangers talking, for we were among friends and strangers, it seemed that she had a position with, worked for, earned her livelihood—was it with the B & O?—sounded pretty much like the B & O, an established transit corporation, no doubt one of the few corporate organizations that had in its title the name of a city *and* a state. It struck me as pretty odd that she should be *with* (that's a nice way of saying that you work for somebody), that she should be with an organization half-city and half-state, a kind of industrial mermaid. She was with them in a capacity, and you can spend an awful (in the sense of long) amount of time with a company if you are with them in a capacity, but it really wasn't so long, it just seemed long because it's an everyday thing, you've got to be there or give an excuse, like a marriage that way. It's a way of paying for your leisure. But she spoke pleasantly of the task (not an ordeal at all), she was not among those who suffered in order to enjoy later, she gave the impression of enjoying the working day (but who knows?), caught it all up in that warm reassuring smile, the one mentioned in Section 1.

3. A CONNECTION

At a certain point, between old friends and between friends newly met there comes a pause. We are all acquainted with that pause: nothing is said—some are embarrassed, some are relaxed, some absolutely relish this pause (enjoy the embarrassment and upset by the relaxation). If the friends are old, and the pauses numerous and lengthy, well, then, the situation requires grave analysis. With old friends newly made, it is always possible to ask, as I now asked: "Do you happen to know Mr. Indleberg, who is connected with your firm?"

"Certainly I know Mr. Indleberg, we are in different departments."

"So you *know* Mr. Indleberg. He happens to be my brother-in-law's cousin."

"Would that be your wife's brother or your sister's husband?"

"My sister's husband, of course."

"Do you know him very well?"

"I've met him exactly twice, on family occasions."

"I don't really *know* him; not only are we in different departments, but the departments have no connection with each other."

"I'd say that he's about 5'8"."

"That's right, he's rather stout, somewhat stooped."

"Obviously the same fellow."

This is a way of making a connection to destroy a pause. Ah, Indleberg, wherever you were at the time (and it would have been nice if you were at a party, enjoying yourself), you surely never understood that you were being used, as a pawn, as a pause-destroyer, between old friends newly met, to establish, for a brief moment (as compared to a lengthy moment) a connection.

4. SURROUNDED BY SOCIOLOGISTS

I yield to no man in my admiration for Thorstein Veblen, that genuine (as opposed to phony) eccentric, that hard-bitten North Woods stylist, and I can read with pleasure many a page of Sumner, but I must say that my blood boils, my gorge rises (not necessarily in that order), when I see a pretty girl surrounded by sociologists. Seeing it now, it struck me as a kind of allegory of the English language (why is a pretty girl like the English language?) in its purity, menaced by the killers of that language. By "purity" I mean the ability of the language to reach what is true and beautiful in experience, and to clothe that truth and beauty in appropriate images and ideas. By "killers" I mean those who smother the newborn truth and beauty (for truth and beauty are always newborn) by an apparatus, an effluvium, gobbledegook, words that have lost all relation to the object, to language itself. How to save her from the sociologists? I assumed that she wanted to be saved from the sociologists (though she was chatting with them in a friendly enough way) because who would not want to be saved from the sociologists? Looking around the room (for support or for weapons) I noticed a set of the English Classic Poets. I picked one of the volumes from the bookshelf—the book was solidly constructed, weighed perhaps two pounds, and had sharp edges. I determined to hurl at the heads of the sociologists these Classic volumes. What would be more fitting weapons, in this new *Battle of the Books,* with which to save this maiden, or in distress? I gripped the volume, got the feel of it, so to speak, and then noticed that she had fled from the foul circle and was wandering alone, in an aimless freedom. I regretfully put the volume back in its place.

5. RESPONSIBILITY

It suddenly occurred to me that I was an engaged man! My fiancée was wearing an engagement ring, *my* engagement ring; there had been an announcement in the metropolitan papers, if not her picture, and only the date had to be set. My fiancée was visiting her grandparents in Kansas City. She is very devoted to her family and has an extensive family, mostly in the Midwest and the Far West. I realized (also suddenly) the *outlandish* and *irresponsible* nature of my behavior. True, my connection with the girl I had just met at the party (I didn't know her name, the introductions were slurred) had not even reached the flirtatious stage. We merely spoke to one another with a more considerable interest than you might statistically expect (equating interest with percentage of meetings over a given length of time), we merely looked at one another (the romantic mixing of the glances) in a manner that bespoke the possibility, circumstances allowing, that we might get into an involvement more personal than the next, though not necessarily very personal. Why, it was very possible that on this very evening, at this very party, a number of people, meeting for the first time, were interested in one another in just the same way. And it was possible that my fiancée, off in Kansas City, if she were at a party, could easily become just so interested in a stranger whose name she had not quite heard. Nevertheless, it being a fundamental law of life that one thing leads to another, I thought that I ought to act more *responsibly,* for it is, if not a law of life, than a fact of it, that we can be *carried away,* and that would take me far from my fiancée, far from my engagement and prospective marriage (though no date had been set) down some turbulent river, into some unknown sea. In order to avoid this fascinating possibility (and responsible behavior, if it does not *have* to destroy fascination, can very easily chill or contract it) I determined to avoid this young woman, whose warm reassuring smile had carried me so quickly down turbulent rapids to unknown seas. I've only known her twenty minutes, I thought, and here I am engaged to my childhood sweetheart (I meant by that thought that I knew my childhood sweetheart ever so much longer). I was pleased with this truly responsible thought.

6. INDLEBERG . . . THE OLD RAZZLE-DAZZLE . . .
CONTACT-CONTINUATION

"He's married to a girl his own size."

"Indleberg's child once came to the office. He's a boy."

"When I last saw him," I said, "we discussed Red China, the four-minute mile, and the soul's immortality."

"He used to be in my office," she said, "that is, before I was there. Then he was moved into another office, then into another section, then into another division, and now I hear his name mentioned occasionally."

"He told me," I said, "that Red China would spill over into Soviet Russia *before* the twenty-first century, that the four-minute mile was in its infancy, and that he was working up evidence for the soul's immortality."

"He told me," she said, "that he loved his work, but wanted to retire."

"He drinks bourbon on the rocks."

"He used to write with a ballpoint pen."

"Did you know that he was married previously?"

"That's incredible," she said, "I mean, he doesn't give that impression."

"His previous wife," I said, "is now married to a man in the diplomatic corps."

"He eats tuna fish for lunch," she said, "with a strawberry float."

"He's sort of nice," I said, "he lets you say so many things about him."

"I didn't know we knew him so well," she said.

"We know him very well," I said, "and why shouldn't we? He's our oldest friend."

"Who?"

7. KINDS OF DOING

To do for the sake of your living parents is filial gratitude.

To do for the sake of dead parents is ancestor worship; otherwise (if they be not parents), it is to honor the mighty dead.

To do for the sake of the work is dedication.

To do for the sake of dear ones is gratitude, for the sake of friends is love, for the sake of strangers is sacrifice.

To do for the sake of the future is alienation, and distrust of one's powers.

To do for the doing's sake is animal joy.

To do for truth's sake is nobility.

To do for God's sake is presumption.

To do for fame's sake is neurosis.

To do for money's sake is tragic.

To do out of fear is degenerative.

To do out of duty is necessary.

To do for beauty's sake is romance.

8. ROMANCE

I lifted a volume of the Classic Poets. If I hurled it at the head of an offending sociologist, and thereby saved a maiden not exactly in distress, would that get me into the arena of Romance? This style of Romance is quite out of fashion, particularly in the metropolitan society which I frequent. Of course, there are girls in trouble—there will always be girls in trouble—but the help they need does not seem to require courage. It might require understanding, it might require the scientific knowledge of a psychoanalyst (plus understanding), or it might require just simple friendship (as compared to complex friendship). The growth of protective institutions—police departments, fire departments, etc.—makes the old kind of courage irrelevant. The emancipation of women has helped to destroy the old Romance. The point is to save someone weaker than you. But men are in trouble, and are saved by women psychoanalysts. Nevertheless I gripped the volume; I felt as though I had the feel of it now, thinking that the old Romance is not dead, that Beauty will yet be saved. Man needs woman, so woman is in trouble. Beauty is menaced in all sorts of ways, by the ogre of uniformity, by the resentment of the ugly in spirit, by the cold Hell of mediocrity. I heaved the volume of Blake at the head of a sociologist (for she was once more in that circle).

9. THE FIGHT

Angered by the unprovoked assault (for the man was unknown to me, so he mistakenly thought that it could not be personal) the sociologist retaliated, the struggle took the form of a fistfight. Neither one of us was particularly skilled in this form of struggle, but we fought fiercely, I for the reasons already disclosed and he (not knowing the provocation) because of what he considered an unprovoked attack. It was the first fistfight I'd had in about ten years, but boxing is a skill that you do not easily lose. I began, as though this were an everyday occurence, to use the old feints and combinations. Now the point about a fistfight is that in all probability no one is going to be killed or seriously injured: it is not a duel, not a struggle to the death. We both observed the Queensberry rules, did not hit under the belt, did not deliver the murderous rabbit punches; it was a clean bitter fight which we were both bound to survive. The overwhelming possibility of mutual survival naturally weakened the romantic conception. Nor was the spirit of romance strengthened by the fact that the girl (whose name I had not caught) was unaware that she represented Beauty encircled as well as the purity of the majestic English language, likewise encircled and endangered. She may have thought that I was jealous, or more likely thought that I was drunk and irrationally combative, but I did succeed in breaking up the circle of sociologists. After some ten minutes of fighting our host hurled himself in between us, cried that our behavior was absurd and that any differences we had ought to be settled in a civilized way.

"What's it all about?" he asked.

"He threw a book at me," said the sociologist, "and for no reason."

I refused to discuss the matter, but the fight having stopped (by the intervention of our host), neither one of us was anxious to continue, the sociologist because he felt that he had retaliated sufficiently (my eye was cut) and I because I did not want to continue in a struggle that was bound to be inconclusive (for nobody would be killed, though his nose was bleeding). But the girl was once more freed from the circle of sociologists, and, catching her glance, I recognized my error in thinking that she was unaware of my motive, for she smiled at me most graciously.

"This is plain stupid," said our host, and added, inconsequently, "You don't even *know* one another."

10. OUR HOST

Our host was upset for two reasons. The first reason for his upset was that he felt concentrically trapped: by his difficult marriage (that is, by his marriage), by the constrictions of his social and professional life, by the apparently irreversible loss of contact with his old friends, by time's tyranny, the slow erosion, body and soul. The second reason for his upset was the feeling that he had been too late to save the girl in distress. Feeling young in heart (the way dissatisfied people often do, having missed the great early experiences) he dreamed often (for Romance dies hard) of a woman who needed to be saved, dreamed of himself, strong, wise, wily, fighting his way to the heart of the maze and taking her off to some place where life was forever real. That dream had died hard, but it had died, not altogether died, for he was young in heart, but for everyday purposes it had died. And he was upset (a third reason) because I had come to the aid of the girl in the grip of the sociologist. He was the only one in the room (with the possible exception of the girl herself) who understood that my act was neither erratic nor drunken: he understood that my hurling the book and the struggle not to the death which followed was an effort to save the girl, and he was resentful that another had come to her aid, he bitter and unable to make the swift move (for it is the young hero who comes to the aid of beauty and the future).

11. OUTSIDE

Standing at a window in the moment before the coming to the end of the party, and then the end of party, I looked out the window. The apartment overlooked the river, though up to this moment I hadn't at all felt that I was in an apartment overlooking the river. The river flowed silent and powerful toward the sea. Across the river the Palisades endured, in their ancient struggle with time and erosion. And in the obscure depths of the sky shone the steadfast stars. I indulged in the traditional melancholy reflection that we and all our chatter would soon disappear but that this river and sea, these cliffs and stars, would go on and on. This is an absolutely inconsequential thought, I said to myself, because nothing follows from it. Thus I had apparently come to the conclusion that in order for a thought to be consequential something should follow from it. These rather pointless reflections were interrupted by a remark addressed to me.

12. THE END

"That's a glorious view," she said, and she smiled reassuringly. "Except for the fact that we're on the fifteenth floor," she went on, "it's the same view that the Indians saw five hundred years ago."

"The rocks and river endure," I said, but refrained from adding that *we* would disappear. The chatter in the room had died down. Most of the guests had gone. The host was wearily serving coffee to the hard core. The volume of Blake had been kicked into a corner. We heard someone tell the joke about the grandma who, walking with her three grandchildren, tells an admiring acquaintance:

This is Albert, nine years old, the doctor. This is Stanley, six years old, the lawyer. This is Gordon, two years old, the accountant.

and: *He is beautiful, but you should see the picture!"*

"Thanks," she said, looking at the book on the floor, in the corner. So she surely had understood my quixotic blow! For had I really meant business, I would have hurled the Wordsworth, a much heavier volume. "Your eye is cut," she said, and passed her hand softly over the bruised area.

"It's only a superficial wound," I said idiotically, for I had never expected that she would touch me. Had her touch not been so soft, I would have been angry at her for touching me, but since her touch was so soft, I was not angry. I have known many people for ten years and longer, and we have never touched one another. There was a pause before the departure. "Remember me to Indleberg," I said. Her smile, following so closely to her touch, reassured me. The age of the Palisade cliffs was somehow not so impressive. "It will all be part of the Great Memory," I said, thankful that she did not shake my hand, for she was leaving with a group (three men, two women) and the other four were impatiently waiting. "It is a phrase of Yeats's," I said.

"I know," she said, *"The last of the Romantics."*

"That was a bit presumptuous of him," I said, "there will always be a last romantic."

She smiled reassuringly.

"Would you like some coffee?" asked our host.

"I certainly would," I replied, thinking of Kansas City, of doing for beauty's sake, of the youthful Palisades. I picked up the volume of Blake and gravely replaced the book in its proper place.

ONE

This is a story about a friend of mine, but first I must say a few words about myself, because of the contrast in our natures, a contrast that was probably the basis of our friendship in college twenty-five years ago.

I am volatile, outgoing, extroverted, eager for new places, new people, new experiences, restless, with a somewhat low attention span, careless, picaresque, libidinous, not under the domination of my superego, a man who is easily infatuated, marries and divorces without making too much of a thing of it, makes and loses friends without making too much of that either.

Dubroff (as I knew him in college) is quiet, timid, introverted, cautious, conscientious, exact, pretty much a stay-at-home, worrisome, holds on, makes changes of any sort only with the greatest difficulty, resists infatuations, falls in love in a kind of somber and eternal way, is under the domination of his superego, fights off experience.

That's how I knew Dubroff in our college days. Two unlikely candidates for friendship? So it would seem, and yet, in our senior year, we were very close. Of course I had other friends, close to me in different ways. I had lots of girls—it all came very easy to me; maybe it wasn't real friendship and it was rarely love, I was in a swirl of curricular and extracurricular activities. But at that time, in that year particularly, there was a kind of intensity to my friendship with Dubroff that set it off from all my other friendships, all my other connections. We'd see each other quite often, take long walks, see each other in company (mostly friends and acquaintances of mine). He came to my home many times, I went to his less frequently (I only remember being there once). It is difficult to describe our friendship, I never tried to understand it, we never confided in each other, and when other friends, puzzled by this friendship, asked about it: "What is it with Dubroff anyway?" I'd throw this question off. I didn't expect these others to be friends of Dubroff, or even to get along with him. He was not the kind of person you "get along with." His back did not invite slapping. If jokes were being told, he was not impatiently waiting his turn. I didn't exactly get along with him myself, but we were close nevertheless, friends nevertheless, and looking back on it, it's quite amazing, for I've never had as a friend, as a close acquaintance, a person so opposite in disposition, in habits, in nature, the way I first put it. My friends, it is true to this day, are invariably like me temperamentally, I usually get bored with people like Dubroff. People like Dubroff. But I've never known anyone like him.

And, in a way, even during that year of friendship I was bored with Dubroff. Nevertheless (I am trying to understand what happened at that time) there was something, how shall I say, comforting in his presence. That's it, he was somehow a source of strength, stability. In the midst of a party to which I had taken Dubroff (another thing, he was not the kind of fellow who took you to parties), getting drunk, screaming, carrying on the way I do at parties, I'd catch a glimpse of Dubroff, silent in a corner, or maybe carrying on a serious conversation, his head quietly nodding in characteristic way. I say his head was nodding rather than he was nodding his head because that was the way it looked, and the sight of him would somehow calm me. I don't know how to put it better. He was a sobering influence in my life: I have a frivolous nature, I am aware of it, and Dubroff made me aware of it, the only one who did, and the only one *who made me ashamed of myself.* Yes, in the midst of all that screaming and drunkenness, the cursing and lewdness, he brought me to a pause.

All this makes it sound as if Dubroff was a wet blanket, one who disapproved of pleasure without enjoying life *because* he didn't enjoy life, but it was not that way at all. The fact is that he had a kind of astringent sense of humor, saw the pretense and pomposity in behavior, could make the telling deflationary remark. I appreciated that in him. I appreciated his steadfastness, his loyalty. I defended him against those who couldn't understand what I saw in Dubroff, who waved off my defense of him as some kind of quirk or abnormality on my part.

I never failed to defend Dubroff; we were close, we trusted and needed one another in that year of turmoil (that is how I remember the year). I turned to him as often as he turned to me, maybe more often; maybe I needed him more than he needed me. We would have long conversations about the problems of society, about the futures of our friends and schoolmates, about good and evil, determinism and free will, the devil remembers what, whatever it is that undergraduates talk about, but no confidences that I remember. And then the school year came to an end. The graduation came and went: I went off to journalism school out West, Dubroff stayed in the city—he had to line up a job immediately, there was no money for further education.

I stayed out West a couple of years, came in occasionally, wrote to Dubroff, heard from him, looked him up a few times the first year away, but then came in less frequently, called him once or twice, didn't get him in. The years passed, I married, found a job in California, Dubroff drifted out of my life, I heard nothing about him. And then, just yesterday, in the city on an assignment, after, as I've said, twenty-five years, I was walking down a street in the West 30s, when I saw a familiar figure walking up the steps of a brownstone house.

"Dubroff!" The figure turned. It was indeed Dubroff—how could it not have been Dubroff?—and in that first glimpse, I saw, and with a sense of foreboding, a kind of terror, even guilt (though what was my responsibility for a man I hadn't seen in a quarter of a century?) that something dreadful had happened to him. It was as though he had moved in on himself; there was a kind of psychic shrinking, I don't know exactly how to describe it, but Dubroff always had that effect on me, of making me stop, be more careful about the accuracy, the honesty of my thinking.

He came down the steps and shook my hand. I was on the way to my hotel room, was coming from a party given by a presidential candidate for a select group of journalists, the ones he considered influential. There was much drinking, I in my usual active, even excited state, with a dinner appointment in an hour's time, all the usual chaos, appointment-mongering of my life, and here was Dubroff, shaking my hand, saying to me, after I addressed him:

"My name is no longer Dubroff. I've changed it to Broff." He asked if I'd like to come up to his apartment for coffee, he didn't say for drinks, and I accepted.

You know how it is when you come into a house and you have a sudden sense of strangeness, a kind of blow, though everything seems to be in such good order. So it was in my old friend's apartment. He lived in one room, with a kitchenette in a corner (where else?). There was a fair-sized window, with a window shade pulled down most of the way. In another corner was a sofa, to which Dubroff (Broff—I naturally keep thinking of him as Dubroff) waved me. There was a kind of plain kitchen chair, which Dubroff pulled up opposite me. There was a television set, on top of which a book was lying, a Goya print on the wall, a narrow bed. The room was certainly furnished in a sparse way, that was my immediate impression.

I told Broff about what I had been doing during these twenty-five years. It was not difficult for me to skim over this period, to tell of my jobs, my marriages, my divorces, my children, some of our mutual college friends that I had run into over the years, all told in the breezy, off-the-top-of-the-head manner so characteristic of me, a kind of headline speech, and then I started to slow down, knowing full well that I was gliding, talking superficially, dodging the troublesome, disguising where it suited me, often witty, mostly insincere, the effect of the presidential candidate's liquor beginning to wear off, I slowed down to a pause, and a wave of *shame* swept over me.

Broff told me that he had never married, and that he was employed in the city audit bureau. The water was now boiling in the kettle over in the kitchenette area (it semed to be on a small burner); Broff asked me how I liked my coffee, and he brought it over to me.

"Aren't you having any?" I asked.

"No," he said. "There is just the one cup."

I sprang to my feet.

"One cup," I cried, "one saucer, one bed, one table, one chair, one window, one TV set, one picture, one book."

I rushed over to the kitchenette.

"One pot," I went on, rapidly, as though proving something, "one burner, one kettle, one knife, one fork, one spoon."

I rushed back to the center of the room.

"One lamp," I cried, "and here one vase with one flower in it."

"So it is," said my old classmate, "one, one, one, one. . . ."

And he kept repeating the word, sitting there on his kitchen chair. I started for the door, and he kept saying, "One, one, one, one. . . ."

When I reached the door, I paused, turned to my old friend, and said, quietly:

"Dubroff, what is it, what?"

He kept saying, in a perfectly even tone: "One, one, one, one, one, one, one, one, one, one . . ." as I left his apartment, and ran down the steps into the street, the evening crowds.

THE GARDEN

What wondrous life is this I lead!
Ripe apples drop about my head;
The luscious clusters of the vine
Upon my mouth do crush their wine;
The nectarine, and curious peach,
Into my hands themselves do reach;
Stumbling on melons, as I pass,
Insnared with flowers, I fall on grass.

Andrew Marvell from *The Garden*

The above lines were read, slowly, by our high school English teacher. Most of us were inclined to be uninterested; a few of us were surprised out of uninterest; I was ravished not only by the lines (the first lines of verse ever to *impress* themselves on me) but by the tone which our teacher adopted in reading them (one of intense detachment).

We were all in love with our high school English teacher—for one reason and another, but mostly because she was young and beautiful, and read poetry with an odd kind of intonation, which attracted us, and perhaps frightened us a little, for we were not used to teachers who had *contact* with their subject matter.

We were made well aware of the futility of our yearning by knowledge of the interest which the principal had in our teacher.

He was an elderly man, gray though not distinguished, and created many a pretext to come into her classroom and interrupt her reading or her analyses, which we followed with dumb interest, our infatuation stilling all criticism.

> *What wondrous life is this I lead!*
> *Ripe apples drop about my head;*

It was not *too* difficult to understand these lines. *Wondrous* was an unusual word, but it was something like wonderful. None of us would have thought of expressing the sentiment in this way, rather: *I am having lots of fun,* and the image of the falling apples (we came to understand that *only* ripe apples fell) we accepted as realistic description, the kind of thing that happens in a well-kept garden, somewhat of a hazard, but certainly less so than the passing automobiles and trucks in our streets. One could always duck, or sidestep, or even catch the apples, eat them or throw them away.

We were prepared to protect our teacher against any hazard or danger, even prayed for hazards and dangers to prove our courage and self-sacrifice, to win her love, to prove our devotion. Now deep in our hearts we considered the principal a real and ever-present danger, but alas! we refused to recognize this openly, for we were aware of our helplessness, and therefore refused to *recognize* him as the danger we knew him to be.

> *The luscious clusters of the vine*
> *Upon my mouth do crush their wine;*

This was puzzling for a while, seemed to activate Nature somewhat excessively, but continued reading made the sentiment more familiar. We began to see that this was a way of describing good fortune, being in luck, that when you were *on,* everything came your way (fell into your lap). We compared this to conditions with which we were familiar: the athlete who was having a good day—the ball bounced true for him, the basket gave, the wall of the handball court surrendered dead spots, the tape came to meet him halfway.

To be *on:* it was luck plus what we called to have *form* even in our petty stealing, where one of us was sure to be caught, while for another the crystal for the radio set, the apple, and the peach fairly flew into his hands, by a magnetism, a relation between the subject and object we called skill, or luck, or form. We began to understand that this man in the Garden was having a good day, but we could not fail to be astonished at the use of the word *crush* —it seemed too strong a word for the setting.

> *The nectarine, and curious peach*
> *Into my hands themselves do reach;*

More of the same, for being fortunate, favored by the gods, all good things incline toward him, offer themselves for his pleasure. Even the *curious peach,* which at first I took to be a type of fruit, like the Georgia peach and only later saw the adjective for what it was—an adjective. Why *curious?* Was the fruit so unknown in the seventeenth century? It is surely no more curious than the unadjectivized nectarine. I repeated these two words to myself over and over—the *curious peach.* I believe this was my first contact with the Unlimiting Adjective.

But our high school teacher did not incline toward us, she did not do that; rather she inclined away from us, a fascinating movement which inclined us all the more toward her. She was not flirting (exactly) for it was a true movement of confused desire.

She had no favorites, or if she had favorites, did not play them; though any one of us, because she favored that one with a glance, or because a line she read made a particular impression on him, fancied that he was the favorite and swelled with impatience, or flushed with shame.

She surely wanted us to fall in love with the poem, and presented the poem as an object of desire. That this presentation made *her* all the more desirable she could not fail to recognize, and this self-awareness made the poem all the more desirable.

You might say the poem was a protection, in the way that any organized activity is a protection; or you might say it was a riddle, whose solution granted an unknown, but surely fabulous prize; or you might say it was a gift, which you accepted as something personal (in lieu of something personal); or you might say it was a created object handed around from one generation to another, to be held and examined and passed on (though retained).

But how pleasing that it was our English teacher, lady of poems, of silences, who, as a protection, handed us this created object as a gift or as a riddle, before whose solution we trembled.

It was not pleasing when another teacher handed us this created object, the way a clerk hands you a package over a counter; no, it was not pleasing to receive the object from those hands, but yes, from our young and lovely teacher of English literature, wedded to the object; but we, in our confusion, were unable to distinguish the one from the other, and so handled the object as though it were a living thing (it is a living thing) and treated the living thing as though she were an object.

And it was pleasing to watch as she read the lines and brought into being images of the past and present, read them in the odd, monotonous tone which had first attracted us, and whose nuances, changes of pace, we came very slowly to understand; for it was difficult to believe that any of these lines, which we had so often memorized and forgot, could have any meaning at all connected with our lives.

For, pursued as she was by the principal, and separated as she was from us, our English teacher was the only one who gave us any sense of hope, for she was wedded to an object of desire which she (somewhat shamelessly) offered to share with us, and which we, confused beyond belief by those objects and by herself as an object, seized at hungrily, in our departmentalized school, the way one reaches for the luscious fruit just out of reach:

> *Stumbling on melons, as I pass,*
> *Insnared with flowers, I fall on grass.*